D1446251

Retrieving a Living Tradition

Angelina of Montegiove

Franciscan, Tertiary, Beguine

Roberta Agnes McKelvie, O.S.F.

The Franciscan Institute
St. Bonaventure University
St. Bonaventure, New York

1997

©
The Franciscan Institute
St. Bonaventure University
St. Bonaventure, New York

October 4, 1997

The book is essentially the same as the author's doctoral dissertation: *RETRIEVING A LIVING TRADITION: THE RECOVERY OF THE HISTORICAL SIGNIFICANCE OF ANGELINA OF MONTEGIOVE AS FRANCISCAN TERTIARY, ITALIAN BEGUINE, AND LEADER OF WOMEN* (NY: Fordham Univeristy, 1996). Overall, some changes have been made for the sake of clarity and readability. Chapter Seven has been re–visited in hope of strengthening the conclusions drawn. I hope that the material in this book opens avenues of further research for scholars. It is also the author's prayerful hope that this book enriches the self-understaning of ordinary Franciscans so that our lives continue to model the Gospel in ever-richer ways.

Cover Design

A contemporary oil painting of Angelina of Montegiove and her community. Artist: Sergio Marini.

ISBN: 1–57659–131–X

Printed in the USA
Bookmasters
Ashland, Ohio

Table of Contents

Acknowledgments

This work began several years ago as an independent study project, an attempt to learn more about a Franciscan woman—any Franciscan woman—other than Clare of Assisi. Not that Clare was unworthy of study; she was the most recognizable woman in Franciscan life. Yet it did not seem possible that she could be the only significant female contributor to the many forms of life experienced by generations of Franciscan women. When I studied at the Franciscan Institute the curriculum had one major gap, provoking in many students a major question: "Where are the women, where are our stories?" When I broached the possibility of pursuing a study of Angelina and the threads of Beguine life I thought were so obviously connected, little did I know the course the pursuit of that story would take.

None of the work that has been accomplished would have been possible if it were not for the encouragement and support of my religious community, the Bernardine Franciscan Sisters. Special thanks go to Sr. Mary Margaret Jackson, whose love of our history has been an immense blessing; Sr. Maxine Porambo, who first fostered my studies at the Franciscan Institute; Sr. Lynn Rachelle Pascoe, who supported my two trips to Europe to pursue necessary materials; Sr. Theresa Ann Rygiel, who served as my translator in Poland, and Sisters Domitian Moscicka and Florence Kruczek, whose dedicated work brought the Polish-language materials into workable English prose.

Also, an immense debt of gratitude is owed to the Sisters of Sacred Heart Convent in Zakliczyn and St. Joseph Convent in Cracow, two Polish Bernardine houses intrinsic to this study. Special mention goes to Sr. Kinga at Zakliczyn and Srs. Elizabeth, Ludwika, and Benigna at Cracow.

Over the years, many others have supported this long-term search, some of whom must be recognized by name: Margaret Carney, OSF, whose challenge and encouragement first led me to Angelina; Regis Armstrong, OFM Cap., in whose class the independent study project first came to light: Drs. Richard Gyug, Ewert Cousins, and Elizabeth Johnson, of Fordham University, who shepherded me through the dissertation process; the staff of the Franciscan Institute at St. Bonaventure University, especially Br. Ed Coughlin, OFM; Noel Riggs; Elise Saggau, OSF; and Br. Tony LoGalbo, OFM, whose enthusiasm and persistence in helping me track down resources was invaluable.

Theresa Schaffer, at the Friedsam Library and Patrice Klausing, OSF, of the Office of Communications of my community, provided detailed and sometimes instantaneous assistance; Sisters at the Generalates of the Francescane Insegnati and the Felician Sisters provided gracious living space during my travels.

When the materials developed to the point where I had to make additional contact with the descendant community of Angelina and visit them as a seeker of texts and truths, Nancy Celaschi, OSF, General Secretary of the International Franciscan Conference of the Third Order Regular in Rome opened the doors of her office to me and facilitated communication with Srs. Clotilde Filannino and Lorella Mattioli of Angelina's community. Not only Srs. Clotilde and Lorella, but all the members of the Tertiary Franciscans of Blessed Angelina whom I have met have offered most gracious hospitality, support, and friendship. We are truly sisters. For this, I am deeply grateful.

In the process of revising the original work into publishable form, Br. Ed Coughlin, OFM, the Director of Publications of the Franciscan Institute, has kept things manageable and motivated me by this unfailing kindness, humor, and energy.

My sisters–in–Franciscan life, from general leadership to local fraternity, supported my research in so many ways—no price can measure the value of such a gift. The shared re–discovery of our roots has been an adventure, a grace, a challenge for the shaping of our future together.

For the many un-named fellow travelers, Franciscan women and men whose lives are also stories worth telling—know that you are appreciated beyond all telling.

Feast of the Sacred Heart
June 6, 1997

LIST OF ILLUSTRATIONS

Abbreviations Used

Concerning the Founders

AP	Anonymous of Perugia
1 Cel	*First Life of St. Francis*
2 Cel	*Second Life of St. Francis*
3 Soc	Legend of the Three Companions
LegCl	Legend of St. Clare
MajLeg	Major Legend of the Life of St. Francis
Proc.	Process of Canonization of St. Clare
RegCl	Rule of Clare
RegInn	Rule of Innocent IV
TestCl	Testament of Clare

Concerning Third Order History

ABFS	Archives, Bernardine Franciscan Sisters
ACSJ	Archives, Convent of St. Joseph, Cracow
AFH	*Archivum Franciscanum Historicum*
AFMC	Archives, Friars Minor in Cracow
AM	*Annales Minorum*
AMSA	Archives, Monastery of Sant'Anna
BF	*Bullarium Franciscanum*
BF n.s.	*Bullarium Franciscanum*, new series
DIP	*Dizionario degli Istituti di Perfezione*
DHGE	*Dictionnaire d'Histoire et Géographie Ecclésiastiques*
KBP	*Klasztory Bernardy-skie w Polsce w Jej Granicach Historycznych*
LBSZ	Library, Bernardine Sisters, Zakliczyn
LSB	*Lives of the Saints and Blesseds of the Third Order of St. Francis*
MPH	*Monumenta Poloniae Historica*

Dedication

To my mother, Agnes H.

and

To the women of the Third Order Regular
who constitute the living tradition of Tertiary Observance,
to those who have walked in this way before,
to those who walk in this way today,
to those who will walk in this way in the future.

INTRODUCTION

Historical Context and Interpretive Issues

The life and experience of Angelina of Montegiove (ca. 1357-1435) reveal in microcosm the major issues of women's identity present in both the Late Middle Ages and early modern period. Known in the "lives of the saints" tradition as Angelina of Marsciano or Angelina of Corbara, she has traditionally been thought of as the "founder" of the Franciscan Third Order Regular for women. In actuality, she was much more than that. Her life combined the ordinary aspects of a young woman born into a family of lesser nobility when feudal power was declining: loss of parents, a forced marriage, widowhood and political turmoil all shaped the first part of her life. Angelina joined the Franciscan Third Order as a widow and freely entered into its program of charitable works. She settled eventually in Foligno in a community which combined the independence of Italian Beguine life and the austerity of the Franciscan Observant tradition in an "open" (unenclosed) monastery. For at least forty years she lived at the Monastery of Sant'Anna. During that time, Angelina reshaped its form of life, founded other open monasteries, and was widely revered as a charismatic leader of tertiary women. From 1428-1435 Angelina was the first papally approved minister general of a group of Franciscan Third Order houses in Italy.

An abundance of Italian sources about Angelina has been available for centuries. She is treated briefly by sixteenth-century Franciscan chroniclers who extol her as a model of holiness while attacking her disciples because of a troubled relationship between them and the Friars Minor. The first work that can be called biographical did not appear until 1627, nearly 200 years after Angelina's death; the biographer portrayed Angelina as the "foundress of enclosed Third Order nuns" and launched an image of Angelina that remained unchanged until this century. Modern scholarship usually presents Angelina in brief "lives" based upon an inaccurate or misleading hagiographic tradition or buries Angelina within fleeting references submerged in the much larger framework of the history of the Franciscan Order. Both kinds of sources rely more upon the viewpoint of the Friars Minor than on a Third Order woman's perspective.

As a result, several difficulties of interpretation remain, particularly in light of feminist scholarly concern with the erasure of women from historical or theological consideration. The first difficulty is that the historical narrative concerning Angelina is both distorted and incomplete: distorted in that it was shaped by the particular perspective of patriarchy; incomplete, in that it did not use internal sources available to it to portray Angelina fully and accurately. A second concern stems from awareness that scholars have not treated Angelina as representative of a particular stage in the development of Italian Beguine, that is, *bizzoche*, houses and semi-religious life. This is a troubling erasure of a significant part of women's history that deserves recovery and analysis. The third area of difficulty is that no study has examined the spread of the "Angelina form of life" beyond the borders of Italy into eastern Europe, although her seventeenth-century biographies indicate that such a dissemination occurred. Such omissions of women and women's history are no longer permissible if we are to honor the *imago dei* in women.

One way of beginning to remedy the deficient tradition entails examining the story of Angelina and the religious movement associated with her from within the tradition and reading source texts about her with a hermeneutic of suspicion and retrieval. Such an assessment produces a greatly expanded and revised perspective of the historical significance of Angelina. Therefore, the study which follows will show, through an examination of hagiographic and historiographic sources, that Angelina of Montegiove was both a Franciscan tertiary and Italian Beguine; that she and the Third Order movement associated with her in Italy and Poland have been misrepresented in hagiographic and historiographic traditions shaped by patriarchy; and that a "history of the history of interpretation" which employs internal, previously unexamined sources provides an immensely different understanding of Angelina's life and the contribution to the Franciscan tradition made by her movement of "tertiary observance."

Undoubtedly, multiple problems confront anyone who attempts an interpretation of Angelina's hagiographic material. First, Angelina's life story was written during the Counter-Reformation, nearly two hundred years after her death, within the ambience of a Church and Order with an agenda for religious life: the exaltation of Christian holiness as embodied in virginity lived out in an enclosed community. Historiographic analysis addresses the imposition of such an agenda and serves not only to clarify the problems extant in her *Vite*; it likewise provides significant opportunity for revision of a part of Church history, Franciscan history, and women's history.

A second problem originates from within Franciscan history. A nuanced historiographic analysis of women in the Franciscan milieu, especially of the place of Angelina of Montegiove, must be situated in a new way in the context of Friar Minor history. Because Franciscan history has been overshadowed by a centuries-long emphasis on the "First Order," an interpretation of Angelina without an understanding of *both* Clare and Francis as founders of the Franciscan *movement* is destined to be flawed. Therefore, the present work includes a survey of the basic elements of that history: the identities of Francis and Clare of Assisi, the origins of their poverty-centered form of evangelical life, and the promise of continuing loving care and solicitude made by Francis to Clare and her sisters, and by association, to later-developing groups of Franciscan women, in order to provide a revised context for the analysis of Angelina.

A third problem in studying Angelina of Montegiove is the impact of a fundamental Franciscan issue, the Poverty Question. An inescapable tension in Angelina's history results from internal problems in the Franciscan movement caused by the fragmentation of the original Franciscan vision with regard to ownership of goods. This tension also results from the emergence of the groups known as Spirituals and Conventuals—but there has not yet been an analysis of Angelina that touches on the Poverty Question in the light of contexts connected to the Poverty Question.

A fourth problem to be assessed is the relationship of friars to women, to the penitential movement, and to the way of life of Italian Beguines; this includes an examination of the role of the institutional church in the above areas. Inclusion of all these elements affords an opportunity for a fundamental enrichment in understanding both Angelina and Franciscan history.

Previous Historical Perspectives

Historical analysis of such background issues before and after Angelina's life is influenced by, indeed limited by, the interaction of Franciscan and secular interpretations of the Order. There is an important caution to be noted with regard to interpreting the circumstances of the establishment of the Franciscan movement: one must be aware of the influence of Paul Sabatier's treatment of Franciscan history.[1] Sabatier raised questions about the nature of the original Franciscan ideal as well as about the relationship of that ideal to the "will of the church"—questions that have yet to be fully answered. According to Sabatier and his adherents, the original ideal of St. Francis "was progressively diluted and smothered" by the legalisms of the institutional church.[2] In a similar fashion, the "institutionalization of a charism" question raised by the Sabatier school about Francis will also be integral in the discussion of the story of Angelina of Montegiove.

In the recent history of interpretation many historians outside the Franciscan tradition have limited their work on the friars and Franciscan women to the "founding period" that ended in 1253 with Clare's death, and have not addressed stories of other women long known but essentially unexamined. Some of these women, like Angelina of Montegiove, have had incorrect interpretations placed on them and on their religious-life experiences. Consequently, a great deal of research needs to be done in examining critically the relationships within various religious movements, especially the relationship of the Franciscan Movement's male First and Third Order groups vis–à–vis women's Second and Third Order groups. This is particularly true if one chooses as a starting point the words attributed to Francis himself: "I resolve and promise for myself and for my brothers to always have that same loving care and

---

[1] Paul Sabatier, *Vie de S. François D'Assise*, trans. L. S. Houghton (New York: C. Scribner's Sons, 1894). This work initiated "the Franciscan Question."

[2] C. H. Lawrence, *Medieval Monasticism: Forms of Religious Life in Western Europe in the Middle Ages*, 2nd ed. (London and New York: Longman, 1989), 245.

solicitude for you as [I have] for them"[3]—words spoken to Clare and her companions at San Damiano, but words also defining a core ideal of the Franciscan movement: an essential relationship of brother-sisterhood. Clare had promised obedience to Francis, it is true; what this promise meant in terms of the effective history not only of Clare and Second Order women but of *all* women the friars encountered remains an area of controversy.

A much broader understanding of the relationship between the Friars Minor and women and the possible fulfillment of the promise of loving care and solicitude can be achieved by looking for connections with the development of the tertiary (Third Order) branch of the Franciscan movement.[4]

In this area, as in others, major problems exist within the narration of Franciscan history. Four instances will demonstrate some broader historiographic problems. John Moorman's history of the Order devotes several chapters to the development of the tertiaries, but provides a generic treatment of Franciscan women.[5] Moorman allots about one page to the Beguine-tertiary connection, and that is within the context of problems that result from friars being held responsible for difficult women and the move toward claustration.[6] He devotes one chapter to fourteenth-century legal issues and to the regularization of tertiary life. However, perhaps the most significant woman in Franciscan tertiary life at the time,

---

[3]*Rule of Clare* VI.4. All source citations from the writings of Clare are taken from *Clare of Assisi: Early Documents*, edited and translated by Regis J. Armstrong, O.F.M. Cap. (New York/Mahwah: Paulist Press, 1988). An expanded and revised edition of this work was published in 1993 by Franciscan Institute Publications, St. Bonaventure, NY.

[4]"Third Order" history involves two branches, not always clearly delineated. "Third Order Regular" refers to groups of tertiaries (male and female) who were committed to following the *Rule of 1289* and ultimately became religious congregations with simple vows. To get at the history of the formation of these communities, however, some significant hurdles must be overcome. First, there is the First Order perspective, and then there is the Sabatier-Spiritual paradigm. Lastly, much recent published material comes from Italy and so has a very different viewpoint from English-language material. "Third Order Secular" refers to the many diverse individuals and groups who followed the *Rule of 1289*, but who did so outside the constructs of institutionalized religious life.

[5]John R. H. Moorman, *A History of the Franciscan Order From Its Origins to the Year 1517* (Chicago: Franciscan Herald Press, 1988; London: Oxford University Press, 1968).

[6]Moorman, 217-18.

Angelina of Montegiove (Marsciano), is covered in only one major paragraph and a few other very brief references.[7]

The second instance is Robert M. Stewart's major study of the development of the *Rule of Nicholas IV* (1289) into the *Rule* of the Secular Franciscan Order, a group formerly known as the Third Order Secular. Stewart's work is a chronological and textual analysis based on the Franciscan ideal found in sources beginning with 1221, but does not address the relationship of friars and women at all.[8] Nor does it offer any assistance with regard to the development of the Third Order Regular women's congregations.

Two volumes by Raffaele Pazzelli cover Third Order Regular history; both interpretations differ from the First Order perspective.[9] The first work establishes the origins of the tertiary movement and locates those origins in the flow of history surrounding the penitents of the late eleventh and early twelfth centuries.[10] In the process of researching and writing this book, Pazzelli realized that he was unable to include any of the story of the women's participation in this movement. He therefore set about doing more detailed research in order to publish a work devoted to the story of Franciscan Sisters.[11] In both of Pazzelli's books, it is clear that the Friars Minor were not always content with their traditional responsibilities of providing spiritual services for the penitents, tertiaries, and sisters who were not Poor Clares. Pazzelli devotes a fairly large segment of his discussion to the life and accomplishments of Angelina of Montegiove (Marsciano) and her struggle with the leadership of the Friars Minor (Conventuals and Observants) over issues of governance and visitation. Although Pazzelli makes

---

[7]Ibid., 420, 558, 562, 566.

[8]See Robert M. Stewart, *De Illis Qui Faciunt Penitentiam: The Rule of the Secular Franciscan Order: Origins, Development, Interpretation* (Rome: Istituto Storico dei Cappucini, 1991).

[9]Raffaele Pazzelli, *St. Francis and the Third Order* (Chicago: Franciscan Herald Press, 1989) and *The Franciscan Sisters* (Steubenville, Ohio: Franciscan University Press, 1993).

[10]Unfortunately, there is a slightly argumentative tone to the book, since in some areas it contradicts and intends to correct First Order interpretations of Third Order history.

[11]In spite of the fact that much of what is contained in the book is gathered from work done by other Italian scholars, it is a meaningful contribution to the history of Franciscan women.

a major contribution to the history of Franciscan Third Order women, his work merely broke open the uppermost layer of investigative possibilities.

In 1984 a group of Italian historians published a volume comprised entirely of essays on Angelina, given as lectures at a historical congress the previous year.[12] The material presented at the 1983 meeting confirmed the fact that enclosure and authority conflicts continued to be a part of the relationship between the Friars Minor and Franciscan women well into the fifteenth century. Although a valuable resource, most of this volume has yet to be translated into English and so has been neither thoroughly analyzed nor used by English-speaking scholars.

Toward a Feminist Reconstruction

If one surveys yet more recent historical literature, it is disturbingly obvious that there has been no attempt to choose a Franciscan woman other than Clare of Assisi as the focal point of major study. Franciscan women's history, whether Third Order or Poor Clare history, clearly is undertold.[13] Recent interpretations grounded in deconstructive feminism have assumed a perspective that presents a history of conflict without any elements of harmony at all.[14] Both of these positions, undertelling the story and total

---

[12]The volume, *La beata Angelina da Montegiove e il movimento del terz'ordine regolare francescano femminile*, ed. R. Pazzelli and M. Sensi (Rome: Analecta TOR, 1984), includes articles on Angelina's iconographic representations; her foundation at Foligno; documents associated with that house, including constitutions; and work on the spirituality of the sisters living that *bizzoche*-Franciscan life. Much of the material in this volume will be referred to throughout the following chapters.

[13]To my knowledge, there is no single work dealing exclusively with the history of the Second Order. Most materials center on Clare herself and were written by men for the limited audience of Poor Clares themselves, such as F. M. Fiege's *The Princess of Poverty* (Evansville: 1909), and E. Gilliat-Smith's *Saint Clare of Assisi* (London: 1914), or Nesta deRobeck's *St. Clare of Assisi* (Chicago: Bruce Publishing Co, 1950). They clearly emerge from a point of view that accepted the monasticized Clare life and promulgated it. Work on the history of Third Order women is at an embryonic stage of development.

[14]See, for example, Noreen Hunt, "Enclosure II," *Cistercian Studies* 22 (1989): 146. Brenda Bolton, "*Mulieres Sanctae*," in *Women in Medieval Society*, ed. Susan Mosher Stuard (Philadelphia: University of Pennsylvania Press, 1976), 151-52; Carol Neel, "The Origins of the Beguines," in *Sisters and Workers in the Middle Ages*, ed. Judith M. Bennett, Elizabeth A. Clark, Jean F. O'Barr et al. (Chicago and London: University of

deconstruction, present a flawed assessment, inconsistent either with the weight of evidence for women's roles and their distinctive spirituality, or with the egalitarian promise made by Francis. Clearly, conflict did exist. What needs to be investigated is the alternation of "loving care and solicitude" and supervision which bordered on domination. This requires a commitment to the wholeness of women's history, a willingness to move beyond purely institutional history into the retrieval of texts for purposes of reinterpretation—in other words, a feminist *reconstruction* which challenges not only the incompleteness of deconstruction but also offers hope for the future.[15]

The story of Third Order Regular Franciscan women is usually presented as congregational history; when an individual person is involved as the subject, the point of view is more often than not an abbreviated narrative of the life of the person as a founder. What results is, often, a sense that so much more could be done; that something, many things, are missing. What would happen if someone were to attempt a "history of the history" of one Franciscan woman, a work that emerges from a "history of interpretation" perspective? What would happen if a feminist historical theologian followed the lead of Rosemary Radford Ruether, Elisabeth Schüssler Fiorenza, and Anne Carr in critiquing the tradition that surrounds Angelina of Montegiove?[16] Would it be

---

Chicago Press, 1989), 240; and Joanne McNamara, "The Need to Give: Suffering and Female Sanctity in the Middle Ages," in *Images of Sainthood in Medieval Europe*, ed. Renate Blumenfeld-Kosinski and Timea Szell (Ithaca: Cornell University Press, 1991), 211. All express a negative viewpoint about the friars' unwillingness to establish or maintain connections to women interested in the Franciscan life. McNamara claims that Francis himself did not regard women "as eligible partners in the preaching mission" and incorrectly implies that he was thwarting Clare's vocation.

[15]See Eleanor McLaughlin, "The Christian Past: Does It Hold a Future for Women?" in *Womanspirit Rising: A Feminist Reader in Religion*, ed. Carol P. Christ and Judith Plaskow (San Francisco: Harper San Francisco, 1992), 93-106 for a fine essay on the viability of retrieving women's history as a sign of hope.

[16]See Rosemary Radford Ruether, *Sexism and God-Talk: Toward a Feminist Theology* (Boston: Beacon Press, 1993) for the fundamentals of a method of correlation; Elisabeth Schüssler-Fiorenza, *In Memory of Her: A Feminist Reconstruction of Christian Origins* (New York: Crossroad, 1983, 1990) for a theory of interpretation and reconstruction based on early sources of a tradition; and Anne Carr, *Transforming Grace: Christian Tradition and Women's Experience* (San Francisco: Harper SanFrancisco, 1988) for theoretical perspectives on women's studies. These works have been primary influences which shape the method followed in the present work.

possible to retrieve and release the *dangerous memory* contained in Franciscan women's history and move toward repairing the imbalance of traditional scholarship in that area?

The work that follows addresses these questions. In order to enter into an interpretation of hagiographic and historiographic traditions surrounding Angelina of Montegiove with the intention of deepening and clarifying our understanding of them, I propose to examine three areas: the story of a religious movement, basing the examination on the *Vite* of Angelina of Montegiove; the various changes in interpretation about her; and the influence of Angelina's tradition on "tertiary observance" in Poland. The method followed springs from Ruether's method of correlation, standing within the tradition and entering into dialogue with the texts in order to illustrate gaps and distortions within them. Beyond correlation, the method of Elisabeth Schüssler-Fiorenza allows an interpretive history which combines historical exegesis with multi-leveled analysis of the texts. Cultural, political, social, and ecclesial factors will be subjected to "creative critical interpretation" in order to identify and respond to androcentric influences.

For this purpose, Chapter One provides background on the central features of early Franciscan history. The second chapter presents an interpretive examination of several accounts of the first portion of Angelina's life, that is, the period between 1357-1395. It focuses on the details of her biography, examining various representative texts with both deconstructive and reconstructive purposes. Chapter Three attempts to contextualize developments within Franciscan history in the *Quattrocento* against a backdrop of concurrent Church history so that clarity is brought to the development of the "Observant Tradition" as a crucial influence on Angelina between 1395-1435. The history of interpretation resumes in Chapter Four, covering what the *Vite* present about Angelina's life after 1395. The reconstructive approach will be extended by inclusion of the "collective memory" of the present community of Sant'Anna, Angelina's Franciscan descendants. Chapter Five breaks new ground in identifying missing pieces in the story, specifically, houses not previously named as part of Angelina's movement—houses of the "Regular Tertiaries of the Observance" in Poland. Both Chapters Five and Six examine internal texts and archival sources of women "Regular Tertiaries of the Observance" in order to delineate the particular development of this movement within the larger Franciscan story, and to note parallels with the story of Tertiary Observance in Italy. The concluding chapter offers a commentary on the significance of the contribution Angelina made to Franciscan women's history, not only in her own era but also, by extension of the charism, to the present historical moment.

By these steps, it can be shown that Angelina of Montegiove (Marsciano) is an erased figure whose historical significance as a charismatic leader of Italian *bizzoche* women and Franciscan tertiaries lies in the living tradition of tertiary observance associated with her, a tradition which stretched across Europe into Poland and the United States and endured through the centuries to the present time.

CHAPTER ONE

The Foundation of the Franciscan Movement

In order to provide the best possible study of the religious movement associated with Angelina of Montegiove, several contextual reference points are needed, beginning with the original Franciscan experience at the "founding moment." Until very recently only one perspective has been presented, that of the Friars Minor. It is they who have had "the history" and the resources with which to tell it; therefore, the narrative has focused virtually exclusively on Francis of Assisi (1182-1226) as the founder of three religious orders. However, in the last twenty-five years or so, a new understanding of the origins of the Franciscan Orders, or what is now being called the Franciscan Movement, has been advanced. This view espouses the belief that along with Francis of Assisi, Clare of Assisi (1193-1253) co-founded the Franciscan Movement.[1]

In general, historical narratives had ignored the role of Clare: Francis and Francis alone was inspired by God to preach penance and shape a new form of evangelical life which eventually mushroomed into the "fraternity" of "lesser brothers."[2] Clare was

---

[1] A succinct summary of the origins of the Franciscan "movement" is found in Lazaro Iriarte, *Franciscan History: The Three Orders of St. Francis of Assisi*, trans. Patricia Ross (Chicago: Franciscan Herald Press, 1982), 1-13. More recently, there is the groundbreaking work of Margaret Carney, *The First Franciscan Woman: Clare of Assisi and Her Form of Life* (Quincy, Illinois: Franciscan Press, 1993), in which she places Clare squarely as co-founder of the movement. For a fine contextualization of the genesis of the Rule of 1221 in relation to the reforms continuing in the church from the eleventh century, see David Flood and Thadée Matura, *The Birth of a Movement*, trans. Paul LaChance and Paul Schwartz (Chicago: Franciscan Herald Press, 1975).

[2] Kajetan Esser comments upon the confusion and absence of "unanimity among the Friars Minor" themselves as to their identity, and provides an explanation of their causes, based on the Rule, Letters, and Testament of Francis as well as other internal Franciscan sources. Esser cites Francis' use of the word *fraternitas* to describe the community which had grown around him, because this word gives expression to an essential characteristic of his followers." See *Origins of the Franciscan Order*, trans. Aedan Daly and Irina Lynch (Chicago: Franciscan Herald Press, 1970), 17, 23. However, Esser writes of only one Franciscan Order, specifically the Friars Minor. This is a limited point of view. A broader understanding can be found in Iriarte, who

merely the "little plant"[3] of Francis; the Poor Clares were a distant relation to the mendicant reality of Franciscans and Dominicans sweeping across Europe in the first half of the thirteenth century, and the Third Order received least recognition of all. But the "return-to-your-roots" mandate of the Second Vatican Council and the 800th centenaries of both Francis and Clare (1982, 1993) radically altered these perceptions, and has led to the re-evaluation of the founders' relationship.

The "Founding Moment"

The Franciscan tradition, both older and revised versions, proposes that the conversion of Francis Bernardone began at the Battle of Collestrada (c. 1202), in the war between Perugia and Assisi.[4] Captured and held prisoner for nearly a year, Francis experienced first-hand the inglorious nature of suffering.[5] Returned home, he could no longer fully enjoy the carefree, spendthrift life of his earlier youth.[6] In 1205 he became an oblate-penitent,[7] rebuilding with his own hands the small chapel of San Damiano below the city of Assisi.[8] In a public dispute with his father, Francis relied upon exemption as a penitent in order to escape civil

---

covers three Orders: the Friars Minor, the Poor Clares, and the Order of Penance (Third Order). For Iriarte on *fraternitas*, see pp. 9-12.

[3] *Testament of Clare* 37. (Hereafter *TestCl*). "Little plant" is an appellation Clare gave herself.

[4] See Thomas of Celano, "First and Second Life of St. Francis with selections from 'Treatise on the Miracles of Bl. Francis'" translated from the Latin, with introduction and notes by Placid Hermann, O.F.M., in *St. Francis of Assisi Writings and Early Biographies English Omnibus of the Sources for the Life of St. Francis*, edited by Marion Habig, Fourth Revised Edition (Chicago: Franciscan Herald Press, 1983). This volume will be cited as *Omnibus* in subsequent citations. Reference to the "First Life" will be as 1 Cel; reference to the "Second Life" will be as 2 Cel. Also see the "Legend of the Three Companions," translated from the Latin and Italian by Nesta deRobeck, in the *Omnibus*. Citations for this source will be as 3 Soc. The specific sources for the war with Perugia are 3 Soc 4 and 2 Cel 4.

[5] 1 Cel 3-4.

[6] 3 Soc 7; 2 Cel 7.

[7] See Pazzelli, *St. Francis and the Third Order*, 30, 87-90. Oblates placed themselves at the disposal of a church or monastery, as part of their personal conversion. This was one model of life for those included in the term "penitent." The latter was an officially recognized "state of life" before, during, and after the life of Francis of Assisi.

[8] 1 Cel 18.

charges.[9] Over the next two or three years, Francis rebuilt two other churches,[10] and was joined by a few other men from Assisi.[11] In 1209 or 1210, the group walked to Rome to ask permission of Pope Innocent III to "preach and do penance," which was granted.[12] For the next year or so, Francis and his "brothers" did just that.

Contemporary historiography broadens the context of the founding moment by recognizing the significant place of the first identifiable woman who became an integral part of the unfolding Franciscan Movement, *Chiara di Favarone di Offreduccio*, Clare of Assisi. On Palm Sunday night in 1212 the eldest daughter of one of the wealthiest noble families of Assisi left her father's house to join Francis and the "brothers."[13] Within weeks she was joined by her younger sister Catherine; within months they were joined by other women, friends or relatives from the region around Assisi, becoming a community living in the re-built church of San Damiano.[14] Before long, other groups of women began to imitate that particular form of life.[15] The "founding moment" includes,

---

[9] 3 Soc 19.

[10] 1 Cel 21.

[11] 3 Soc 27-29; 1 Cel 24-25; 2 Cel 15.

[12] 1 Cel 32-33; 2 Cel 16-17.

[13] The primary sources for biographical information on Clare are the "Legend of St. Clare" and her Process of Canonization. The abbreviation for the "Legend" is LegCl; for the Process the abbreviation is Proc. For the story of Clare's entrance into Francis' group, see LegCl 7:2; Proc 12:4; 16:6; 17:5; 18:3; and 20:6. Recent scholarship includes, in addition to Armstrong and Carney, the work of Ingrid Peterson, *Clare of Assisi: A Biography* (Quincy, Illinois: Franciscan Press, 1993).

[14] LegCl 24-26; Proc. 1: 3; 2: 1-2.

[15] This is an especially difficult historical topic. The other groups of women may have been partly the result of the preaching effectiveness of the friars, or partly the result of the earlier and continuing manifestation of the larger women's religious movement of the time. An excellent resource discussing the complexity of this material is Mario Sensi, "Incarcerate e recluse in Umbria nei secoli XIII e XIV: un bizzocaggio centro-italiano," in *Il movimento religioso femminile in Umbria nei secoli XIII-XIV*, ed. Roberto Rusconi (Regione dell'Umbria: La Nuova Italia Editrice, 1984), 85-122. For an English language translation see: "The Women's Recluse Movement in Umbria during the 13th and 14th Centuries," trans. Edward Hagman, O.F.M. Cap., *Greyfriars Review* 8 (1994): 319-45. Subsequent citations will be taken from the translation and identified as Sensi-Hagman, unless otherwise indicated. Sensi focuses as well on the role of Card. Hugolino deSegni, later Pope Gregory IX, in the "regularization" of the so-called Damianite Movement. Two other excellent sources are the works of Giovanna Casagrande and Anna Benvenuti Papi, which will be

therefore, Francis *and* Clare equally, as leaders of rapidly increasing groups of followers.

One of the most important sources from which to take the measure of the earliest years of the movement is a letter of James of Vitry, who was an important supporter of one of the many women's religious movements at the time, the Beguines.[16] In 1216 he reported on a trip that had taken him through the Umbrian Valley, in which Assisi is located:

> I found one consolation in those parts, nevertheless: many men and women, rich and worldly, after renouncing everything for Christ, fled the world. They are called the Lesser Brothers and Lesser Sisters. . . .They have already borne much fruit through the grace of God, and have converted many, so that whoever hears them says, "Come" (Rev 22:17; Jn 1:46) and one circle of hearers draws another.
>
> They live according to the form of the primitive Church. . . .They go into the cities and villages during the day, so that they convert others, giving themselves to active work; but they return to their hermitages or solitary places at night, employing themselves in contemplation.
>
> The women live near the cities in various hospices. They accept nothing, but live from the work of their hands. . . .[17]

"Lesser brothers" and "lesser sisters" is a literal translation of *fratres minores* and *sorores minores*; "minor" indicates a fundamental aspect of the kind of relationships Francis envisioned for his followers. Lazaro Iriarte writes that "Friars Minor" was the culmination of a process of finding "some name by which people would know them and that 'Brothers' and 'lesser' summed up the Gospel ideal in a nutshell."[18]

---

cited in later chapters.

[16] See Armstrong's introduction to the excerpted letter, *Early Documents*, 245. James of Vitry was intimately associated with the Rhineland Beguines and was the biographer of Marie of Oignies.

[17] "Testimony of Jacques de Vitry (1216)" in Armstrong, 245-46. Armstrong cites as the original text source R.B.C. Huygens, *Lettres de Jacques de Vitry* (Leyde, 1960), 75-76.

[18] See Iriarte, 7. Fraternity and minority were essential elements of the early movement. For a brief summary of the values embodied in the first years of the Friars

A most interesting area of scholarly discussion concerns the continuing relationship between the "lesser brothers" and "lesser sisters" in the years after the death of Francis (d. 1226). Within both her *Testament* and her *Rule*, Clare emphasized her understanding of the essential commitment: "And moved by compassion for us, he [Francis] bound himself, both through himself and through his Order, to always have the same loving care and special solicitude for us as for his own brothers."[19] In the *Rule*, the language is even stronger; Clare quotes Francis' own words as "I resolve and promise for myself and for my brothers to always have that same loving care and solicitude for you as [I have] for them."[20] Clare might be seen here as explaining how she and Francis circumvented Canon 13 of the Fourth Lateran Council which had forbidden the establishment of new religious orders by mandating adherence to an already approved Rule, since the promise includes her and her companions in the original approbation given Francis by Innocent III in 1209-10.[21] But Margaret Carney maintains that there is much more than juridical necessity involved in this promise. There was loyalty to the ideal of poverty;[22] there was the promotion of an orthodox alternative to heretical penitential groups, and there was a sense of shared vocation.[23] And, I would propose that there is an extended sense in which the promise can be said to cover *all* members of the Franciscan Order, since many thousands of men and women also followed the teaching and example of Francis while remaining in their secular lives. The

---

Minor, see Iriarte, 10-12.

[19] *TestCl* 29. Armstrong, [1993] 58.

[20] *Rule of Clare* VI.4.

[21] The applicable section of Canon 13 states: "The founding of new religious orders is forbidden. New monasteries must accept a rule already approved." See H. J. Schraeder, *Decrees of the General Councils Texts, Translation, and Commentary* (New York: Herder, 1937), 254.

[22] In 1216 Clare requested and received from Pope Innocent III the "Privilege of Poverty," which was renewed by Pope Gregory IX in 1228. The most significant element of the Privilege is the statement that "no one can compel you to receive possessions" (Priv. 7; see Armstrong, [1988] 84). This document is the first (and possibly most important) papal approval of the austere poverty lived by the earliest members of the Franciscan Movement. Here, at least temporarily, the cultural imperative against female mendicancy was overcome.

[23] See Carney, 132-35.

promise implies that the Friars Minor will continue to teach, care for, and be brothers to other Franciscans.

Those who were inspired to follow the Gospel according to the preaching of Francis of Assisi could choose one of several ways to implement Franciscan-Gospel values. Men who joined the Friars Minor as clerics or as lay brothers are referred to as the First Order; women who joined Clare at San Damiano or imitated the form of life there are called at first Damianites, and later, the Second Order. And there is also a Third Order, sometimes called the Order of Penance, whose members are often called tertiaries; they have the least clear and most decentralized history of the groups founded by Francis. The earliest Franciscan accounts indicate the immense success of the friars' preaching and refer to thousands who "converted" and committed themselves to the Gospel.[24] One source says that after hearing the preaching of Francis and the first friars, "many women" asked what they could do because "we cannot be with you" —without explaining why they could not, although cultural imperatives against vagabond women certainly would have been operative.[25] The same source also indicates that the friars established monasteries of recluses for doing penance in every city possible.[26] St. Bonaventure, in his re-telling of the life of Francis, mentions great numbers of people who adopted a "rule of penance" given by Francis, including men and women, clerics and laity, married and single.[27] The last reference, encompassing several levels of medieval society, clearly points to the groups later covered by the umbrella term "tertiaries." Given the rapid increase in the number of followers of the particular forms of penitential life modelled by Francis and Clare, then, the term "co-

---

[24] Anonymous of Perugia (hereafter AP) 41 b,c ; 3 Soc 14:60. The AP manuscript was listed in an inventory of manuscripts at the *Sacro Convento*, Assisi, in 1381; it was later lost. The author is thought to be Brother John, a disciple of Brother Giles, one of the First Companions. Among Franciscan scholars, AP is treated as a source for the Legend of Three Companions (3Soc).

[25] See Lawrence, 264.

[26] AP 41C.

[27] St. Bonaventure, Major Legend IV:6. See "The Life of St. Francis," trans. Ewert Cousins, in *Bonaventure*, The Classics of Western Spirituality (New York: Paulist Press, 1978).

founders" is not an exaggerated one, even when applied to the Third Order.

The Poverty Question

The second contextual problem from early Franciscan history affecting Angelina of Montegiove is the Poverty Question, which impinges on the history of the Franciscan Movement well into the fifteenth century. This is especially pertinent with respect to the rise of the "regular observance" with which her communal life is associated (see Chapter Three). By 1230, only four years after the death of Francis of Assisi, friars were seeking mitigations of the strict poverty that had characterized the earliest years of the movement. Time and expansion had established that the literal poverty of Francis' original vision was not possible for a large group of itinerant preachers. In Francis' lifetime, friars could accept food and lodging, but not money, and not fixed places of residence. Once friars moved beyond the Umbrian Valley, however, a series of legal stratagems evolved with the result that "voluntary poverty" quickly changed.[28] Because the Church had found the mendicants to be useful "direct agents of papal action,"[29] it was to the advantage of the Church to relax the severity of the Franciscan ideal. This "Poverty Question" developed into a critical component of change in the Franciscan movement, not only for the friars but for Poor Clares and tertiaries as well. Voluntary poverty quickly became a political issue rather than a vocational ideal.

Promulgation of *Quo elongati* in 1230 delineated the increasing disparity between two views of Franciscan life.[30] On one side stood the question of faithfulness to the original ideal; on the other, the question of adaptation in response to the needs of the larger Church. *Quo elongati* annulled the binding force of Francis' *Testament* and allowed the use of money on behalf of the friars, so long as the spending was done by an agent of the benefactor. In reality, this quickly became a legal fiction by which Rome blessed

---

[28] Philip F. Mulhern, *Dedicated Poverty: Its History and Theology* (New York: Alba House, 1973), 101-03.

[29] *Cambridge Illustrated History of the Middle Ages III 1250-1520*, ed. Robert Fossier (Cambridge: Cambridge University Press, 1986), 139.

[30] BF I, 67–70.

those favoring a broad interpretation of the original ideal. These friars became known as "the Community" or, later, the "Conventuals." For this group, adaptation was the will of God; opportunity for expansion, evidence of Divine Providence. Those objecting to such an interpretation became known as the *zelanti* or "Spirituals."[31] Included among this group were the "First Companions" of Francis: brothers Leo, Giles, Rufino, and Masseo, and Clare herself. For them, adherence to the original austerity of early Franciscan life was God's will; reliance on Providence, not on benefactors' agents, constituted fidelity. From 1230 onward, Franciscan life was shaped by this issue and by a recurrent tendency to reform that life from within. The "spirituals" eventually became, by the early fifteenth century, the "Observants" —whose impact on the communal life of tertiary women at the time of Angelina constitutes a major consideration in Franciscan history and spirituality.[32]

As far as external factors are concerned, some historians place the issue of poverty against past problems with heretical penitential groups such as the Cathars, Waldenses, and Humiliati, as well as against the influence of Joachimite eschatological ideas, citing the extremism of the ideal of absolute poverty as disturbing to the Church.[33] Other historians identify as a pertinent factor the Church's struggle with avoiding heresy and controlling the laity, especially laywomen.[34]

---

[31]Here I follow a broad sense of meaning for this term; that is, the Spirituals/ Spiritual Tradition refers to a tendency to more rather than less faithful observance of the Rule (either 1st, 2nd, or 3rd Order Rule) rather than a narrow meaning taken from an association with the "Spiritual Party" of Angelo Clareno, Peter John Olivi, Ubertino of Casale, or John of Parma. I agree with Rosalind B. Brooke's objection to use of terms such as "parties" when speaking of the origin of the Spiritual Tradition. See her work, *Early Franciscan Government* (Cambridge: University Press, 1959), 5.

[32]See Chapters Three and Four below.

[33]See, for example, Jacques LeGoff, *Medieval Civilization*, trans. Julia Barrow (Cambridge: Basil Blackwell, 1989), 88ff; 86; and Little, 113-28 and 134-45.

[34]Brenda Bolton, "Vitae Matrum: A Further Aspect of the Frauenfrage," in *Medieval Women*, ed. Derek Baker (Oxford: Basil Blackwell, 1978), 262. See also Caroline Walker Bynum, *Holy Feast and Holy Fast: The Religious Significance of Food to Medieval Women* (Berkeley: University of California Press, 1987), especially chapter 1; and Diane Owen Hughes, "Invisible Madonnas? The Italian Historiographical Tradition and the Women of Medieval Italy," in *Women in Medieval History and Historiography*, ed. Susan

With regard to Franciscan women living out the ideal of poverty, the Poor Clares are generally perceived as the most faithful custodians of Francis' legacy of poverty.[35] Yet by 1247 Innocent IV had promulgated a *Rule* which stripped the group at San Damiano of its right not to own property and tried to impose ownership of land. Innocent's text regarding this reads: ". . . you may be permitted to receive, to have in common, and to freely retain produce and possessions." This is a direct contravention of the Privilege of Poverty, which stated that no one could compel Clare and her sisters to receive possessions (see note 22, page 15). Further, Innocent wrote that each monastery could have a procurator "to deal with these possessions in a becoming way."[36] Innocent was extending, or trying to extend, the principle of *Quo elongati* to San Damiano. Clare's response was to compose her own *Rule*, for which she obtained Innocent's approval in 1253.

As far as women tertiaries living a common life are concerned—a reality in various places by the mid-thirteenth century—not making a vow of poverty was an integral element in their identity. It also allowed them to use their financial resources for care of the sick or other corporal works of mercy. Tertiary works of charity required freedom not possible for enclosed women who had vowed poverty. But the tendency of tertiary women, especially widows, to live very simply and to use their financial assets in a "new" way meant they were subjected to ecclesiastical suspicion and repeated attempts to curtail their perceived independence—primarily through imposition of the vow of poverty and the vow of enclosure.

What aspects of the "founding moment" lead us to an examination of the life of Angelina of Montegiove? The Franciscan founding experience was built on two touchstones: fidelity to one's individual vocation, and absolute orthodoxy, manifested in service to the Church. It is the successful linking of these traits which distinguished Franciscans, whether First, Second or Third Order members, from heterodox penitential groups of the thirteenth and fourteenth centuries. As the story of Angelina unfolds in the

---

Mosher Stuard (Philadelphia: University of Pennsylvania Press, 1987), 24-57.

[35] See, for example, Walter Nigg, *Warriors of God: The Great Religious Orders and Their Founders*, ed. and trans. Mary Ilford (New York: Alfred A Knopf, 1959), 245.

[36] RegInn 11; see Armstrong, [1993] 119.

following chapters, each of these areas—fidelity to one's vocation, absolute orthodoxy based upon literal imitation of Franciscan values, and service to the Church "in the world" —provide a perspective for analysis and contribute to a new level of interpretation for her story.

CHAPTER TWO

ANGELINA OF MONTEGIOVE:

The Interpretive Tradition

I. Angelina's Personal Life

Having situated Angelina of Montegiove within the framework of the first two centuries of Franciscan history, it is now suitable to examine the resources pertaining to the first half of her life, in which the issues are largely personal and biographical, and not the matters of her communal life to be considered in later chapters. In discussing the history of interpretation of the hagiographic tradition that defines the story of Angelina, a chronological approach moves through various selected resources in sequence. Material has been arranged in five sections: (1) the earliest sources, those of Mariano of Florence,[1] Mark of Lisbon,[2] and Luke Wadding,[3] Franciscan chroniclers all; (2) a composite version of Angelina's biography extracted mainly from two of Ludovico Jacobilli's works; (3) historiographic reactions to Jacobilli, including the genealogical revision by Ferdinand Ughelli;[4] (4) a few nineteenth and early twentieth-century (pre-World War II) forms; and (5) some post-World War II interpretations. For each source in each section, the areas of discussion will be limited to the topics of Angelina's birth-family names; her marriage; her adherence to the Franciscan Third

---

[1]Mariano of Florence, "De Sanctis et Beatis Tertii Ordinis iuxta codicem Mariani Florentini," ed. A. Van DenWyngaert, AFH XIV (1921), hereafter cited as "Tertii Ordinis." Another work, "Compendium Chronicarum Fratrum Minorum," contains a brief mention of Angelina and is found in AFH III (1910): 708.

[2]Mark of Lisbon, *Delle Croniche de'Frati Minori, del Serafico Padre S. Francesco,* Italian translation by Horatio Diola (Venice: Erasmo Viotti, 1591) terza parte, 27-28. Hereafter cited as *Chroniche* III. For text, see Appendix A, Part I.

[3]Luke Wadding, *Annales Minorum seu trium Ordinum a S. Francisco institutorum* (Ad Claras Aquae, 1932), IX: 2-3, 129-33; X: 159-60, 279-80; XI: 123-25.

[4]My focus will be the lineage of Angelina and Ughelli's clarification of earlier persons "collapsed" into the Angelina story, and the threads of familial involvement in political unrest.

Order; an accusation of witchcraft against her; her pilgrimage to Assisi and subsequent move to Foligno; her connection to the monastery of Sant'Anna in that city; and her death, with ensuing veneration. The limit involves conscious elimination, for the moment, of Angelina's role at the monastery and her affiliation with the Observant tradition within Franciscanism, especially regarding juridical problems or the *bizzoche* form of life. It also postpones discussion about Angelina as the figure in a widespread "movement" within Third Order communities. Both topics pertain to later chapters of this study.

The methodology used in presenting the content of these selected hagiographic sources involves analysis of the links, if any, among authors, as well as pointing out the shifts and gaps in various works. The texts will be interpreted with a hermeneutic of suspicion, that is, going underneath the traditional meaning in order to extract a new level of understanding of who Angelina was and what she accomplished. To that end, questions will be raised about the possible intentions or agendas of any given writer at the time of authorship.

The hagiographic sources concerning Angelina of Montegiove present several problems, the first of which is identity. An immediate difficulty arises from the modern tendency to identify her based upon her place of birth (Montegiove) and the hagiographic use of family names: due to her membership in the families of the Counts of Marsciano and Corbara she is most frequently referred to as Angelina of Marsciano or Angelina of Corbara. But these are not exclusive forms of identification. In some cases her first name is shortened to Angela, and she has been called *Angela of Marsciano,*[5] *Angelina of Foligno,*[6] or *Angela of Civitella.*[7] This produces an additional problem, giving her a homonymous name with Angela of Foligno (1248-1309), another famous Franciscan tertiary associated with Foligno. Further confusion results from the fact that both Angela of Foligno and Angelina of

[5]*Rule and Constitutions of the Bernardine Sisters of the Third Order Regular of St. Francis* (Reading, Pennsylvania, 1963), article 9.

[6]Wadding, AM IX: 133.

[7]Mariano of Florence, *Tertii Ordinis*, f. 142v; AFH 29. Civitella is a place associated with her husband's family; Angelina is called "Countess of Civitella" in a number of sources, including Mark of Lisbon, below.

Montegiove are interred in and venerated at the same church: the church of St. Francis in Foligno.

The Earliest Sources: Franciscan Chronicles

Our foundational sources consist of relatively brief references in sixteenth-century Franciscan chronicles, annals, and compendia. The oldest source is that of Mariano of Florence (d. 1523), the *Compendium Chronicarum Fratrum Minorum* (compiled between 1519-23), which places Angelina in Foligno in 1415 and calls her the "most blessed Angelina, Countess of Civitella."[8] A later work by the same writer which treated the saints and "blesseds" of the Third Order, cited above, provides expanded information about Angelina: she was the Countess of Civitella from Abruzzo, was exiled by an unnamed king, and donned the attire of a member of the Third Order.[9] All of this is revealed in the first sentence of Mariano's entry. Sant'Anna is mentioned at the beginning of the next sentence, but as the name of a congregation, not the name of a monastery.[10] The remaining material in this entry, contained in some eighteen sentences,[11] refers to areas eliminated from consideration in this chapter—life at Sant'Anna as part of the Observant Tradition, and juridical issues—and reserved to Chapters Three and Four.

The second source is the mid-sixteenth-century chronicle of Mark of Lisbon, published in 1556.[12] Mark (d. 1591) complained that there was no *legenda* for Angelina; he then proceeded to synthesize a rudimentary one. In this work there is more focus on Angelina herself than in Mariano's work. Angelina is still identified as the "Countess of Civitella in Abruzzo," [13] but a motive is supplied for her arrival in Foligno: she and some relatives were inspired by the Holy Spirit how to live "a strict and holy life,

---

[8]Ibid.

[9]Ibid. I use "attire" rather than "habit" in order to avoid retrojection of a formal kind of garb associated with vowed religious women onto Angelina. She was never a solemnly professed nun. *Habito* in Italian is defined as "dress," "garment," or "clothes."

[10]Ibid.

[11]Ibid., 142v-144r; AFH XIV, 29-31.

[12]See note 2, above. Full text is in Appendix A, part I.

[13]Mark of Lisbon, *Chroniche* III, 27r.

with the attire and Rule of the Sisters of Penitence."[14] Mark correctly identifies Sant'Anna as a monastery, not a congregation, and reveals that Angelina is interred "in the church of the Friars Minor" there.[15] Then he adds a new element, that "before she took the attire of the Third Order," Angelina was accused before the King of Naples, to whom she demonstrated her innocence by carrying before him coals of fire in the folds of her clothes, without anywhere burning her clothes (see fig. 1, p. 26).[16] Mark does not specify what kind of accusation was made against Angelina. In addition, Mark relates that after "receiving the attire" of the Third Order (apparently after exoneration by the King), Angelina was persecuted and beaten for devoting herself to "works of piety" such as visiting the sick and restoring many to health.[17] He identifies neither her persecutors nor assailants. Lastly, it is in this source that Angelina is first credited with a miracle of reviving "a dead boy through her prayers," as well as with other miracles.[18] Both incidents are represented in an oil painting from the seventeenth century, currently preserved at the Monastery of Sant'Anna in Foligno (see figure 2, p. 27).

In the fourth part of Mark's *Chronicles*, continued by other friars after his death, we read:

> In the province of St. Francis in the Monastery of Sant'Anna in Foligno lies the body of the Blessed Sister Angelina, formerly Countess of Corbaria (sic) who, after her husband's death, renouncing the world, and distributing her goods to the poor, enclosed herself in this sacred place, putting on the habit of the Third Order of St. Clare, where by fasting, by prayer, and by afflicting her body, she reached such great perfection that she deserved to have

---

[14]Ibid. 27r. "Sisters of Penitence" or "Sisters of Penance" is a common way of identifying Franciscan Third Order women, just as "Brothers of Penance" identifies Franciscan Third Order men.

[15] Ibid. 27v.

[16]Ibid. This incident with the burning coals became a core element of the Angelina tradition, and provided an image that remains her iconographic symbol. See Servus Gieben, "L'iconografia di Angelina da Montegiove," in *La beata Angelina da Montegiove e il movimento del terz'ordine regolare francescano femminile*, ed. R. Pazzelli and M. Sensi (Rome: Analecta TOR, 1984), 181-201.

[17]Mark of Lisbon, *Chroniche* III, 27v.

[18]Ibid.

Our Lord perform many miracles for her, both during her life and after her death, and she is held in great veneration by all the people.[19]

There are two significant errors in this piece: first, Angelina is not interred in the Monastery of Sant'Anna; and second, the "Third Order of St. Clare" did not exist,[20] although a Third Order of St. Francis did. Perhaps the mistaken use of "St. Clare" helps explain the statement that Angelina "enclosed herself" at Sant'Anna. In any case, this is the earliest indication that an outside agenda, enclosure, has infiltrated the hagiography.

As had Mariano, so Mark of Lisbon presents material on the history of Sant'Anna and Angelina which is pertinent to Chapter Four of this work.

The third Franciscan chronicler to be cited, Luke Wadding (1588-1657), wrote contemporaneously with Ludovico Jacobilli, and used not only Jacobilli's material but also that of Mariano of Florence and Mark of Lisbon. Wadding's *Annales Minorum* is a monumental history of the Franciscan Order from the birth of St. Francis to 1540. It was compiled between 1625-54; references to Angelina are scattered through several volumes.[21] In Wadding's work, chronology and event determined what was written, not biographical considerations. Therefore, Wadding copied directly a large part of Jacobilli's material covering Angelina's birth, marriage, residence in Abruzzo, the pilgrimage to Assisi and move to Foligno, her death, and the first indications of veneration.[22]

---

[19]*Chroniche*, (Naples, 1680), 130, cited by D'Alatri-Pieper, note 30, pp. 99-100. I have kept the translation of "habit" used by this source only because it is used in association with the Order of St. Clare.

[20]See Lorella Mattioli, "Le Tertziarie Regolari Francescane della Beata Angelina e le loro Costituzioni," an unpublished dissertation submitted to the Istituto Superiore di Scienze religiose di Assisi (Assisi: 1992), 20; she attributes the earliest errors of this type to other works, such as Francisco Gonzaga, *De Origine Seraphichae Religionis* III, (Venice, 1603), 3. However, there is an interesting historical reality to be considered: at some point, the extern Poor Clares began to live according to the Rule of the Third Order Regular, even making profession according to its formula rather than that of the Urbanite Rule, given to the Poor Clares in 1263.

[21]See sources identified in note 3, above.

[22]Mattioli, 20. Raffaele Pazzelli, *Franciscan Sisters*, 65, states that Jacobilli follows Wadding's date with regard to Angelina's arrival at Foligno. This may be a translator's error, or may perhaps be correct. In the margins of the *Vite dell'Umbria*, however,

Since Jacobilli provides a more thorough and unified view of Angelina, Wadding's *Annales* receive attention in this study only when cited by other sources.

At this point, the existence of another source of hagiographic and historical tradition must be acknowledged, even though it will be mentioned very briefly in this chapter. The source is the tradition about Angelina as found within the unbroken history of the Tertiary Franciscans of Blessed Angelina, the religious congregation that descends from her reform of the monastery of Sant'Anna in Foligno. This tradition contains both oral and archival elements, and will be considered more fully in Chapter Four.

Fig. 1: Illustration of Angelina from the 1737 edition of Jacobilli's *Vita*. (With permission of Director of Friedsam Library, St. Bonaventure University)

Jacobilli does not cite Wadding, and gives the date 1385 for the foundation of Sant'Anna. *Vita* I gives 1395 as the date.

Fig. 2: Oil, dated from some time after Jacobilli's first *Vita*, located at Monastery of Sant'Anna. The scene recessed on the left side (behind Angelina's right hand) portrays the burning coals incident; the scene recessed on the right side (behind Angelina's back) portrays the resuscitation incident. (Photo by author; reproduced with permission.)

The Works of the "Official" Biographer: Jacobilli

Blessed Angelina of Montegiove was venerated by the people of the city of Foligno immediately upon her death,[23] yet no canonization process was ever initiated for her.[24] Ludovico Jacobilli did not publish the first edition of her *Vita* until 1627, nearly two hundred years after her death.[25] He later revised his work several

---

[23]See citation from *Croniche degli Frati Minori, dal P. S. Francesco*, parte quarta (Naples, 1680), 130, found in note 30, page 99 of Mariano D'Alatri, "Leggenda della beata Angelina da Montegiove: Genesi di una biographia," in *La beata Angelina da Montegiove e Il movimento del Terz'Ordine Regolare francescano Femminile*, ed. R. Pazzelli and M. Sensi (Rome: Analecta TOR, 1984), 33-46. Translation by Lori Pieper published as "The Legend of Blessed Angelina of Montegiove: Genesis of a Biography," *Greyfriars Review* 7 (1993): 95-107. Citations for this work will be designated as D'Alatri-Pieper.

[24]D'Alatri-Pieper, 105.

[25]Ludovico Jacobilli, *Vita della beata Angelina da Corbara, Contessa di Civitella, institutrice delle Monache Claustrali del Terz'Ordine di S. Francesco e Fondatrice in Foligno del Monastero di S. Anna Primo delli Sedici Che Ella Eresse in Diverse Provincie* (Foligno: A. Altieri, 1627). Hereafter cited as *Vita* I. Reissued by Francesco Medina (Montefiascone, 1737) as *Vita della Beata Angelina di Marsciano, Contessa di Civitella*

times.[26] All subsequent biographies of Angelina relate in some manner to Jacobilli's works. Most writers simply echo him; some add to the basic story; a few contradict him, particularly in regard to Angelina's family lineage.[27]

In Jacobilli's first edition, the portrait of Angelina is developed primarily through an ideological consideration: Jacobilli is promoting her importance as a woman "fiercely in love"[28] with virginity. He is no different from other hagiographers about whom Hippolyte Delehaye would offer the following caution:

> the hagiographer "shares the ideas of history current in his day. But he writes history with a special, clearly defined object in view . . . for he writes above all to edify [people], to 'do them good.' And so a new form of literature is born, part biography, part panegyric, part moral lesson."[29]

There is likewise "a community which has definite expectations concerning the outcome of the biographical record."[30] The purpose of sacred biography is to teach the truth of the faith by means of analysis of the example of a given individual; therefore, it has a

---

nella Provincia di Abruzzo nel Regno di Napoli Istitutrice delle Monache Claustrali del terz'Ordine di S. Francesco, hereafter cited as *Vita* IV.

[26]Ludovico Jacobilli, "Vita della B. Angelina Contessa di Civitella d'Abruzzo, Institutrice delle Terziarie Claustrali di S. Francesco. . . ." *Vite de'Santi e Beati di Foligno, e di Quelli, i Corpi de' Quali Riposano in Essa Città e Sua Diocesi* (Foligno: Alterii, 1628), 188-208; herafter cited as *Vite di Foligno*. This is Jacobilli's second version of Angelina's life. The third version of Angelina's life is found in Ludovico Jacobilli, "Vita della B. Angelina Contessa di Civitella d'Abruzzo, Institutrice delle Terziarie Claustrali di S. Francesco. . . ." *Vite de Santi e Beati dell'Umbria, e di Quelli i Corpi de 'Quali Riposano in Essa Provincia, con Le Vite de Molti Servi di Dio dell'Istessa*, II (Foligno, 1652), 33-35; herafter cited as *Vite dell'Umbria*. It is this latter work which holds most significance for this study. (See Appendix A, part II for the full text.) And a final set of corrections by Jacobilli is contained in *Additione e corretione alli 3 tomi de'Santi dell'Umbria posta al termine delle Vite de Beati dell'Umbria*, III (Foligno: Alterii, 1661).

[27]Especially F. Ughelli, *Albero et Istoria della Famiglia de'Conti di Marsciano* (Rome, 1667) and C. Simoni, *Il Castello di Monte Giove 'de Montanea* (Rome, 1925), who relies on Ughelli.

[28]D'Alatri-Pieper, 95.

[29]H. Delehaye, *The Legends of the Saints*, trans. Donald Attwater (New York: Fordham University Press, 1962), 54.

[30]Thomas J. Heffernan, *Sacred Biography: Saints and Their Biographers in the Middle Ages* (New York & Oxford: Oxford University Press, 1988), 20.

"catechetical imperative."[31] Jacobilli's work demonstrates all of these aspects of hagiography.

Not only was Angelina's *Vita* written for edification, it had a more practical purpose. Just prior to its publication, Rome had issued in 1625 "guidelines" governing the veneration of persons not officially recognized by the Holy See, that is, persons (including Angelina) for whom the formal process of beatification or canonization had not been accomplished. Cults for such individuals were prohibited, unless the cult had existed "from time immemorial."[32] Jacobilli's work may be construed, and probably *should* be construed, as an effort to demonstrate that Angelina, among many others, was an individual whose cult had existed both for a long time and with the approval of the Ordinary of Foligno, thus fitting the newest papal criteria.

The most concise version of the Jacobillian Angelina stories is the one contained in *Vite de Santi e Beati dell'Umbria*, published in 1652 and it serves as my primary reference. It is supplemented, as is helpful, with references to the 1737 edition of the first *Vita*, and secondary citations found in Mariano D'Alatri, Mario Sensi, and Lorella Mattioli or others.

According to Jacobilli, Angelina was born in Montegiove, not far from Orvieto. She was the daughter of Giacomo Montemarte of the Counts of Corbara and his wife Anna of the family Bugari, Counts of Marsciano of Perugia.

In the 1627 version, the earliest by Jacobilli, Angelina's date of birth is given as 1377. Although all of Jacobilli's works provide some basic details concerning her family lineage and the spiritual qualities of Angelina's life, many complications develop because

---

[31]Patrick Geary, *Living with the Dead in the Middle Ages* (Ithaca: Cornell University Press, 1994), 15.

[32]D'Alatri-Pieper, 105, note 61, gives the text from *Bullarium diplomatum et privilegorium santorum Romanorum Pontificum Taurinensis editio*, XIII, Augustae Taurinorum 1868, 309. The decree allows continued veneration according to the following criteria: "Declaring that . . . the [Holy See] does not wish in any way to prejudice or refer to those who have been honored, either by the common consent of the Church, and from time immemorial . . . or for a long time with the knowledge and tolerance of the Apostolic See or of the Ordinary." D'Alatri claims that Jacobilli's work was a great service to Angelina's followers, since her cult was clearly threatened by the 1625 decree. See D'Alatri-Pieper, 106.

he changed her date of birth several times in his revised writings.[33]

A later writer identifies five children, but Jacobilli mentions only Angelina.[34] Little that is verifiable is written about her childhood; the most important claim is that at the age of 12, Angelina made a secret vow of virginity.[35] Some time later, her father arranged for her marriage, which she opposed; in response, he threatened to allow her to starve.[36] At prayer, she is inspired to obey her father;[37] on her wedding night, she is visited and consoled by an angel.[38] Her husband is identified as Giovanni of Termis, Count of Civitella of Abruzzo.[39] She persuades her husband to also vow virginity, and they live in continence until his death.[40] As a widow, Angelina began to wear the attire associated with the Third Order of St. Francis. She also distributed all of her inheritance in pious works for the love of God.[41] She began to travel through the region exalting virginity, inducing "many young girls to make this vow."[42] Few of the events described by Jacobilli or his claims, however, can be verified.

Because of the number of young women following her exhortations, Angelina was denounced to the King of Naples (to whom she was subject) as a threat to the Kingdom, and called to the court of

---

[33]In the first version and in *Vite di Foligno*, the date of birth is 1377; in *Vite dell'Umbria* 33, the date of birth is 1367; and in *Additione e corretione*, 1357. Jacobilli gives no justification for making the changes. This is one of the more serious defects in his work. Mario Sensi proposes that the revisions were caused by Jacobilli's recovery of new source material, but offers no real proof. See "Documenti per la Beata Angelina," in *La beata Angelina da Montegiove e il movimento del terz'ordine regolare francescano femminile*, ed. R. Pazzelli and M. Sensi (Rome: Analecta TOR, 1984), 60; Appendices, 76-122. Hereafter cited as Sensi, "Documenti." Another major difficulty lies in Jacobilli's identification of Angelina's parents; her mother is incorrectly named Anna and connected to a Perugian branch of the Counts of Marsciano. This was corrected by Ughelli, as will be illustrated below.

[34]Ughelli identifies them as Notto, Niccolò, Mariano, Francesca, and Angelina; see *Albero et Istoria*, 58-60.

[35]Jacobilli, *Vita* IV, 4; *Vite dell'Umbria*, 34.

[36]Jacobilli, *Vita* IV, 6.

[37]Ibid.

[38]Ibid., 10.

[39]*Vite dell'Umbria*, 34; *Vita* IV, 5 identifies the husband as "Giovane, Count of Civitella."

[40]*Vite dell'Umbria*, 34; *Vita* IV, 12-13.

[41]*Vite dell'Umbria*, 34; *Vita* IV, 18.

[42]*Vite dell'Umbria*, 34; *Vita* IV, 20.

King Ladislas.[43] As she travelled to Naples, God revealed to her the King's intention to burn her at the stake. The means by which she could escape such a judgment was also revealed, hence, the burning coals.[44] Angelina was exonerated. And, while and while in Naples, she "resuscitated the only son of a Lady of Naples and did other miraculous acts."[45] Eventually she was exiled. In company with other young women committed to virginity, she made a pilgrimage to the tomb of St. Francis in Assisi, arriving there 31 July 1395.[46]

While in Assisi, according to Jacobilli's first telling of the story, Angelina was again inspired by "a voice from heaven, which said to her, 'Angelina, go to Foligno with your companions, because God wants you to build there a monastery of the Third Order of St. Francis.'"[47] This is the monastery of Sant'Anna.

These various inspirations are one way in which Jacobilli attempts to illustrate the holiness of Angelina. He also provides an image of piety and asceticism, as expected in a work of edification: Angelina is "the most clear mirror of every virtue," reflecting highest charity, prudence, humility, practicing daily fasts and continuous prayer, possessing the gift of tears and contemplative rapture.[48] According to all of Jacobilli's biographies of Angelina, she died 14 July 1435. Her body was transported to the church of St. Francis amid "much pomp and concourse of the people."[49]

---

[43] *Vita dell'Umbria*, 34; *Vita* IV, 21.

[44] *Vite dell'Umbria*, 34; *Vita* IV, 23.

[45] *Vita dell'Umbria*, 34; cf. *Vita* IV, 28. The incident of resuscitation is the second iconographic symbol for Angelina, but it is less frequently used than the burning coals.

[46] *Vita* IV, 36.

[47] *Vita* I, 52, cited by D'Alatri-Pieper, 97. In the third edition, however, Jacobilli made two important modifications in his information: he changed the "build a monastery" to "institute the reform of the nuns of the Third Order of St. Francis in enclosure with the three essential vows," and he changed the date from 1395 to 1385. (See *Vite dell'Umbria*, 34.) This illustrates Delehaye's point about a given hagiographer sharing the ideas current to the history of his day: in the first half of the 17th century, enclosure of religious women had been forcibly imposed in many places (including the monastery of Sant'Anna in Foligno). By the time Jacobilli wrote *Vite dell'Umbria*, he was undoubtedly promoting the "enclosed" life of Angelina as well as her cult.

[48] *Vite dell'Umbria*, 34-35; *Vita* IV, 58.

[49] *Vita dell'Umbria*, 35; *Vita* IV, 62.

At the end of his treatment of Angelina of Montegiove in the *Vite dell'Umbria*, Jacobilli offered a paragraph in which he discussed a mixed-identity problem concerning her. Already in 1652 two different women named Angelina were being treated by some authors as one: Angelina of Montegiove and "Sister Angelina of Teramo," a city in the Abruzzo region, whom Jacobilli identified as a member of the Second Order of St. Clare. Angelina of Teramo lived for a time in the monastery of Santa Lucia in Foligno, and died in Rome, 24 December 1459.[50] The issue of conflated biographies has remained a problem throughout the history of texts about Angelina of Montegiove even into the twentieth century.

A Partial Response of Historiography to Jacobilli

At this point, it is necessary to address, at least partially, four major questions about Jacobilli's work: the issue of Angelina's actual year of birth; her marriage; the trial at Naples; and the date of her arrival at Foligno. As has already been indicated (note 33), Jacobilli gave three different dates for Angelina's birth, moving backwards from 1377 to 1367 to 1357. Consequently, two vital problems are affected by the date: (1) Angelina's age at the time of her marriage and trial, and (2) the identity and age of the person before whom she was tried.

As to the first problem, historiographic research cited by Mario Sensi has produced four testaments of family members written between 1357 and 1363 which allow us to place 1357 as the correct date with relative certainty.[51] A testament dated 21 March 1357, given by Giacomo di Binolo, Count of Montegiove, gravely ill with the plague, named as heirs three sons and no daughters.[52] Further, Angelina is not named in a codicil written the next day.[53] The second testament is that of Angelina's grandmother, Fiandina,

---

[50]*Vite dell'Umbria*, 35. See pages 33-34 and 49, below, for other examples of conflated material.

[51]Sensi, "Documenti." Original testamentary documents (first identified in Ughelli, 62-63), are found in Orvieto, the Archives for the Work of the Duomo, n. 39, *Testamenti*, (1348-1363), cc. 90v, 109 (olim 90v, 111).

[52]Ibid., 50-51; the document itself is item I.e in Sensi's Appendix, 78, in "Documenti." The same text is found in Ughelli, 60.

[53]Ibid., Appendix I.a, 76. Sensi also cites Ughelli, 62.

dated 20 December 1360. In this document, Fiandina names the same three sons of her son Giacomo, but does not name her son, nor his daughters.[54] Sensi deduces from this that Giacomo of Binolo, father of Angelina, had died by this date.[55] But the two daughters, Francesca and Angelina, *are* named as heirs, with only two of their brothers (the eldest having died), in the testament of their mother, Alessandra, dated 20 September 1363.[56] Sensi therefore concludes that Angelina's date of birth was probably before March, 1357, when her father apparently died of the plague.[57] It is also significant that Mattioli warns that no conclusions ought to be made from the detail that daughters Francesca and Angelina are not mentioned in the father's testament and codicil, since the documents' legal purpose was to name those responsible for fulfillment of financial obligations to the Duomo, and given that there were three sons, no obligations were incumbent on the daughters.[58]

These documents also raise a second major question about Angelina's eventual marriage. Based upon the testaments just cited, if 1357 is both the correct date of Angelina's birth and of her father's death, and if other relatives died by 1363, then by the age of six or seven Angelina had lost both parents, a brother, and her paternal grandmother. Who, then, would have had the authority to arrange a marriage for her? Furthermore, the tradition surrounding Angelina's "virginal marriage" to Giovanni of Termis presents other problems. There are simply no extant historical records that the marriage ever occurred. For this reason, Mattioli proposes that Jacobilli's focus on the lifelong virginity and so-called "white marriage" of Angelina may be his particular method of using a contemporary hagiographical model that juxtaposes

---

[54]Sensi, "Documenti," 51 and Appendix I.b, 76-77; Ughelli, 59, 63.

[55]Sensi, "Documenti," 51.

[56]Alessandra's will is found in Sensi's Appendix I.d, pages 77-78. This is a family line proposed by F. Ughelli, not by Jacobilli. The details of the discussion follow in the next section of this chapter.

[57]Sensi, "Documenti," 51.

[58]Mattioli, 34, note 78. Felice Rossetti, in *La Beata Angelina dei Conti di Montegiove* (Siena: Industria Grafica Pistolesi, 1976), 42, cites the cultural tradition of not "over-dividing" inheritances as the explanation for not mentioning the daughters. He claims it would be a "grave error" to assume that they had not yet been born in 1357.

"defense of virginity" and marriage.[59] Sensi seems to think that proof of the marriage may yet be found, even though he noted that the Sacred Congregation for Rites had removed any expressions concerning the virginal marriage of Angelina from the texts of the Mass and Offices for her feast.[60] He also thinks that the story of the marriage may be the result of the conflation of stories about two distinct Franciscan tertiaries: the subject of this study *B. Angelina comitissa de Thermis Aprutii"*(Blessed Angelina, Countess of Termis of Abruzzo) and *"B. Angelina Fulginea comitissa Corbarae"* (Blessed Angelina of Foligno, Countess of Corbara).[61] There is also *Angelina of Teramo* mentioned by Jacobilli in *Vite dell'Umbria.*[62] Although Sensi does not mention this Angelina, his judgment about conflated biographies is most likely correct.

Jacobilli's wavering chronology also creates a third problem, the date for the episode of the trial at Naples and for Angelina's arrival in Foligno (assumed to be closely related chronologically). If the trial occurred in 1385, (also the year Jacobilli cited in *Vite dell'Umbria* as the founding year of Sant'Anna's monastery) Ladislas of Durazzo was only 8 years old and not yet King of Naples. In 1385, Angelina would have been 28, if born in 1357; or 18, if born in 1367. Pazzelli has offered the opinion that if we accept 1385 as the date of Angelina's alleged founding of Sant'Anna, then we must "discard the 'legend' of the trial in Naples at the Court of King Ladislas in 1384-1385."[63] If, however, Ladislas reached his majority in 1393,[64] this provides a more realistic date for the

---

[59]Mattioli, 39.

[60]See Sensi, "Documenti,' 52, n. 13.

[61]Sensi, "Documenti," 52, n. 13; the source of the two names is A. De Sillis, *Studia, originem, provenctum atque complementum Tertii Ordinis de poenitentia S. Francisci Concernentia* (Naples, 1621), 48.

[62]See above, page 32.

[63]Pazzelli, *Franciscan Sisters,* 65, n. 9. Pazzelli also identified the years between 1381-85 as "years of battle between Charles III (Ladislas' father) and Louis I of Angio (sic) for control of the Kingdom of Naples." See Pazzelli, 64, citing D'Alatri's *"Genesi di biografia,"* 42. Charles of Durazzo seems to have acquired the throne by murdering Queen Joanna I in 1382, and Ladislas was apparently equally ambitious: "In 1409 and again in the year of his death, 1414, Ladislas seemed about to swallow up the entire Papal States. . . ." Denys Hay, *Europe in the Fourteenth and Fifteenth Centuries* (London: Longmans, 1966), 180-83.

[64]See Sensi, "Documenti," 55, n. 18. Pazzelli, *Franciscan Sisters,* 65, n. 9, gives 1399 as the date of Ladislas' majority. Another source gives additional conflicting

inquisition of Angelina. Since in his first biography Jacobilli gave the date for Angelina's arrival in Assisi (*after* the trial at Naples) as 31 July 1395, the problem of the child-king raised by Pazzelli can be avoided.

One could, perhaps, consider the political connections surrounding Angelina, and attribute her summons to the King to a family connection to the *Angiobulli*[65] and the civil unrest of the time.[66] The larger historical context involves the rise of the communes against the feudal lords (*signori*) as well as the Guelf-Ghibelline conflict between the papacy and the Emperors. The family of Angelina seems for the most part to have supported the papacy.[67] In addition, it has been proposed that some of Angelina's family sided with the King of Naples while others fought against him in the early part of the fourteenth century.[68] Ughelli's work contains significant material about continuing problems of political intrigue in which the males of the various parts of the Marsciano family were involved during the 1380s.[69]

---

information, identifying 1386-1414 as the dates for Ladislas' reign as King of Naples, and 1390-1414 as dates for his reign as King of Hungary. According to this source, two branches of the house of Anjou were at war with each other. See *Webster's New Biographical Dictionary* (Springfield, MA: Merriam Webster, 1988), 575. See also Yves Rènouard, *The Avignon Papacy*, trans. Denis Bethell (Hamden, CT: Archon Books, 1970), 22, note 1. See also *A Short History of Italy from Classical Times to the Present Day*, ed. H. Hearder and D. P. Waley (Cambridge: University Press, 1966), 61-62.

[65]This is a name used by Jacobilli in *Vita* I, apparently an Italian reference to the house of Anjou.

[66]Pierre Péano, "*Angioni e Spirituali e la beata Angelina,*" in *La beata Angelina da Montegiove e il movimento del terz'ordine regolare francescano femminile*, ed. R. Pazzelli and M. Sensi (Rome: Analecta TOR, 1984), 29.

[67]Rossetti, *La Beata Angelina* 31. Orvieto is identified as one of the cities with Guelf loyalties; see Daniel Waley, *The Italian City-Republics*, 2nd ed. (London and New York: Longman, 1978), 121.

[68]See Rossetti, *La Beata Angelina*, 35, but he is without notes for the source of this information.

[69]Ughelli 60. Rossetti also describes the history of fratricidal wars waged for supremacy in Orvieto. See *La Beata Angelina*, 47-48. John Larner presents material on the conflict between the communes and the *signori* in the 13th century which might be applicable even in a later century to the Counts of Marsciano; the *signoria* was the rule of one man or family as the principal form of government in northern and central Italy. Larner claims that throughout central Italy, in the Papal States, the *signori* were virtually independent. See *Culture and Society in Italy 1290-1420* (London: B.T. Batsford, 1971), 16, 64, 98, 127. The independence of the *signori* may be at least partially attributable to the fact that the Avignon Popes had not been in Rome since 1305, when Clement VII left.

Whatever the political realities may have been, when both of Angelina's remaining brothers died of the plague in 1394, without heirs, there was a brief interval of anarchy and the political overthrow of Angelina's family, after which the *castello* passed to a collateral branch of the family, the Counts of Montemarte of Corbara.[70] Given such varied familial political entanglements, it seems more than likely that Angelina, if unmarried and still living in Montegiove, would have had to leave by 1395 because of the loss of male relatives who could inherit the title of "Count of Marsciano." In light of this, a most intriguing possibility arises: the trial before Ladislas did actually occur, perhaps in 1394-95, with the motive for the trial a political rather than religious one.

As to our fourth historical problem, the date of Angelina's arrival in Foligno, records indicate that the Monastery of Sant'Anna had been established by Paoluccio Trinci, not Angelina herself. Sensi presents documents which apparently substantiate this. One document from 1394 is a testament in which Angelina is not named and the place is called "the monastery of the countesses, or truly of friar Pauluccio (sic). . . ."[71] Another is the text of a letter to Paoluccio granting approbation for the building of a monastery. Sensi writes: "That place had been founded *ex novo* [from scratch] by Friar Paoluccio Trinci before February 14, 1388, as we deduce from the letter of approval" written by "Emilio Alferi of Asti, the Minister General of the Order of Friars Minor."[72] The monastery was intended to be for "all those women he [Trinci] judged capable of persevering in the life in a praiseworthy manner" and allowed

---

[70]Concerning the brothers' deaths, see Sensi, "Documenti," page 55, note 19, who cites Ughelli, 36 and Simoni, 69. For the period of anarchy, see Sensi, "Documenti," 55-56. Fourteen years before the deaths of Angelina's last two brothers, they had submitted their property to the commune of Perugia, on 9 June 1380. Ughelli, page 60, mentions an annual "tribute" of ten gold florins owed to Perugia as a result of this submission. Rossetti (*La Beata Angelina*, 56) asserts that the change occurred because when the commune of Orvieto had discontinued exemptions, privileges, and the like, it weighed down the family Marsciano with taxes and collections.

[71]Sensi, "Documenti," Appendix IIB, page 79, from the will *of "Marianus, qn. Puccipti Mactioli Gerardoni de Gerardonibus."* According to Sensi, the original document is found in the State Archives of Foligno, I/C Rinaldo di Cagno di Simone (1364; 1394).

[72]Sensi, "Documenti," 61. Text of letter is found in Appendix IIA, 79. Extracted from *AM* IX, under year 1388, 81-82, n. 3.

Paoluccio "to admit them under the title of the Third Order until such time as the Holy See should decide otherwise."[73] If there seems to be a measure of obscurity here, it is because the monastery was actually a *bizzocaggio*, a house of Italian Beguines, who had been forbidden in the bull *Sancta Romana* to live a common life under the Third Order Rule.[74] Here, again, we touch material to be treated in greater depth in subsequent chapters.

Given the kinds of problems associated with the biographies written by Ludovico Jacobilli, a revision or clarification by later authors was inevitable. Approximately forty years after the publication of Jacobilli's first *Vita* of Angelina (and fifteen years after Jacobilli's final revision in *Vite dell'Umbria*), Ferdinand Ughelli, an Orvietan related to the family Marsciano, published in 1667 an extensively researched family history: *Albero et Istoria*.[75] His work established a difference in both paternal and maternal titles, most especially in the identification of the family of Angelina's mother. Whereas Jacobilli called her "Anna, daughter of Giacomo of Angiolello Burgari of the Counts of Marsciano of Perugia,[76] Ughelli identified Angelina's mother as "Alessandra," possibly of the Salimbene family of Siena.[77] Subsequent writers are divided between the two genealogical lists; it is not without importance that the religious community at Sant'Anna, descended from the time of Angelina without interruption, uses Ughelli's lineage.[78] Ughelli's text indicates that Angelina died in 1439, but this most likely is an editor's error.[79]

Equally important, an examination of citations from Ughelli also supplies an interesting feature concerning the widowhood of

---

[73]Pazzelli, *Franciscan Sisters*, 66, citing Pierre Péano, *Les Religieuses Franciscaines Origines, Histoire et Valeurs Constantes*, ed. J. De Schampheler and Jean-François Godet (Lens, 1981), 24. Also cited by Rossetti, *La Beata Angelina*, 90.

[74]*Sancta Romana* made explicit reference to members of the "Third Order of Penance of St. Francis living in community;" see Sensi-Hagman, 341. In another interpretation, Pazzelli claims that this document was directed toward the *Fraticelli*, a heterodox group, and was later misapplied to orthodox tertiaries, both men and women. See *Franciscan Sisters*, 45.

[75]See note 27, this chapter.

[76]*Vite dell'Umbria*, 33; *Vita* IV was edited by Medina to include the names provided by Ughelli.

[77]Ughelli, 62. See also Mattioli, 23-24; and Sensi, "*Documenti*," page 49, note 4.

[78]See Mattioli, 35.

[79]Ughelli, 64; Mattioli, 53.

Angelina. He identified the Lady Lucretia of Simone of Genga (an important associate of Angelina) as the widow of Count Federico of the Counts of Montegiove, while he said nothing as to the status of Angelina of Giacomo of Montegiove as a widow although he would have known that the earlier literature had identified her as such.[80] This may mean that he does not affirm the tradition of her marriage to Giovanni di Termis.

In many of the biographies of Angelina that have been written since publication of Jacobilli's biographies and of Ughelli's *Albero et Istoria*, two main streams emerge: those which follow the familial identifications and hagiographic tradition of Jacobilli, and those which follow the familial identifications and historiographic tradition of Ughelli. Cross-currents of these two streams will be discernible in works discussed in the next two sections.

Nineteenth and Early Twentieth Century Interpretations[81]

It might be expected that by the end of the nineteenth century the impact of historicism had carried over into the "lives of the saints" tradition. But one work very clearly demonstrates such an expectation would have meant disappointment. Rather than a historical revision of Jacobilli, the next work to be examined is found in a more specifically Franciscan adaptation of the stories of Angelina: it is contained in the multi-volume *L'Aureola Serafica*.[82] This is an Italian translation of a work of French origin, useful in that it was published by the Franciscan friars at Quaracchi, the

---

[80]Cf. Mattioli, note 95, p. 38. The document to which she refers is found in *Albero et Istoria*, 66. Lucretia is named also as founder and inhabitant of a monastery in Todi, "of the Third Order of St. Francis, under the Institute of the Lady Angelina" and Angelina is identified as an "inhabitant of Foligno."

[81]The gap of over a century is due to the fact that the only major work about Angelina in the 18th century was Francisco Medina's re-publication of Jacobilli's first *Vita*.

[82]L. deClary and G. C. Guzzo, "*Beata Angelina di Marsciano, vedova . . .*" in *L'Aureola Serafica: Vite dei santi e beati dei tre ordini di S. Francesco*, vol 3. Italian edition, trans. Marino Marcucci (Quaracchi: Collegio San Bonaventura, 1899), 76-90. Material translated from the French edition by de Clary: *L'Auréole séraphique*, t. III, (Paris, 1897), 71-83. Another work on Angelina, an 1882 text of Antonio Cristofani, purported to be the edited *Leggenda* by Nicolas of Prato, although cited by some later writers, was said (by Cristofani's secretary) to be fraudulent, and so receives no consideration in this study. See Mattioli, 25; confirmed in conversation on 14 October 1995, in Foligno.

foremost *locus* of hagiography in the Franciscan world (whose work may be said to be comparable to that of the Bollandists). *L'Aureola* can be used, therefore, to interpret some parts of the story of Angelina's life up to her arrival in Foligno, both for purposes of a fuller sense of the narrative and for analysis of underlying truths buried within an admittedly historically-flawed account. This is appropriate because the last page of the *L'Aureola* material makes specific mention of Jacobilli's name as the source of its information.[83] While it relies heavily upon Jacobilli's first *Vita*, using much of the same material found there, it also contextualizes Angelina in terms of the Third Order and the Franciscan Observance.

L'Aureola introduces the story of Angelina with two pages of explanation concerning the birth of the Third Order of St. Francis and its evolution into two distinct branches, "Secular" and "Regular."[84] Within this context, the authors identify Angelina as having been ordered by God to propagate the Third Order Regular form of life.[85] As in Jacobilli, Angelina is portrayed as the founder in Italy of the Third Order Regular monasteries with enclosure and three solemn vows.[86] Biographical narration then begins, following closely the first *Vita* by Jacobilli. Angelina's father is Giacomo Angioballi and her mother is Anna, descended from the Counts of Corbara. At twelve, Angelina both loses her mother to death and makes the vow of virginity; she "consecrated her whole life to prayer, penitence, and works of charity."[87] At fifteen, she opposes a marriage arrangement (to Giovanni of Termis, Count of Civitella) that would "increase the luster of the house." Angelina is described as "most resolute to have no other spouse than Jesus Christ" and initially refusing to marry because of her private vow of chastity.[88]

The story continues to follow Jacobilli in various episodes, including the heavenly voice telling Angelina to obey her father, the angelic consolation on her wedding night, and the vow of her

[83]Ibid., 90.
[84]Ibid., 76-77.
[85]Ibid., page 76, note 1.
[86]Ibid., 77.
[87]Ibid., 77-79.
[88]Ibid., 79.

husband to live in perpetual chastity.[89] He dies two years later; Angelina adopts the clothing style of the Third Order, "openly makes a profession to renounce all the vanities of the world," and turns her home into a "school of virtue."[90] She and those who join her become involved in works of charity such as aiding the poor, visiting the sick, and assisting widows; in what perhaps reveals a post-Enlightenment and contemporary nineteenth century mentality, the gift of working miracles is deemed secondary to the "more precious" one of converting souls.[91] To this end, Angelina is clearly portrayed as making a kind of preaching tour, going from city to city in the Abruzzo region, converting sinners and inviting young girls to "complete hatred of vice and love of virtue."[92]

The charges of heresy which prompted the trial before Ladislas have quite specific components as enumerated in *L'Aureola*: wasting the patrimony of her husband, condemning matrimony, instructing to her own advantage the companions with whom she surrounded herself, going around like a vagabond, and being a cause of discord in families by inspiring the girls to abhor marriage.[93] Given these specific charges, one might ask on what theological basis the heresy issue was raised, since other than "condemning matrimony" most of the items listed are cultural imperatives rather than theological ones.

The trial before Ladislas, the miracle of burning coals, the resuscitation of the only son of one of the noble families of Naples are all recounted. After the latter miracle, Angelina secretly leaves Naples and returns to Civitella. On the way, however, she resumes her "work for the salvation of sinners and preaching virginity,"[94] with the result that many more young ladies place themselves under her direction and follow her to Civitella. This

---

[89]Ibid., 79-80.

[90]Ibid., 80.

[91]Ibid., 80. This perspective may be one of the effects of Vatican Council I (1869-70).

[92]Ibid., 80-81.

[93]Ibid., 81. These are not the same charges recounted by Jacobilli, who did not mention the wasted patrimony, the vagabondage, or an abhorrence of marriage. See *Vita* IV, 21.

[94]Cf. Wadding, IX, 132.

provokes new accusations and persecutions, and Ladislas "issued a decree of exile against Angelina and her company."[95]

L'Aureola also presents a richly-textured account of the start of the journey to Assisi. Angelina sells all her goods and distributes some of the money to the poor, "reserving the rest to supply the needs of her company."[96] Seemingly all of Civitella turns out for the farewell, full of admiration for her virtue and tearful that they are losing one so dedicated to the care of the poor, widows, and orphans.[97] And in what is unmistakably a completely imagined episode, Angelina and her entourage go to Montegiove, stopping at her father's *castello* to say farewell.[98] We are told that the old man was "profoundly moved by the virtue and courage of his daughter" and offered the *castello* as a place of asylum. Grateful though she was, Angelina obeyed her commission from God to journey to Assisi, arriving there with her companions on the thirty-first of July, 1395.[99]

Following an additional inspiration, Angelina and her group are reported as moving to Foligno on 3 August 1395. She immediately visited the church of St. Francis, "in order to implore his protection and that of Bl. Angela of Foligno, whose body reposes there."[100] She next presented herself to the bishop of Foligno, Giovanni de Angelo, and asked permission to establish a monastery, although as we have seen, she in fact entered a house already established by Paoluccio Trinci. According to the account in *L'Aureola*, the bishop "heard favorably" Angelina's request, and petitioned Pope Boniface IX for "the necessary faculties." The bishop also obtained land from Prince Ugolino Trinci, feudal lord of the city, land on which to construct the monastery.[101] When it was ready two years later, Angelina, supposedly at the age of 20, became abbess of the new community "and the following year the

---

[95]*L'Aureola*, 83.

[96]Ibid.

[97]Ibid.

[98]Ibid., 84. Cf. Jacobilli, *Vita* IV, 35.

[99]Ibid., 84. That *L'Aureola* fixes the year of the pilgrimage as 1395 once again gives evidence of heavy reliance on the first *Vita* by Jacobilli. See note 46 above.

[100]Ibid.; cf. Jacobilli, *Vita* IV, 39.

[101]Ibid., 84-85.

young women were allowed to make solemn vows of religion, to which they added the vow of perpetual enclosure."[102]

Here, too, the enclosure agenda, whether merely a repetition of Jacobilli's idea or the imposition of a late-nineteenth century one, is present. The monastery at Sant'Anna was an open monastery, one clearly *not* founded with enclosure, and it is historically demonstrable that it was one of the last in Foligno to submit to enclosure.[103] With regard to this particular issue, however, historical criticism would not have been applied by deClary because the writer would mirror both the attitudes of his era and the strictures of canon law, which still heavily supported perpetual enclosure for all religious women. Realistically speaking, it seems that there is limited use of the historical method anywhere in *L'Aureola Serafica*. Exact identification of "corrective writing" is limited to a few footnotes, none of which give primary source citations.

By the time *L'Aureola* was published, hagiographers and historians had long since begun to reexamine their relationship to each other. Even if evidence of historicism is minimally present in deClary's biography, the consequences of criticism founded in scientific exactness and a search for verifiable truth were moving beyond the texts of sacred scripture into the texts of lives of the saints. The historical-critical method became one of the tools that, if employed, could help unravel the tapestry of so-called amplifications woven together by writers such as Ludovico Jacobilli.[104]

Consequently, many of the texts (but not all, as already shown) about Angelina from this time period reflect the impact of historical criticism: the use Jacobilli made of the resources available to him came under scrutiny, while any of the "miracles" attributed to Angelina were also subjected to what Delehaye called the "straight path of scientific criticism."[105] In addition, two aspects of

---

[102]Ibid., 85. The age of 20 given here is again taken from *Vita* I, which gives Angelina's date of birth as 1377.

[103]The monastery of Sant'Anna did not accept papal enclosure until 1617. *Regola*, fol. 29, at the Archives of the Monastery of Sant'Anna, cited by Mattioli, 99.

[104] Delehaye, 172.

[105]Delehaye, 170. Geary, 9, states that the nineteenth century "positivist concern to separate 'fact' from 'fiction'" in hagiography has "largely subsided in modern hagiographic studies."

a more modern use of hagiographic sources emerge: they are seen as "a privileged source for the study of social values" and as possessing "an essential political dimension."[106] The material contained in *L'Aureola Serafica* clearly allows us to examine the story of Angelina from such perspectives, even if it represents an uncritical approach to the earlier writings.

The remaining examples within this chapter will examine several pieces which illuminate how historiography sometimes acted as a corrective to inexact practices of hagiographers. Two small encyclopedic entries are to be examined as representative of the body of material that exists. A century after the 1737 reprinting of Jacobilli's first *Vita*, and already 54 years before the purely hagiographic *L'Aureola* Life, the following entry by G.M. Romano appeared in the *Dizionario di Erudizione Storico-Ecclesiastica*:

> Angelina, blessed. Born in the year 1357, in Montegiove of Alfina,[107] in the territory of Orvieto. Ever since her early years, she began to enjoy the sweetness of intimate union with Jesus Christ, and when only 12 offered him a vow of virginity. In accord with the will of relatives, she was joined in matrimony, but never violated the obligation which she first made with the Lord. Her husband passed to a better life; she gave her earthly goods to the poor, wearing the dress of a Franciscan tertiary. Exercising the higher virtues for some years, she thought to reform the *monache* [nuns] of the Third Order of St. Francis, and in 1385, backed by pontifical authority, erected the first monastery in Foligno. . . . Finished with her mortal career, crowned with glorious virtue, she died in the embrace of God on 14 July 1435, in the 78th year of her life. Her body

---

[106]Geary, 12-13.

[107]With reference to the location of *Alfina*, and even its use, we have here an indication that historiography could cause problems as well as solve them. Felice Rossetti says that Romano, whom he calls Moroni, followed the work of F. Siri, *Sommario della vita della B. Angelina Monte Marte de'Conti di Titignano* . . . (Foligno, 1663); and Lorella Mattioli holds that Siri produced a work which caused much confusion by mixing up familiar names. See Mattioli, 23; and Rossetti, *La beata Angelina*, 12.

was buried in the church of St. Francis in Foligno, in a place of distinction.[108]

Romano appears to have combined elements of Jacobilli and Ughelli, but this is an assumption, since he provided no bibliographical references or notes. Jacobilli's ideology of virginity is clearly present, as are the identification of Angelina as a Franciscan tertiary, the idea that she was to reform Franciscan tertiary life, and the 1385 foundation date of the Foligno monastery. The style of presentation, what might be called "semi-edifying" language, evokes a sense of hagiography. At the same time, however, there are indications that a modern tone of historiography has influenced the shaping of this text. For example, Angelina's marriage is an arrangement "by relatives," an editorial decision presumably based on awareness of the accepted dates of Angelina's parents' deaths. "Passed to a better life" might be interpreted as a rational way of defining a theological notion of heaven. Similarly, rather than list specific ascetical practices or virtues of Angelina, Romano uses an inclusively simple phrase "Exercising the higher virtues. . . ."

In his brief text Romano avoided completely the problems of family lineage. And he provided an interesting nuance for at least one chronological aspect of Angelina's life: he said that Angelina "thought to reform" the Third Order nuns *after* exercising virtue "for some years." According to his chronology, Angelina was 28 when she arrived in Foligno. For our purpose, this interpretation reinforces the possibility of a political cause for her move from Civitella, for her itinerant preaching and the attraction of other women to her way of life, as suggested above.[109] At the very least, I interpret this to mean that Angelina did not necessarily go to Foligno immediately after either her husband's death or the trial at Naples (this last, a topic which Romano avoided.) There is also an interesting alteration with regard to the motivation behind Angelina's presence in Foligno: to **reform** *monache* (nuns)—but not enclosed nuns. Romano omitted the use of *claustrali* that appeared

---

[108]Gaetano Moroni Romano, "*Angelina* (b)," in *Dizionario di Erudizione Storico-Ecclesiastica*, 1840 ed. See Appendix A, part III for text.

[109]See pp. 39-41 above.

in every edition of Jacobilli's work; perhaps this is due to the influence of Ughelli's work.

A second example which illustrates cross-currents of hagiography and historiography shaping its content is another "encyclopedic" entry, taken from the *Dictionnaire d'Histoire et de Géographie Ecclésiastiques*. In the account by L. Oliger, published in 1924, the "edification factor" is greatly reduced and the writer seems to be moving (however well or badly) toward a quasi-historical point of view. In the bibliography for this entry, the first item cited is the original French version of the *vita* found in *L'Aureola Serafica*, and the contrast between that source and Oliger is remarkable. The entry is for "Angelina of Marsciano (Blessed)":

Angelina of Marsciano (blessed) foundress of a Third Order congregation of St. Francis, born at Montegiove (Umbria, Italy) in 1377—died in Foligno, 14 July 1435. Her father was Count of Marsciano and her mother was from the Counts of Corbara. Raised piously, Angelina at the age of 15 was given in marriage to Count Giovanni, Lord of Civitella in the Abruzzo, with whom she had lived for two years when death took him away. A widow at 17, she was received into the Third Order of St. Francis and devoted herself to a retired life with [other] honorable women looking to comfort the poor. By her example and her exhortations, many young noble women entered the religious life, and for her influence upon them she was accused of witchcraft to Ladislas, the King of Naples, who wanted to burn her as a witch. When she made her way to the court of Naples, Angelina was able to convince the king of her innocence. But some time later she was nonetheless exiled from the kingdom. In 1395 she went to Assisi with her companions. There she was inspired to found the monastery of Sant'Anna. . . . Angelina died in the 58th year of her life; she began to be venerated soon and Leo XII confirmed her cult. Her feast is fixed on July 15th.[110]

The chronology and genealogy cited come directly from Jacobilli, with the details of family heritage omitted. The marriage to Giovanni of Termis (although it is not treated as

[110]L. Oliger, "Angéline de Marsciano (Bienheureuse)" in *Dictionnaire d'Histoire et de Géographie Ecclésiastiques*, 1924 ed. See Appendix A, Part IV for full text.

"virginal") and the trial before Ladislas are also retained, which is noteworthy in light of the difficulties of chronological accuracy and historical verification. But two small segments of this entry signal what seems to be a shift in the presentation, if not the understanding, of the source texts. Although Angelina is identified as the founder of a congregation, which is historically inaccurate in one sense,[111] the use of the term implies a recognition of the unbroken history of the group of women descended from Angelina and the transformation of the group into a "religious congregation." Secondly, Oliger openly uses the term witchcraft, not heresy; this is the most significant aspect of Oliger's entry, since it implicitly admits the historical reality of European witchcraft trials.

From a feminist perspective, it is possible to suggest that Oliger's witchcraft interpretation of Angelina's story is consistent with an early manifestation of the vengeful inquisition that engulfed Europe in the sixteenth century.[112] A consideration may be once again proposed: the incident of Angelina's trial as a heretic-witch would have been consistent with social attitudes and possible within an historical narrative and is not merely a hagiographic device, although the "miracle" of Angelina's escape from the flames enhanced the edification paradigm that governed Jacobilli's work. The eventual banishment of Angelina was not unusual after trial at a secular court, and effectively rid the Kingdom of Naples of a "dangerous individual."[113] If one accepts the suggestion that the role of witch was often ascribed to those who deviated from set societal roles or those whose power was feared, it is not difficult to see why Angelina would have been suspect.[114]

The possibility becomes even more intriguing if one applies the concept of boundary maintenance to both the issue of witchcraft and to the socio-political realities of Angelina's world. Nachman Ben-

---

[111]See material on Mariano of Florence, page 23 above.

[112]Richard Kieckhefer, *European Witch Trials: Their Foundations in Popular and Learned Culture 1300-1500* (Berkeley: University of California Press, 1976), 10. For years between 1385-94, Kieckhefer indicates a doubling in the number of trials in Europe, from five to ten per year: see graph, page 11.

[113]Brian P Levack, *The Witch-hunt in Early Modern Europe* (London & New York: Longman, 1987), 83-84.

[114]Cf. Mary Daly, *Beyond God the Father* (Boston: Beacon Press, 1985), 64.

Yehuda, citing the work of Durkheim on boundary maintenance and social deviance, proposes that the multi-layered changes—social, institutional, intellectual—within European society in the fifteenth century were so significant that they completely altered the "dominant outlook" which gave order to society.[115] The hierarchy of nobility, lords and vassals—unquestionably the dominant outlook—was rapidly breaking down. Part of the breakdown stemmed from unbalanced demographics: a higher number of women married at a later age, or never married at all.[116] A second acknowledged factor in social change was the devastation resulting from repeated episodes of the plague throughout the fourteenth century.[117] Although figures vary widely, and are only estimates, it is thought that Italy may have lost half its population as a result of the 1348 plague.[118] In the adult years of Angelina, the Black Death contributed to a population imbalance in which women outnumbered men. More "unattached women" —those not subject to a husband or a father—led to preachers' questioning of just how so many women escaped the plague. And the answer that often emerged was that "the Devil protected his own".[119]

The applicability of the historical background to the biography of Angelina is startling. She belonged to a family that was involved in political change and upheaval in Orvieto; she espoused virginity and publicly preached its efficacy, thus

---

115 Nachman Ben-Yehuda, "Witchcraft and the Occult as Boundary Maintenance Devices," in *Religion, Science, and Magic In Concert and In Conflict*, ed. Jacob Neusner, Ernest S. Frerichs, and P. V. P. M. Flesher (New York & Oxford: Oxford University Press, 1989), 235-36.

116 For data on the average age of marriage in Tuscany in the late Middle Ages, see S. Shahar, *The Fourth Estate: A History of Women in the Middle Ages* (London and New York: Routledge, 1983), 180; also, David Herlihy and Christiane Klapisch-Zuber, *Tuscans and Their Families: A Study of the Florentine Catasto of 1427* (New Haven and London: Yale University Press, 1985), 87, table 3.10.

117 Ben-Yehuda, 237.

118 See Orville Prescott, *Lords of Italy: Portraits from the Middle Ages* (New York: Harper and Row, 1972), 285. John Larner cites other years of severe plague as 1360-1363, 1371-1374, 1382-1384, 1398-1400, and 1410-1412, and comments on consequent economic decline and political instability. See *Culture and Society in Italy 1290-1420* (London: B. T. Batsford, 1971), 125. Samuel K. Cohn, Jr., *The Cult of Remembrance and the Black Death* (Baltimore & London: Johns Hopkins University Press, 1992) presents an interesting study of post-plague patterns of bequests in six Italian towns/cities.

119 G.R. Quaife, *Godly Zeal and Furious Rage: The Witch in Early Modern Europe* (New York: St. Martin's Press, 1987), 88.

undercutting marriage, a major social-political-economic institution; she disbursed her inheritance rather than use it to attract power or prestige; she travelled freely from place to place without apparent male supervision; and she was not intimidated by the anger of the feudal lords, gathering around herself other women who had responded to her example and exhortations. Ben-Yehuda uses an immensely clear designation for the kind of dichotomy Angelina represents: decentralized individuals vis-à-vis centralized authority and institutions.[120] She moved beyond every boundary of her day, unquestionably acting as leader of "decentralized individuals" in conflict with the centralized authority of the King of Naples. In light of such interpretive possibilities, an acceptance of the accusation of witchcraft as historically plausible is not without merit.

Post World War II Works

For the most part, the works to be discussed in this section continue along the trajectory of Jacobilli's work, but in a more succinct way. Generally speaking, historical perspective rather than spiritual edification had become the controlling principle of ecclesiastical historiography in the second part of the twentieth century, and with the possible exception of the work by Felice Rossetti, what H. Jedin calls the "regalistic and rationalistic concepts" of the church of the nineteenth century had been expunged.[121] However, as in the preceding section of this chapter, there are exceptions which demonstrate the complex nature of the confusion surrounding Angelina as well as the subjective agenda or recalcitrant outlook within some of the pieces selected.

The first example, an entry in the *Biliotheca Sanctorum* by Germano Cerafogli, immediately demonstrates continuation of a mis-identification that first appeared in the fourth part of the *Chroniche* of Mark of Lisbon and in Gonzaga in 1603:[122]

> Angelina of the Counts of Marsciano, blessed. Clarisse, foundress of the women's Third Order Regular, born in

[120] Ben Yehuda, 241-42.

[121] H. Jedin, "Historiography, Ecclesiastical," in *New Catholic Encyclopedia*, 1967 ed.

[122] See notes 19 and 20 above.

> 1377 in the *castello* of Monte Giove (Orvieto). Orphaned of her mother at 12, she made a vow of virginity, and when in 1393 her father forced her to marry, God sent her, on the evening of her wedding, his angel to reassure her. Surprised by her husband while in conversation with the heavenly messenger, she told him the secret of her pure soul, and he swore to imitate her. After a year, Angelina became a widow; she distributed all her goods to the poor and wore the humble habit of St. Francis, making herself a promoter of virginity and purity of attire, followed by other young women who abandoned the world for God. This instigated the anger of the feudal lords, who induced Ladislas, King of Naples, to decree her exile, together with her companions. Departing with these women from Civitella on 31 July 1395, they went together to Assisi to visit the tombs of St. Francis and St. Clare; from there she took herself to Foligno, where in 1397, with her followers, she promised the three evangelical vows. The first nucleus of regular Franciscan tertiaries issued from these [beginnings]. . . .[123]

Angelina is identified as a "Clarisse, foundress of the women's Third Order Regular." Somehow, the distinction that evolved between the 17th and 20th centuries between Second Order women and Third Order Regular women is ignored. The error is all the more problematic since Cerafogli reiterated that "the first nucleus of regular Franciscan tertiaries issued from" Angelina's monasteries.[124] The key phrase is "regular Franciscan tertiaries." As subsequent chapters will demonstrate, an earlier extension across Europe of the kind of life associated with tertiary monasteries occurred before Angelina, and of "regular tertiary monasteries" as a result of her influence.

It is also evident that the entry was written for hagiographic purposes more than historical ones: the apparition of the angel on the wedding night is retained, and the motive for her distribution of her wealth to the poor is attributed as a *fuga mundi*—flight

---

[123]Germano Cerafogli, "Angelina dei Conti di Marsciano, beata," in *Bibliotheca Sanctorum*, 1961 ed.

[124]Ibid., 1232.

from the world, while the least likely date for Angelina's birth (1377) goes uncorrected.

Nevertheless, there is an important indication in the text which lies closer to the truth about Angelina as a member of the Third Order than some earlier texts. Cerafogli describes Angelina as making herself a "promoter of . . . purity of attire." That phrase is probably the most accurate description used in the texts with regard to what it meant for Angelina to be recognized as having joined the Third Order. The *Rule of Nicholas IV* in its chapter "On the Manner of Dress" states that women members were to wear clothing that was of common cloth; they could wear a black or white skirt, but without pleats; they should wear no ribbons or silk cords, use only lambskin fur, and should not wear any "ornaments of the world."[125] These details constitute the kind of "purity of attire" that would have proclaimed Angelina's membership in the Third Order.

In conspicuous contrast to most of what Cerafogli wrote is another 1961 publication, the entry on Angelina in the *Dizionario Biografica degli Italiani* by Alessandrini.[126] The author reprises the biographical information about Angelina in clear historical terms, consulting (according to his bibliography) not only the chronicles, Jacobilli, and Simoni (who used Ughelli), but adopting a twentieth-century historical perspective as well. Consequently, he moves through a detailed explanation of the date-of-birth discussion and settles on "most probably between 1357-1360" as the solution.[127] Alessandrini gives a full explanation of the family testaments covered above, although he holds that Angelina must have been born after her father's death, or else her father would have mentioned her.[128] Alessandrini explains that his dating corrects both Wadding and the "apologetic, romantic biography" by Jacobilli.[129] He attributes to the hagiographic tradition the specific aspect of a *chaste* marriage to Giovanni of Termis, but he

---

[125]*The Rule of Nicholas IV*, Chapter III, nos. 2-4, as found in Stewart, 176-77.

[126]A. Alessandrini, "Angelina da Montegiove (A. da Marsciano, A. da Corbara), beata," in *Dizionario Biographica degli Italiani*, 1961 ed.

[127]Ibid., 207.

[128]See pp. 32-33 above.

[129]Ibid., 208. Regarding Alessandrini's disagreement with Mattioli on Angelina's probable date of birth, I tend to agree with the latter rather than with Alessandrini.

seems not to deny the fact of the marriage itself. He accepts the role of Angelina as preacher even as he acknowledges that it as both "dangerous to feudal institutions" as well as the cause of the accusation of witchcraft.[130] In discussing the move to Foligno, Alessandrini omits the aspect of an *enclosed* monastery, one of Jacobilli's accretions, holding only that Angelina was inspired to establish a "true and proper women's monastery for tertiaries."[131]

There is, however, one strange element to Alessandrini's work: he gives a different date for the death of Angelina: 4 July 1439, basing the date on an entry in the *Bullarium Franciscanum.* He and Ughelli are the only two sources which use this date, which must be explained as an error of the type Jacobilli warned against in the text of *Vite dell'Umbria.*[132]

Both Cerafogli and Alessandrini are pre-Second Vatican Council texts. A post-conciliar representation of Angelina might be expected to present something akin to Alessandrini's work, with perhaps some additional corrections. However, this did not happen. In what can be judged to be the result of a facile consultation of very limited sources, Mariano D'Alatri produced in 1974 a brief, somewhat vague biographical description:

> Angelina of Marsciano, blessed. Foundress of a congregation of Tertiaries of St. Francis called the Franciscans of Blessed Angelina. Born in Montegiove (Grosseto) in 1377 to the count of Marsciano and the countess of Corbara, died at Foligno (Perugia) 14 July 1435. Educated piously, at fifteen she was married to Giovanni, Count of Civitella in Abruzzo. Became a widow at 17; joined herself to the Franciscan Third Order and together with her ladies in waiting *(dame d'onore)* took to living *ritiramente* (retreatedly, in seclusion) dedicating herself to works of piety and mercy toward the poor. In 1395 she took herself on pilgrimage to Assisi, to be inspired there to establish a monastery of tertiaries, then going to that of Sant'Anna in Foligno. . . .

---

[130]Ibid. With reference to the age of Ladislas, Alessandrini notes that in 1385 he was a child of eight, and in Hungary with his father, not at Naples sitting at court. Alessandrini opts for 1395 as the year Angelina went to Foligno and Sant'Anna.

[131]Ibid.

[132]*Bullarium Franciscanum* I (1929), n. 3. See also page 57 above, for Ughelli's use of the same date and Appendix A, Part II for the text of *Vite dell'Umbria.*

Died at Foligno, in the monastery of Sant'Anna. Her cult as blessed was confirmed on March 8, 1825.[133]

D'Alatri affirms that Angelina founded a congregation of tertiaries of St. Francis and then very briefly repeats the main facts of her life, giving the 1377 date of birth, avoiding the problems of genealogy and accepting without comment her marriage and widowhood. He accepts her connection to the Third Order, the pilgrimage to Assisi, and the inspiration to go to Foligno. At first reading, D'Alatri seems not to have had any critical awareness of Sant'Anna's having pre-dated Angelina's presence there, and appears to have accepted at face value the Jacobillian picture of Angelina. It is tempting to use this text as a "worst case scenario" for inadequate scholarship. Except for one thing. There is one line that can be said to be more striking than any other, and it has significant meaning: as a tertiary, Angelina took to living *ritiramente*, that is, in seclusion, while dedicating herself to works of piety and mercy toward the poor.[134] D'Alatri here picks up on a thread that existed in the very earliest Franciscan chronicles and was also used by Oliger: "separateness" from the world, but not with the connotation of the monastic *fuga mundi*–flight from the world paradigm found in Cerafogli or Jacobilli.[135] There is distinct value in mentioning the concept of seclusion because we shall see that it is a constitutive element of the life of Angelina at Sant'Anna, and of the houses which were part of the movement of her form of life to other monasteries throughout Europe.

These brief encyclopedic descriptions of Angelina provide adequate illustrations of post-World War II sources. However, one more source must be commented upon, briefly. It is a full-length, twentiethth-century work on Angelina Montegiove published by Felice Rossetti in 1976. Although cited above several times, there are major difficulties with the work. First of all, it is controlled by

---

[133]Mariano D'Alatri, "Angelina da Marsciano, beata," in DIP, 1974 ed. This is the same Mariano D'Alatri whose "Genesis of a Biography" has been repeatedly cited in my first chapter. Obviously, his understanding of Angelina has gone through major change.

[134]Ibid.

[135]For Mark of Lisbon, see pages 23-25, above; for Oliger, see page 45 above.

a point of view that is hagiographic and exhortatory, more reminiscent of Jacobilli than of a critically insightful narration or analysis of Angelina's story. Secondly, it does not distinguish between hagiography and historiography. Sr. M. Clotilde Filannino, currently the Minister General of Angelina's congregation, has written that Rossetti "badly used" Filannino's thesis in his biography of Blessed Angelina and caused more confusion about her existence. He did not keep in mind the peculiar character of the phenomenon which took place in the sphere of the Franciscan Third Order between the end of the 14th century and the beginning of the 15th century. Filannino also criticizes Rossetti because he "gathered together every item, very often second-hand, without worrying about its historical reliability, placing every source on the same level."[136] Consequently, I have used Rossetti's work mostly as a supplementary source for documentation.

Conclusion

What endures in the story of Angelina, then, after initial applications of the historical-critical method to the work of her biographers? At this point, her literary history reveals a number of foundational elements: (1) Angelina of Montegiove was a member of an Orvietan family of noble status and some power; (2) she was orphaned as a child; (3) she may have been married to a nobleman from the region of Abruzzo and if so, the marriage likely remained virginal; (4) she became a Franciscan tertiary; (5) she was joined by other women who responded to her preaching about virginity; (6) she and her companions were exiled from the Kingdom of Naples towards the end of the fourteenth century; (7) she became connected to and lived at the Monastery of Sant'Anna in Foligno; and (8) upon her death, she was immediately venerated by the people of that city.

---

[136]Published under the name of Anna Filannino, "La Beata Angelina dei Conti di Marsciano e le sue fondazioni (communicazione)," in *Prime Manifestazione di Vita Communitarie Maschile e Femminile nel Movimento Francescano della Penitenza (1215-1447)*, ed. R. Pazzelli and L. Temperini (Rome: Analecta TOR, 1982), 451. Filannino and Mattioli have edited and published a compilation of primary texts and commentaries: *Biografie Antiche della Beata Angelina da Montegiove: Documenti per la storia del monastero di S. Anna di Foligno e del Terz'Ordine Regolare di s. Francesco* (Spello: Centro Italiano di Studi sull'Alto Medioevo, 1996).

In terms of a new interpretation, a core of truth can be extracted about the qualities and character of Angelina herself. Underneath the texts cited, once the rhetoric of edification is peeled back and the specious certainty of dated events is challenged, a significant number of consistent insights and probable relations remain. Obviously, Angelina was, even as a laywoman without any connection to life in a monastery, a highly effective itinerant preacher. Her message bore fruit in the cities and towns of Abruzzo, so much so that she provoked the wrath of the noble lords of the kingdom of Naples. It bore fruit as well, we are told, in Orvieto, and on the way to Assisi. Angelina was an undeniably charismatic person, one who could attract and keep followers in spite of persecution and exile; other women were willing to follow her regardless of her status as an outcast, so she had to have possessed leadership qualities of some kind.

The element of *ritiramente* or seclusion referred to by some writers as part of Angelina's life at Sant'Anna provides an entry into a revised picture of her life there. First of all, it could be the element that allowed Jacobilli's imposition of the ideal of full enclosure onto the story of the early life at Foligno, even though it is now clear that full enclosure at Sant'Anna in Angelina's lifetime is a historical inaccuracy. Secondly, the "retired life" of Angelina is a link to an important aspect of the roots of the Franciscan movement. That link is found in the life and work of Paoluccio Trinci, a Friar Minor. It was Trinci who became, before his death in 1390/1391, one of the more important reformers within the heritage of the Friars Minor that flowed from the Spirituals and ripened into what became known as the Observant Reform.[137] A "retired life," the eremitical aspect of Franciscan life, and a communal life mixed with works of service to one's neighbor emerged in the Franciscan world once again just as Angelina left Civitella and settled with her companions among the *bizzoche* at Foligno. The integration of these several concepts within the Observant tradition shall now be examined.

---

[137]In light of the promise (See Chapter One) of "loving care and special solicitude" made by Francis as a foundational aspect of life at the inception of the Franciscan movement, one might wonder why Angelina's connection to Paolo Trinci or other friars after Trinci's death is not recorded in the context of her biography by Jacobilli or deClary.

CHAPTER THREE

The Third Order and The Observance

Because the preceding chapter covered only those parts of the interpretive tradition relevant to Angelina's personal life, it deferred discussion of three areas: the hagiographic materials which treat Angelina's role at Sant'Anna, that monastery's association with the friars of the "Observant Tradition," and a form of governance that would today be called a federation of Third Order women. Those topics will be discussed in the next chapter; but in order to address that material in the most lucid way, it is first appropriate to establish a broader framework in terms of ecclesial and cultural circumstances and a narrower framework within Franciscan circumstances. Therefore, the present chapter briefly considers four areas and illustrates the connections among them: the presence of the Beguine phenomenon in Italy; the desire of the Church to regulate that phenomenon; the transition of the Friars Minor into two *de facto* branches, "Conventuals" and "Observants"; and the place of Paoluccio Trinci in the formation of the ideals that eventually animated life at the Monastery of Sant'Anna. Once these contextual parameters are established, the discussion will move, in Chapter Four, to Angelina's life at Sant'Anna and the movement of "tertiary observance" that arose in consequence of Angelina's leadership.

Italian Beguines—Or Tertiaries?

The first chapter cited Franciscan sources which indicated that the preaching of Francis and the earliest friars had had a wide impact on men and women who remained "in the world" but desired to adhere to the Gospel more closely than ordinary Christians. These people eventually became known by several different names, including Penitents of St. Francis, members of the Third Order of St. Francis, and so on. From this last name derived the designation "tertiaries." Also present "in the world" at the same time was an immensely widespread and diverse manifestation of renewed religious fervor among laity which pre-dated the Franciscan movement. A variety of labels described such people; the most perduring one is "Beguines and Beghards." It is to the relationship between "tertiaries" and Beguines that we turn our attention.

In its simplest sense, Beguine life refers to a phenomenon that surfaced across Europe in the latter part of the twelfth century which was gradually and only partially institutionalized by the end of the fourteenth century. Beguine women lived a "more religious" life (either singly or in small groups) in their own homes, retaining their personal property. They did not vow poverty and were self-supporting. But they used their financial resources for the good of others, and in this way lived in imitation of the Gospel poverty of Jesus and the apostles. Beguine life can be viewed as a specific adaptation of the *vita apostolica* to cultural conditions which governed women's lives in the High Middle Ages, yet at the same time stretched the limits of those conditions, at least for a while.

Technically not nuns, these laywomen lived a semi-religious life that definitely broke the mold of "true" religious life as it was understood by a patriarchal church and society. Often, Beguines exempted themselves from the cultural imperative of male supervision. As urban women they were receptive to new ideas, including the "ideas of charity, renunciation and mendicant poverty in opposition to the avidity of riches."[1] A provocative combination operates here: not mendicant in the literal sense, as were the Friars Minor and the Second Order, Beguines viewed poverty as a means to an end. Their reaction against the wealth and ostentation of secular society meant for them a life of service to the poor and sick. Service in response to social need became, in many instances, their primary form of work.[2]

Until recently, little attention, if any, has been given to connections between the Beguine phenomenon and the Franciscan movement because it was thought that the Beguines were a northern reality, absent from the Italian peninsula. Many writers followed Grundmann and McDonnell in limiting their discussion of

---

[1] Bolton, "Frauenfrage," 261.

[2] See Fiona Bowie, Introduction to *Beguine Spirituality*, trans. Oliver Davies (New York: Crossroads, 1990), 24. See also C. H. Lawrence, 231-32.

Beguines to the Rhineland and Brabant.[3] Lester K. Little, for all the work he has done on Franciscan social influence, does not recognize an Italian Beguine situation.[4] More recently, however, scholars have re-examined the "absence" of Italian Beguines. Less than twenty years ago Denys Hay questioned where the beguinages in Italy were, suggesting that they might have been overlooked by historians; he saw the *case sante* in Rome (up until then thought of as houses of Dominican and Franciscan tertiaries) as possibly being incorrectly labeled.[5] His hypothesis finds support in the work of Brenda Bolton, who has accepted the reality of the Italian Beguines. She writes of Innocent III bringing all *bizoke* (sic) women in Rome into a *universale cenobium monialium* in the 1190s.[6]

More specifically, Romana Guarnieri unequivocally grouped together as part of the same phenomenon the *begijnen, beguines*, and *Beginen* of the Low Countries, France and Germany *and* the *pinzochere, beghine*, and *bizzoche* of Italy.[7] The *Dizionario Degli Istituti di Perfezione* entry for "pinzochere" describes late twelfth-century pious, devout men and women almost always living in the world, singly or in groups, leading lives of piety and penance.[8] In the 1940s Heribert Holzapfel had referred to Angelina's group as *bizzochae* and claimed that the common name for lay tertiaries was *pinzocare*.[9] The *DIP* also includes *pinzochere* among the various names used for people who exemplify a penitential,

---

[3] See the landmark works of Herbert Grundmann, *Movimento religiosi nel Medroevo* (Bologna: Mulino, 1980) and Ernest W. McDonnell, *The Beguines and Beghards in Medieval Culture with Special Emphasis on the Belgian Scene* (New York: Octagon Books, 1969).

[4] See Lester K. Little, *Religious Poverty and the Profit Economy in Medieval Europe* (London: Paul Elek, 1978), 128-34. Perhaps this is due to his focus on the work of James of Vitry concerning Marie d'Oignes, a northern European phenomenon.

[5] Denys Hay, *The Church in Italy in the Fifteenth Century* (Cambridge: Cambridge University Press, 1977), 98. It seems that they could have been *bizzoche* (Italian Beguine) houses which evolved into tertiary communities.

[6] Brenda Bolton, "Daughters of Rome: All One in Christ Jesus," in *Women in the Church*, ed. W. J. Shiels and Diana Wood (Cambridge, MA: B. Blackwell, 1990), 101-16.

[7] See Romana Guarnieri, "Beghinismo D'Oltralpe e Bizzochismo Italiano tra il secolo XIV e il secolo XV," in *Analecta TOR* (1984): 1-13.

[8] Romana Guarnieri, "Pinzochere," *Dizionario degli Istituti di Perfezione*, 1980 ed.

[9] H. Holzapfel, *The History of the Franciscan Order*, trans. A. Tibesar and G. Brinkmann (Teutopolis, IL: St. Joseph Monastery, 1948), 547.

reformist aspect of the Church at that time. Characteristics assigned them include penance, poverty, continence, and connection with a particular charitable work, usually involving the sick.[10]

If one examines literature about the Beguines, their characteristic dress was grey[11]; at one time they were ordered to stop wearing the "habit of the Minors" (which was also grey); they did not take vows; and one of their chief forms of charitable activity was hospice work. In reality, *bizzoche*, *pinzochere*, and *tertiary* are virtually untranslatable into English as separate terms; in Italy, do they not mean essentially the same thing?

Therefore, one of the presuppositions of the remainder of the present study is that multi-layered combinations of varied aspects of *bizzoche*-tertiary patterns of life constitute part of the rich heritage of Franciscan Third Order women; these patterns heretofore have been insufficiently recognized. Accepting "Beguine" as inclusive of the Italian *bizzoche* phenomena has major implications in any study of the relationship of women to the Friars Minor.

These women often lived a common life but maintained a certain independence and private "space." Group participation was limited to spiritual events such as the Mass, vocal prayer, and "chapter" meetings regarding the discipline of the house. Reexamining the tertiary-*bizzoche* affiliation in light of recent historical findings regarding the institutionalization of women's religious movements in the late fourteenth and early fifteenth centuries has significant implications, especially in light of the

---

[10]There is also an intriguing *possible* etymological link of *bizzoche* to the Franciscan movement. The *Cambridge Italian Dictionary* defines *bizzoco* as "a Franciscan tertiary." See *The Cambridge Italian Dictionary*, gen. ed. Barbara Reynolds (Cambridge: Cambridge UP, 1962), 572. The *DIP* also includes *pinzochere* among the various names used for these people. A more interesting definition appears in an earlier source, *An Italian Dictionary*, published in 1925, in which the entry reads: "*Pinzochero-a* (It. *pizzochero*, lengthened form of *Pizzoco*, i.e., *Bizzoco*, a corruption of *Bigio*, from the grey dress of the Franciscans); devotee, one who wears the habit of an Order, but has taken no vows." See *An Italian Dictionary*, ed. A. Hoare (Cambridge: University Press at Cambridge, 1925), 458. The entry for *pinzochere* in *DIP* says that the terms *bizzoco*, *pinzochero*, *monaca de casa*, and tertiaries living in common were not clearly delineated and were used for one another "indiscriminately." See *DIP* 6, 1723. see also A.G. Matanic, "Bizzochi e Bizzoche," *Dizionario degli Istituti di Perfezione*, 1974.

[11]Bowie 12.

story of Angelina of Montegiove and her leadership role at Sant'Anna.

Representative writers who have dealt with *bizzoche*-tertiary relatedness include Caroline Walker Bynum, who refers to tertiaries as individuals living in the world affiliated with one of the great mendicant orders (usually the Franciscan or Dominican) and following a life of "penitential asceticism, charitable activity, and prayer."[12] Michael Goodich refers to people from various classes of society—nobility, commoners, and laity—who were attracted to the ministry of Francis of Assisi but could not "leave the world." Goodich seems to make an explicit connection, saying that endowment of leprosaria and hospitals was a "characteristic common to the beguines, unaffiliated saints, Franciscans, Servites, and tertiaries."[13] The comments of Bynum and Goodich spring from a point of view external to the Franciscan tradition. Among Franciscan historians, William Short discusses Beguines who accepted the 1289 *Rule of Nicholas IV*[14] for the Third Order as protection from civil and ecclesiastical persecution, describing them as tertiary communities whose members professed religious vows and worked in apostolic endeavors, without enclosure, in autonomous "federations," "congregations," or "chapters."[15] Mario Sensi identifies tertiaries as groups of non-institutionalized urban penitents.[16] Both sets of descriptions—external and internal to Franciscan history—are applicable to our topic.

In illuminating the history of *bizzoche*-tertiary women, Nicholas IV's 1289 *Rule* for Third Order members holds a critical

---

[12] See Bynum, "Religious Women," 124.

[13] See Michael Goodich, *The Ideal of Sainthood in the Thirteenth Century* (Stuttgart: Anton Hiersemann, 1982), 165-77.

[14] This *Rule*, promulgated in 1289, was originally intended to meet the needs of laity living secular lives in their own homes "in the world," while pursuing their own occupations, and gave them guidelines for such a life according to the ideals of Francis of Assisi. As the first universal *Rule* for Third Order Franciscans it was not intended for life in community. See Pazzelli, *Franciscan Sisters*, 27-30.

[15] William F. Short, O.F.M. *The Franciscans* (Wilmington: Michael Glazier, 1989), 17. On page 88 Short also identifies as tertiaries communities of women "already formed in the Thirteenth Century [sic] in France, Germany, and Italy."

[16] Sensi-Hagman, 341. Although not a friar, Sensi is a diocesan priest whose immense contribution to Franciscan history causes one to think of him as a "Franciscan historian."

place. At the very least, a significant series of questions about Third Order history converges in the proximity of the 1289 *Rule of Nicholas IV* and the 1298 decree *Periculoso*. The latter document imposed perpetual enclosure on all nuns (*monache*). Did some Church authorities try to apply the prescriptions of *Periculoso* to tertiaries immediately? Did some groups voluntarily choose enclosed life? When did tertiaries in community begin to profess "religious vows"? What was attractive about the Third Order *Rule* to Beguines and *bizzoche*?[17] At the very least, both tertiaries and *bizzoche* remained at least partially free of strict ecclesiastical supervision for some time; both later suffered in their attempts to maintain autonomy. The particularities of these questions must be examined against the larger background of ecclesial developments in the appropriate centuries.

The Church's View

From the very first years of the Franciscan Movement, the place of the founding charism was not always clear within a church moving toward greater centralization of authority and institutionalization of many diverse forms of religious expression. As the Friars Minor had become more and more a clerical order,[18] as the church had tried to alter Clare's understanding of the Privilege of Poverty, so too, there were efforts to "organize" the Beguines and tertiaries. One form of "organization" included affiliation with an approved *Rule*; another was the imposition of enclosure. A typical mid-thirteenth-century attitude is that of Matthew of Paris: although basically positive toward Beguines, in writing about them he adds an important *caveat*: ". . . nor are they as yet confined within a cloister."[19]

During the papacy of Innocent IV (1243-54), the supervisory role over semi-religious women (including *bizzoche* and tertiaries)

---

[17] See Moorman, Chapter 19, for some pertinent examples regarding these questions; he cites the history of men's tertiary groups as well as women's groups in the twelfth and thirteenth centuries.

[18] See Lawrence F. Landini, *The Causes of the Clericalization of the Order of Friars Minor: 1209-1260 In the Light of Early Franciscan Sources* (Chicago: Franciscan Herald Press, 1968).

[19] Matthew of Paris, *Chronica Majora* IV, 278, quoted in Bowie, 17.

had been returned to local bishops for a variety of reasons.[20] The process of regularization of *bizzoche*-tertiaries and other religious women (such as recluses) continued, but under the auspices of local authorities.[21] It is worth noting, as part of the larger perspective, that Giovanna Casagrande connects the decline of the urban reclusion movement in the thirteenth and fourteenth centuries to the following conditions: (1) the "ever more numerous and imposing presence of Tertiaries"; (2) the need for organization in various women's religious groups (tertiaries or *bizzoche*) living communally as recluses; and 3) the need for guaranteed status not dependent upon only provisional sources.[22]

By the end of the fourteenth century, the move toward regularization appears to mean monasticization, if directed by Rome; but differences of locality and episcopal attitude apparently prevented universal implementation. That this monasticization was not everywhere the norm can be inferred from the various decrees requiring enclosure. A major event in the institutionalization process had occurred in 1298 with the issuance of the apostolic constitution *Periculoso*. But only eleven years later, in 1309, a stronger expression of the same restriction was enjoined through the bull *Apostolicae Sedis*.[23] Application of these decrees was uneven, to say the least, since an interpretation of "nuns" (*monache*) did not necessarily pertain to *bizzoche* or tertiaries, and often women in these latter groups were not willing to accept enclosure. Many bishops also recognized such a distinction and allowed *bizzoche*-tertiary life to continue. It is more than likely that such was the case in Foligno when Angelina arrived at the *bizzocaggio* that was Sant'Anna.

---

[20] Sensi-Hagman, 329. One wonders about the influence exerted on this turn of events by the refusal in 1247 of Clare of Assisi and other "Damianites" to accept a Rule written by Innocent himself.

[21] Sensi-Hagman, 330-32; 336.

[22] Giovanna Casagrande, "Forms of Solitary Religious Life for Women in Central Italy," trans. Nancy Celaschi, in *Franciscan Solitude*, ed. André Cirino and Josef Raischl (St. Bonaventure, NY: The Franciscan Institute, 1995), 91, 105. It must be stated, however, that Casagrande does not think that *bizzoche* and recluses were indicative of the same lifestyle, perhaps because she works more directly with 11th-12th century material. She does, it seems, equate *pinzochera* and tertiary.

[23] Sensi-Hagman, 338, note 8.

Friars Minor and Tertiaries

Because the varieties of expression of religious faith had expanded radically during the fourteenth century, tertiary life became a problem to both secular and ecclesial authorities. Secular authorities did not want to accept such a large segment of the population making vows (private though they were) which precluded the bearing of arms (a cause for persecution of male tertiaries) or swearing of oaths, part of the tertiary commitment.[24] For women tertiaries, public activity such as care of the sick in hospices challenged prevailing cultural norms. Another way in which the tertiary movement was seen as detrimental to social structure stemmed from the fact that tertiaries were often exempt from taxation. Given that they were in some ways secular, in others religious, tertiaries endured a long struggle to gain status as "ecclesiastical persons."[25] Due to pressure from civil authorities the Church was not always protective of this way of life, and John Moorman points out that the friars "repeatedly tried to rid themselves" of pastoral responsibility toward tertiaries.[26] Such changeable status became a continuing problem; in all probability, it contributed to the development of tertiaries living a community-style life in what very-much resembled monasteries and assuming responsibility for their own governance.

Eventually two clearly-delineated branches of Franciscan tertiaries developed, those who remained secular (Third Order Seculars) and those who developed into another form of religious life (Third Order Regular congregations, both men and women). Developing Third Order Regular communities faced the same basic issue: the changeable attitudes of the Friars Minor and the official Church toward them. The difficulties resulting from such

---

[24] Across Europe, the number must have been in the hundreds of thousands; in the middle of the fifteenth century one estimate placed the number at 600,000 in Italy alone. See Moorman, 560.

[25] For one perspective on the difficulties up to 1289, see Pazzelli, *Third Order*, especially pages 145-50. For material covering later issues, see Atanasio Matanic, "Il 'Defensorium Tertii Ordinis beati Francisci' da san Giovanni da Capestrano" in *Il Movimento Francescano della Penitenza nella Societa Medioevale*, ed. Mariano D'Alatri (Rome, Istituto Storico dei Cappuccini, 1980), 45-57.

[26] Moorman, 218.

unreliability are unquestionably visible in the story of Angelina and Sant'Anna.

"Regular Observance" and Paoluccio Trinci

The unwillingness of the Franciscan friars to act as guides, mentors, or directors for *bizzoche* or tertiary women must be seen as having been conditioned by the internal struggles of the First Order, i.e., institutionalization and the Poverty Question, as much as by any other factors from that time. Two primary issues had been carried forward from the "founding moment" of the Order of Friars Minor: the immediate, incipient division over how strictly to interpret Francis' *Rule* (and the later *Testament*); and, the Poverty Question, with alternating focus on either money or property.

Almost immediately after the death of Francis, two positions took shape among the friars. The adaptive group became known as "Conventuals" while the more austere group became known as "Spirituals."[27] The so-called "Spiritual Tradition" endured decades of disaffection and persecution, even to the extent of friars being imprisoned and suppressed.[28] But throughout Franciscan history the seeds sown by Francis and the First Companions survived, and every so often a new voice would be heard calling for "reform" and "return to the primitive values" or literal observance of the "regula."[29] So it was into the fourteenth century.

At the mid-point of that century a reformist tendency arose not just in the Franciscan world, but in all areas of society. In a world of chaos and dissolution brought about by the Avignon papacy, troubled Church Councils, virtually uninterrupted wars, and the Black Death, troubles in the microcosm of the Order of Friars Minor mirrored society itself.[30] The turmoil of the Black Death in its first

---

[27] See note 31, Chapter One.

[28] See Duncan Nimmo, *Division and Reform in the Medieval Franciscan Order From St. Francis to the Foundation of the Capuchins* (Rome: Istituto Storico dei Cappuccini, 1987), 109-138, 193-201; and Moorman 188-204, 320-338 for two views of this material.

[29] Hence, the terminology "regular observance."

[30] Giulio Mancini, "Memoria di frate Paoluccio Trinci," *Forma Sororum* 6 (1992): 300. Between 1378-1415, Councils were held at Constance, Basle, Vienne and Florence. By 1415, there were three Popes, three anti-popes, and three Ministers

two outbreaks, 1348-49 and 1361, had wreaked havoc on the Order (which lost perhaps two-thirds or 20,000 of its members) and thereby set up an abridged process of admission into the Order. Because of the urgent need to re-populate the convents, standards were loosened. One result was grave compromise with regard to money and property.[31] According to Giulio Mancini, the period between 1300-1450 was the most dissension-filled and troubled interval in the entire history of the Order; this merely reflected the European macrocosm. Such was the prevailing environment as Paoluccio Trinci entered the Order in 1323.

Historiographic material presented in Chapter Two revealed that Paoluccio Trinci can be considered the founder of what became the Monastery of Sant'Anna in Foligno. Familial connections were undoubtedly part of his emergence as a leader of reform. The Trinci family had ruled Foligno for generations. Trinci's two eldest uncles were bishops; there were two cardinals on his mother's side of the family.[32] With such beneficial family connections, he would appear to be the ultimate "insider." As a friar, however, Paoluccio knew the experience of being an "outsider": he remained a lay brother, committing himself in his youth to an austere life and literal observance of the Rule.[33] In a milieu which favored the "laxity" of the Conventuals, he adopted the stance of the Spirituals. And new reform came to fruition through his example.

According to Duncan Nimmo, the move to re-establish literal observance of the *Rule* began to take shape about 1368-70.[34] In the first phase of reform Trinci was approximately sixty years old, when, after some years of virtual imprisonment, he received

---

General in the Friars Minor simultaneously.

[31] Ibid.

[32] Nimmo, 366. For a *Vita* of Paoluccio Trinci, see one of several Jacobilli versions: a section of *Vite de'Santi e Beati di Foligno* or of *Vite dell'Umbria;* or *Vita del Beato Paolo detto Paoluccio Trinci* (Foligno, 1629).

[33] Moorman, 371. Paoluccio was born in 1309, entered the Order at the age of fourteen, and spent a number of years in the hermitage at Brogliano before it was suppressed. For biographical sources, see "Il B. Paoluccio Trinci da Foligno," *Miscellanea Francescana* VI (1896): 97-111. A registry of documents concludes the article, 111 ff.

[34] Nimmo, 395. There is much that lies behind the "taking shape" of the movement, but that goes far afield from our topic. For the missing pieces, see either Nimmo or MacVicar.

permission at the close of the Chapter of 1368 to return to a hermitage at Brogliano with five companions. It was not long before they left him there alone, but they were replaced by others who desired to live in "regular observance," that is strict poverty and austerity based upon interpretation of the *Rule* "to the letter." Within five years at least eleven hermitages of "regular observance" had been opened in Italy[35] In 1373 they received papal permission to choose a confessor from among themselves who would have authority to grant a plenary remission of sins in the hour of death. Nimmo interprets this as the first step to spiritual autonomy for the Observants. By the following year the literal observance movement seems to have been accepted into the mainstream of the Order and the larger Church; this is at least partially due to Trinci's insistence that the hermitages remain canonically united with the Conventual leaders.[36]

The movement flourished mostly in Umbria, and achieved a certain measure of autonomy. By 1384, Paoluccio had received authority to accept novices for the Observance and to receive laity "to a proper Third Order."[37] Although lost, this authorization bears major relevance to an accurate interpretation concerning establishment of the monastery in Foligno. Chapter Two cited Mario Sensi's use of a similar type of permission granted in 1388, with regard to the establishment of Sant'Anna; the latter document specifically mentioned accepting women into a new monastery "under the title of the Third Order" which suggests that Trinci's authorization extended to parallel foundations for tertiary women. Also in 1388, Trinci received further authorization to extend the Observance beyond Umbria. This may be presumed to include

---

[35]Ibid., 397; 406. Brogliano is the location of an ancient hermitage which became the central locus of the observance at this time. Iriarte thinks that is the link between Trinci and Angelina of Montegiove is the hermitage at La Scarzuola, outside Montegiove. The hermitage had been built by her grandfather, Count Nero, who had joined the Observance in 1373. See *Formazione Permanente*, 12.

[36]Cf. Nimmo, 411.

[37]Mancini, 305. He says that Trinci received "religiosae mulieres" attracted to the Gospel-focus of Observance and taught them to live the Rule of 1289 "sine glossa." Unfortunately, Mancini does not provide specific reference data. The registry of documents about Paoluccio listed in *Miscellanea Francescana* VI (1896) indicates that there once was a document dated 12 February 1384, mentioned by Mariano of Florence in his *Vita* of Paoluccio; see p. 115.

houses for both men and women of the Observance. According to Mancini, the Observant movement among women soon included communities at Sant'Anna in Foligno, St. Quirico in Assisi, St. Mary in Visso, and St. Elizabeth at Camerino. Hence, Trinci can be said to be responsible for the birth of what Mancini calls an "Order of Tertiaries Regular of the Observance." Mancini interprets the group as consisting of religious women who lived the Gospel in open communities in the world, coming almost always from noble families, of whom Blessed Angelina became the "rector."[38] Later, we will see the various ways in which the hagiographic tradition treats the development of tertiary observant communities.

In its second phase, after the death of Trinci, the "Regular Observance" itself split into rival factions, one supporting an Avignon obedience, the other supporting a Roman obedience. Each side had its own General Minister, held its own chapters, issued its own decrees, and denounced the other side.[39] Among those who joined the First Order on the side of the Observance were Bernardine of Siena and John Capistran, both later canonized. These two "pillars of the Observance" played a significant part in the story of Angelina's unfolding tertiary movement, as did specific items adapted from Trinci's ideals. The "second generation" of the Observance, however, suffered from inconsistencies just as severely as had the "first generation."

Conclusion

Although controversy remains regarding several issues, a number of generally accepted points form the background of Angelina's communal life as a Franciscan tertiary: (1) the Beguine movement did have an Italian manifestation; (2) there are positive similarities and correlations in the appearance and evolution of *bizzoche* and tertiary women living in community in what are called "open monasteries"; (3) the Church alternated between approval and disapproval of both kinds of semi-religious life; (4) the internal problems of the Friars Minor contributed to the difficulties experienced by *bizzoche* or tertiary groups affiliated

---

[38] Ibid.

[39] Nimmo, 439.

with them to any extent; (5) at approximately the same time in which Angelina moved from the status of married woman to widow to Franciscan tertiary and accused witch, Paoluccio Trinci moved from "outsider" within his Order to leadership of the Regular Observants; and (6) the divisions within the Order of Friars Minor, first between Conventuals and Observants, and then between two opposing groups of Observants, ought not be forgotten as the material in the next chapter unfolds.

CHAPTER FOUR

Angelina of Montegiove:

The Interpretive Tradition

II: Angelina's Communal Life

Through examination of many of the same hagiographic sources used in Chapter Two, this chapter will demonstrate that the second half of the life of Angelina of Montegiove follows a course comparable to the first part. The present focus is directed toward those portions of the hagiographic texts related to Angelina's life at the Monastery of Sant'Anna (1395-1435), the evolution of a federation of monasteries of tertiary women affiliated with Sant'Anna, and the relationship of this group of monasteries with the Friars Minor. Sources reveal that Angelina's charismatic leadership did not disappear when she moved to Sant'Anna and communal Third Order life. In truth, she eventually became the first papally recognized minister-general of a group of tertiary monasteries—a very significant achievement for the early fifteenth century.

For the sake of consistency, the source material will be treated in the same sequence as used in Chapter Two. One or more additional items will be examined when they advance the discussion of the "history of interpretation." And, once again, when necessary, an attitude based upon the hermeneutic of suspicion has been assumed, so that in appropriate places a historical corrective will be cited. At the close of the chapter, an interpretive conclusion will be proposed.

The Earliest Sources: Franciscan Chronicles

As before, the very first source consists of a few lines by Mariano of Florence (d. 1523) in the *Compendium Chronicarum Fratrum Minorum*, under the year 1415. In this brief entry Angelina is named as a *reformer of* the Third Order of St. Francis and the founder of nine monasteries: Sant'Anna, Foligno; St. Onofrio,

Florence; St. Quirico, Assisi; St. Margherita, Ascoli; St. Agnes, Viterbo; St. Anthony, Perugia; St. Elizabeth, L'Aquila; St. Mary, Ancona; and St. Clare in Rieti. No dates are given for any of the foundations, and there is no stated reason for including the information in the year 1415.[1] It is noteworthy that Angelina is identified as both reformer and founder. The question of "founder of Sant'Anna" has already been addressed in Chapter Two. "Reformer" of the Third Order may be a reference to the fact that by the late fourteenth century numerous houses of tertiaries living a common life dotted the landscape of Franciscan life, as indicated in Chapter Three. Or it may mean that Angelina brought to this particular group the tenor of a "literal observance" of the *Rule of Nicholas IV*.[2] Mariano does not give any indication of why he refers to Angelina as both reformer and founder.

However, a more detailed portrait of the "progress" of the congregation founded by Angelina is contained in his work on the lives of the saints and blesseds of the Third Order.[3] There Mariano identifies the same nine houses, says that they "were joined together and the sisters who lived in them lived under certain Constitutions and privileges Blessed Angelina implored from Pope Martin V and Pope Eugene IV."[4] According to these Constitutions, the local ministers of the monasteries met in chapter every three years, together with their "discreets" [council members] and "elected one of their number minister general."[5] The minister general and her companions were empowered to visit during the

---

[1] It is very possible that Mariano chose 1415 because that is the year in which the Council of Constance recognized the right of Observant Friars Minor to establish houses in every Province of the Order. See Iriarte, 66-67. In 1415 was also the year in which St. Bartholomew in Foligno was completed and placed under the leadership of Paoluccio Trinci; this place became the center of his movement. See Mancini, 307. Another house under the aegis of Trinci's Observants was the one at the Portiuncola in Assisi, to which Angelina had made her significant pilgrimage before going to Foligno.

[2] Pazzelli, *Franciscan Sisters*, holds that some communities of women tertiaries were opposed to enclosure and others were cloistered by choice. See notes 3 and 4, page 39, in that work for source material on specific examples from the late thirteenth century.

[3] See note 1, Chapter 2.

[4] Mariano of Florence, "*Tertii Ordinis*," 142v; AFH XIV, 29-30.

[5] Ibid.; AFH XIV, 30.

next three years the various monasteries, appointing or removing sisters from office, and "correcting the insolent and transferring a sister from one monastery to another."[6] This seems to be a straightforward narration; except for inclusion of the phrase "correcting the insolent," no negative judgment is expressed by Mariano concerning the material he advances here. The role of minister general seems to be unquestioned and uncriticized.

But Mariano immediately and unexpectedly switches into a bitter invective against the sisters associated with the federated houses, saying that the care and direction of these monasteries was "no small care and burden to the friars of the Observance," describing the relationship as one filled with "frictions and disturbances" because the women wanted to keep their privileges;[7] this no doubt is a reference to the rights of self-governance and mobility granted by Popes Martin V and Eugene IV. Mariano attacks the integrity of the women, saying they have retained from Angelina only "a certain exterior ornament of dress" and that they are "dangerous and deficient" when compared to "honest religious." This is an attack upon the integrity of these women, since "honest" in the linguistic context of the time meant chaste or sexually virtuous. According to Mariano, "even more" of a problem was the journeying of young women moving from Viterbo to Ascoli to Florence and to L'Aquila. Consequently, the friars "decided to deprive them at least of the privilege of celebrating chapter and electing a minister general." To this purpose, Louis of Vicenza, the Vicar General in 1461, with the sanction of Pope Pius II, "deprived them of the said privileges."[8] The obvious underlying issue involves the question of authority and women's autonomy.

The revocation of these so-called "privileges" was not well-received among the monasteries, especially those in Foligno, Florence, Perugia, and L'Aquila, and the aftermath was an outright break between the friars and sisters. Mariano writes: "There was little love lost in the said sisters toward the friars . . . and one by one they began to rebel against their obedience and rule

---

[6]Ibid.

[7]Ibid.

[8]Ibid.

themselves as new congregations" from that time forward.[9] Ultimately, the internal effect of the dissension on Angelina's congregation was the severance of at least some of the ties which united the monasteries as a "federation."

Mariano continues to editorialize, further claiming that the houses of disobedient sisters were not as successful as the ones which lived "according to the ordering and will of Saint Francis," that is, the Third Order life which was intended for "married persons or those who had some other hindrances and could not enter any monastery."[10] Mariano identifies the core problem of Third Order history: how did a way of life for people "in the world" apply to tertiaries (men or women) living in community? In making such a statement Mariano exposes another element of the conflict: if women wanted to enter monasteries, they should go to those for which Francis had "instituted the Second Rule of St. Clare."[11] This sending of women to the Clare life was one of the more frequently repeated complaints made by women tertiaries against the friars.

Finally, Mariano adds a most telling comment which offers a significant insight into the rudimentary problem with regard to *bizzoche* women and friars: "Whence certain congregations were not ordered by St. Francis. They are, however, almost like a fourth Order."[12] The "fourth Order" connotes an entity that fits no acceptable pattern and has no ecclesial status. Also pertinent to Mariano's historical perspective are the three papal documents ("Periculoso" in 1298, "Apostolicae Sedis" in 1309, and "Sancta Romana" of 1317) which had been intended to impose enclosure on all religious men and women.[13] "Sancta Romana" specifically

---

[9] Ibid.; AFH 31.

[10] Ibid.

[11] Ibid. Mariano is a bit inaccurate here, in that he mixes up his terms. Francis did not write a "Second Rule of St. Clare," although by the time Mariano was writing the followers of Clare's form of life were being called the Second Order.

[12] Ibid.

[13] The 1298 decree of Pope Boniface VIII was originally directed, it seems, against Benedictine wanderers but eventually was invoked against any itinerant women religious. The text reads: "Desiring to provide for the perilous and detestable state of certain nuns, who having slackened the reins of decency and having shamelessly cast aside the modesty of their order and their sex, sometimes gad about outside their monasteries in the dwellings of secular persons, and frequently admit suspected

condemned those "who said they belong to the Third Order of Penance of St. Francis and yet were living in community" because living in community was understood to *require* profession of the three essential vows, and the *Rule of Nicholas IV* for tertiaries did not permit that kind of profession (nor did Angelina's congregation) at the time Mariano was writing.[14] The importance of long-standing conflicts over supervision, contemporary historical issues of the early sixteenth century and the strong pride of the First Order concerning both the intentions of Francis of Assisi and the importance of the First Order (in a hierarchical sense) govern Mariano's criticisms.

The next Franciscan chronicler, Mark of Lisbon (d. 1591), writing in the mid-sixteenth century, gives essentially the same account, but in a somewhat less disparaging manner. He identifies the same nine monasteries named by Mariano of Florence, but places tertiary life within the context of a similarity to those who made "the profession of the three essential vows," because by the time of Angelina and her related monasteries, the Third Order, in the words of Mark, "began to become a 'religion'."[15] The connotation of "religion" is that of religious order, as used in canon 13 of the Fourth Lateran Council.[16] It seems likely, although this is not probable, that Mark's use of "three essential vows" may be the source of Jacobilli's emphasis on Angelina's sisters as *monache claustrali*. In part, some of the difficulties of identity probably

---

persons within the same monasteries, to the opprobrium of religion and to the scandal of very many persons; we by the present constitution, which shall be irrefragably valid, decree with healthful intent that all and sundry nuns, present and future, to whatever order they belong and in whatever part of the world, shall henceforth remain perpetually enclosed within their monasteries." Quoted and translated, Eileen Power, *Medieval English Nunneries ca. 1275 to 1535* (Cambridge: The University Press, 1922), 344, cited in Graciela S. Daichman, "Misconduct in the Nunnery," *That Gentle Strength: Historical Perspectives on Women in Christianity*, ed. Lynda L. Coon, Katherine J. Haldane, and Elisabeth W. Sommer (Charlottesville and London: University Press of Virginia, 1990), 110-11.

[14] Sensi-Hagman, 341. This was affirmed in an interview with Sr. M. Clotilde (Anna) Filannino, of the Tertiary Franciscans of Blessed Angelina in an interview in Rome, 27 May 1994. The community had no standard vow formula until after enclosure was imposed in the early 17th century.

[15] *Chroniche* III, 27r.

[16] This decree has been cited in Chapter One, note 21.

were established during the papacy of John XXII, who had issued in 1323 the decree *Altissimo in divinis* to "Brothers of the Order of Penance throughout Italy." Its text, as cited by Pazzelli, reads:

> The practice of making a profession of vows, started by you, is very useful and praiseworthy and in accord with the will of blessed Francis. We now approve this practice and declare that it is not contrary to the *Rule of Nicholas IV*. While understanding that this order was instituted by St. Francis for people living in the world, there is nothing to prohibit a more perfect life to those who wish to enter this Order.[17]

Pazzelli claims the document was never widely disseminated, since it had been written for a small group of "Umbrian hermits." Although directed toward male tertiaries, the Brothers of the Order of Penance, the text gives a measure of insight into the contradictory information about tertiaries as vowed persons "in religion."

In addition to his treatment of the issues of vows and enclosure, Mark of Lisbon places greater emphasis on the Observant tradition as part of the story; Angelina and her companions

> . . . in a short time they created a numerous congregation, living in a monastery called Sant'Anna.
>
> Because they placed themselves under obedience to the friars of the Observance, they received assistance and protection; wherefore in a few years there arose in many places other monasteries of the Observance, and imitators of the Order and Rule of [the monastery of] Sant'Anna in Foligno.[18]

One could propose that Mark's intent was to attribute the growth of Angelina's form of life to the assistance and protection provided by the Observant friars. He even seems to praise those things which had so annoyed Mariano: the election from among the sisters of a minister general who would visit all the "subject monasteries" and

---

17 Pazzelli, *Franciscan Sisters*, 45-46.

18 Ibid. Jacobilli uses the same idea of assistance and protection; see page 80 above.

correct all those in office who needed such correction, "as did the Minors their brothers, which was done with great edification of all the sisters."[19] It appears that in this material, however briefly, there is evidence of an attitude reminiscent of Francis' promise of "loving care and special solicitude," and of a relationship of brother-sisterhood between the friars and the congregation at Sant'Anna. But in the very next sentence the tone changes radically:

> The care and thought for these religious was no small aggravation to the Observant Friars, since many times they caused afflictions and disturbances to religion, as has always been [the case]. And therefore Blessed Bernardine of Fossa wrote, saying:
>
> > Other grievances the friars bear on their shoulders, that is, the care of Monasteries of nuns of the Third Order, who give them the greatest distress. . . . To be thoughtful of religious is good and meritorious, but also very grave and dangerous.
>
> These words left in writing by this good religious were a strong warning to the friars, the prelates of the Observance, for several reasons, but particularly [for] the pride which ruled in these religious because of the privileges they had obtained . . ..[20]

Once again, the "care" of these women was perceived as a burden to the friars, and the privileges obtained by Third Order members encompassing rights of self-governance and moving from monastery to monastery were identified as a problem, because, in Mark's view, they led to "arrogance."

Mark continues his criticism: concern about itinerancy is unmistakable. He censures the sisters for their visits and chapters and acknowledges that the friars had sought the revocation of two specific privileges, election of the minister general and her permission to visit the monasteries. The sub-text was enclosure: if the privilege of travelling between monasteries were to be revoked, it

---

[19] Ibid., 27v.

[20] Ibid.

would mean that "from that time they [had to] begin to live as other religious. The nuns were displeased by such a prohibition, wherefore they did not fail to trouble the friars; and so a few of these monasteries cut themselves off from obedience to the friars."[21] Mark's narrative offers some insight into two issues raised in the analysis of Mariano's work: to be true religious was to be enclosed, and women who lived in common and were itinerant were *not* like "true religious" nor like the Third Order founded by St. Francis.

Both chronicles suggest that some unidentified difficulty is involved. Mariano and Mark sharply criticize the women of the various monasteries for what was perceived as unfaithfulness to the will of Francis or the example of Angelina, but that hardly seems adequate cause for the stinging tone of their words. At the same time, both writers admit involvement of the leaders of the First Order in achieving the revocation of papally approved rights. As one reads the texts critically, an intuition changes to certitude: not all the truth has been told, and in addition to stated negative comments, at least some pivotal information has been omitted.[22] Some of the missing information can be extracted from the texts of Jacobilli.

The Works of the "Official" Biographer: Jacobilli

In his earliest treatment of Angelina's life, Jacobilli provides many details about the establishment of Sant'Anna. Upon her arrival in Foligno Angelina was aware of the need for ecclesial approval, and she went virtually immediately to the city's bishop to request authorization for what Jacobilli calls an enclosed Third Order group with "solemn profession of the three vows."[23] Jacobilli points out that this was a new phenomenon, that never before had there been "tertiaries of St. Francis enclosed in monastic *clausura* with the profession of the three solemn vows; rather [there were tertiaries] living in their own homes, or freely in other places and

---

[21] Ibid.

[22] If material was deliberately omitted, a probable cause may be that the disagreement between the friars and sisters was part of a continuing problem even at the time Mark of Lisbon wrote his chronicle.

[23] *Vita* IV, 40. *Vita* IV, it must be recalled, is the re-publication of the 1627 *Vita* I, unchanged except for the corrected family names.

without formal vows. . . ."[24] It seems logical to conclude that the very last part of this passage accurately describes the *bizzoche* women living in Foligno at the time of Angelina's arrival, including those at Sant'Anna.

Jacobilli continues his narration with the information that the bishop requested from the Pope (who is not named) approval for Angelina's project, and gave space in his own residence to Angelina and her companions as temporary quarters. It may have been that the support of the bishop was more significant than papal approval, since the 1388 approbation of Paoluccio Trinci's project had been only partial.[25] For the first time in the hagiographic tradition, Jacobilli's *Vita* indicates that Angelina also received civil support. According to Jacobilli, the *signore* of Foligno, Lord Ugolino dei Trinci, gave her a site contiguous to the old walls of the city and to "the fraternity and hospital of the Trinity," as well as a garden, on which site Angelina could build a monastery and a church.[26] One is tempted to ask why the site was located next to a hospital—unless the expectation of Angelina and Lord Ugolino had been that the tertiaries would minister to the sick and the dying. But Jacobilli makes no reference to this probability, and again affirms the enclosed nature of life at Sant'Anna.[27] The new monastery was finished in the spring of 1397. It was, according to Jacobilli, the "first monastery of nuns of the Third Order of St. Francis, who would restrict themselves and live in enclosure, and from this same monastery all the others of the Third Order in all of Italy have had their origins and dependence."[28]

If Sant'Anna was a *bizzocaggio*, and the monastery itself had been established by Paoluccio "under the title of the Third Order" (as seen in Chapters Two and Three), we still lack clarity about what shape "reform" took under Angelina's leadership. Sensi believes that the *Rule of Nicholas IV* "was the only avenue that allowed newly forming women's penitential groups to avoid

---

[24] Ibid., 41.

[25] Cf. Mattioli, 45.

[26] *Vita* IV, 42.

[27] Ibid., 43.

[28] Ibid., 44-45. The statement about all Third Order monasteries in Italy originating from Sant'Anna's exemplifies Jacobilli's tendency to overstate an opinion.

becoming nuns bound by enclosure." He also claims that Third Order groups following the *Rule of Nicholas IV* were "the final institutional development of the Beguine movement."[29] Gabriele Andreozzi holds that this same *Rule* was the unique "norm of life" for many monasteries, but that at Sant'Anna, it was the "breath of the Holy Spirit" that was the true guide of governance.[30] He also claims that Angelina's vocation was that she "desired to remain in the Third Order and to profess the evangelical counsels in communitarian form," with modified enclosure and the interpretation of the vow of poverty left to the generosity of each sister.[31] This is not the picture Jacobilli drew in his *Vita*.

Jacobilli says that the way of life at Sant'Anna achieved instant renown in various provinces of Italy because of the obedience of the sisters to Angelina and because of her charity and piety.[32] Here again, underneath his obvious hagiographic intention we find a kernel of an alternative interpretation. What if attention were to be placed upon the *obedience of the tertiaries to Angelina* rather than upon her virtues? It is certainly possible that one of the attractions for noble women to join Angelina at Sant'Anna could have been an awareness that here was an out-of-the-ordinary situation protected by both civil and ecclesial leaders, a situation in which women were free to make a promise of obedience to another charismatic woman without concern for undue external pressures.

In addition, Jacobilli specifically mentions the "perfect observance *to the letter* of the Rule which they professed."[33] The desire to live the text of the Rule literally is a thread that flows from Angelina's connection to the life of Paoluccio Trinci and the "observance" he desired to establish in Italy. It is remarkable that Jacobilli gives no role at all to Paoluccio Trinci in the *Vita* of Angelina, even though he does mention Trinci as one of the gifts

---

[29] Sensi-Hagman, 341-42.

[30] Gabriele Andreozzi, *La Beata Angelina de Montegiove e la coscienza unitaria nel Terz'Ordine di San Francesco* (Rome: n. p., 1984), 25 and note 2.

[31] Ibid., 19.

[32] Ibid., 45.

[33] Ibid., 45. Here, again, the idea of "regular observance" refers to observance of the *Rule*.

God had bestowed on the city of Foligno.[34] It seems to me that the comment about obedience to Angelina is another example of historical truth filtering through hagiographic inaccuracy.

The fame of Angelina and Sant'Anna attracted many young noble women to the monastery, and at the same time inspired many Folignese nobles to send their female relatives to Angelina. The phrase used by Jacobilli is an unexpected one: *che volendo monacar quivi le loro Figlie, o Nepoti*, thatis, that is, "who wanting *to make nuns* therein of their daughters or nieces."[35] According to Jacobilli, the number was so great that the nobles raised funds to buy a site contiguous to the Cistercian hospital, St. Mary of Bethlehem, on the same street as Sant'Anna. Angelina had promised to provide a suitable leader for the new house, which was named for St. Agnes and dedicated in 1399.[36]

Regarding the governance issue, Jacobilli writes that Angelina was elected local minister with the knowledge of the bishop.[37] He also refers to a papal brief from Martin V (dated 1421) that allowed the sisters to leave Foligno for other cities and places in Italy in order to establish other similar monasteries.[38] Jacobilli

---

[34] *Vita* IV, 38. At least one other author considers Trinci's interest in the reform of tertiary life as one of the gifts. He also calls Angelina the "twin soul" of Trinci entrusted by him with the task of reforming the "movimento femminile." See Marino Bigaroni, "*Prime fondazioni di monasteri di terziarie Francescane in Assisi*," in *La Beata Angelina da Montegiove e Il Movimento del Terz'Ordine Regolare Francescana Femminile*, ed. R. Pazzelli and M. Sensi (Rome: Analecta TOR, 1984), 512.

[35] Ibid., 47. It seems completely unrealistic that Angelina would agree to or participate in the foundation of a monastery so that women could be "made nuns" by the will of their male relatives. Sr. M. Clotilde (Anna) Filannino agrees with this assessment, and holds that the foundation of St. Agnes in Foligno preceded even the foundation of Sant'Anna. She considers Jacobilli's error on this point to be "an invention." Interview by author, 14 October 1995, Foligno.

[36] Ibid., 47. Sensi, "Documenti," pp. 62-63 seems to disagree with Jacobilli's attributing the foundation of the house to Angelina. So, too, does the entry in *DHGE*, vol. 18, p. 761, which cites 1382 as the date of the first mention of this convent in historical sources.

[37] Ibid. 45.

[38] Only one other author I have examined refers to such a 1421 document (see deClary, *L'Aureola*, III, 86). It is especially significant that Sensi includes no reference to it, nor a text, in the many documents he has brought forward. A search of the *Bullarium Franciscanum* was also unsuccessful in locating such a document. It is possible that it once existed but has since been lost.

names St. Quirico in Assisi (1421), St. Onofrio in Florence (1429) and St. Agnes in Viterbo (gives no date) as directly established with connections to Sant'Anna. Within a short time, says Jacobilli, eleven other monasteries were erected by Angelina in the following places: Ascoli, Città di Castello, Rieti, Ancona, Todi, Spoleto, L'Aquila, Piacenza, Perugia, and two houses in Rome.[39] The "company" of sixteen monasteries were all "under the Third Rule and attire of St. Francis, and under obedience of the Monastery of Sant'Anna in Foligno and its minister general, who was the same blessed Angelina."[40]

At this rather late point in the narration Jacobilli explicitly mentions the relationship of these monasteries to the Observant friars: they "placed themselves under the care of the Observant Fathers, called *zoccolanti* of St. Francis, and were paternally protected and favored by them."[41] An important connective fragment occurs here, through use of the word *zoccolanti*, which are wooden clogs worn by both men and women Observants. Earlier in *Vita* IV, Jacobilli had referred to the "institutor of the Observant Fathers, called *zoccolanti*" but did not directly designate Paoluccio Trinci in that role.[42] However, one of the most frequently reproduced iconographic representations of Angelina shows her with *zoccolanti* on her feet, and the standard iconography for Trinci also had him wearing *zoccolanti* (see figures 3 and 4, p. 81).[43] As far as Jacobilli's comment that the tertiaries of Sant'Anna were "paternally protected and favored" by the Observant friars, historiography demonstrates this optimistic comment constitutes a major misinterpretation, as will be shown below.

While there is no indication of rancor between the tertiaries and friars in Jacobilli's account, it is noteworthy that both Mariano

---

[39] Ibid., 49-50. *Vite dell'Umbria* contains more dates, and some different dates for some of the monasteries cited here.

[40] Ibid., 51. Note again, the monasteries place themselves under obedience to Angelina.

[41] Ibid.

[42] *Vita* IV, 38.

[43] Reprints of Paolo and Angelina in very similar garb and both with *zoccolanti* are taken from Mario Sensi, *Le Osservanze francescane nell'Italia centrale (Secoli XIV-XV)* (Rome: Istituto Storico Cappuccini, 1985) 34f. and 50f.

Fig. 3: Paoluccio dei Trinci wearing *zoccolanti*

Fig. 4: Angelina of Montegiove wearing *zoccolanti*

and Mark report on it. Jacobilli had used essentially the same information as Mariano in presenting the details of the election of ministers; he referred to the statutes and constitutions given Angelina by Martin V and Eugene IV; he offered the same material about the process of visitation and correction. Jacobilli even echoed Mark of Lisbon's comment on the similarity between the friars' mode of visitation and the sisters' mode in their own visitations.[44] But Jacobilli's purpose, it must be re-stated, was to uphold Angelina and the spread of her movement, not attack them. This is achieved through selective excerpting from other sources.

In telling this part of Angelina's history, Jacobilli overlooked a number of significant events between 1428-30, thereby omitting information which greatly augments our understanding of the struggle over governance and the eventual abolition of the office of minister general. In August 1428 Pope Martin V had issued *Sacrae Religionis,* addressed to six tertiary-*bizzoche* houses federated with Sant'Anna; it provided authorization to elect a *ministra* in each house, as well as authorization for her to receive the profession of novices.[45] Pazzelli claims that this document was an endorsement of an already-existing practice, not something new. What is new is that *Sacrae Religionis* established the office of minister general for the congregated houses, as well as the right of visitation; it is undoubtedly the source from which Mariano of Florence and Mark of Lisbon drew the accounts cited above. Within a few months, however, a contradictory decree was issued by the same Pope. On 9 December 1428 *Licet inter coetera* placed all tertiaries, men and women, "regular" or not, under obedience to the ministers provincial or general of the Friars Minor. In fact, *Licet inter coetera* was issued as a response to a specific request from the Minister General of the Friars Minor.[46] Over the next eighteen

---

[44] Ibid., 52.

[45] Pazzelli, *Franciscan Sisters,* 67; the decree can be found in BF, VII, n. 1826, pp. 706-07. For a translated text, see Appendix A, part V below. Iriarte, in *Formazione Permanente* (p. 13), claims that the chapter which elected Angelina general minister was conducted by the Bishop of Todi.

[46] Ibid., 68-69. The General, Anthony of Massa Marittima, had expressed complaints about the diversity of those claiming to be Third Order members, especially those either living in community or those "leading a religious life according

months the question of enforcement occupied the Friars Minor, and certainly many tertiaries.

Jacobilli omits the events of 1428-30 at first, but in the next part of the *Vita* he does give a more precise source of the troubles in the relationship between the Friars Minor and sisters affiliated with Angelina. He records that at an unspecified moment before 1430 some of Angelina's monasteries had placed themselves under obedience to the local bishop or to their confessor [a possible response to *Licet inter coetera*], but that ultimately, in August 1430 Martin V ordered the minister general (Angelina) to "promise obedience in her name, and in the name of all the others then living in the monasteries subject to her, to the ministers of the Observant friars in the Province of St. Francis."[47] As a result, the Minister General of the Friars Minor, William of Casale,[48] sent the Conventual Provincial of the Umbrian province, Galasso of Naples, to Foligno with the papal brief. Galasso was charged with insuring that Angelina put into effect everything contained in the document. Jacobilli describes the scene: "prostrating herself at the feet of this prelate, [Angelina] promised [this obedience] most promptly in her own name and that of those juridically subject to her." Subsequently, a public promise of obedience was made and authenticated in writing on 3 November 1430.[49]

Again, Jacobilli does not provide more than a portion of the circumstances involved. Major events within the Observant-Conventual sphere between June and August 1430 reverberated within Third Order life. In June a General Chapter had been held in order to implement *Licet inter coetera* and to arrive at some agreement as to a "moderate reform" of the entire First Order. By

---

to their own whims without due reverence and obedience." For a translation of this text, see Appendix A, Part VI below.

[47] *Vita* IV, 52-53. This is the letter "Pervigilis more," BF VII, n. 1892, p. 737. See Pazzelli, *Franciscan Sisters*, 69-70 for background. It is addressed to the "nuns of the order of S. Clare, S. Damian, [and] Minoresses," as well as to all other places where women follow a rule—hence, the impact on Angelina's monasteries.

[48] Jacobilli calls him Vicar General of the Observants; Nimmo and Pazzelli call him Minister General. Once again we encounter evidence of either Jacobilli's inaccuracy or misinterpretation.

[49] *Vita* IV, 53. Sensi, "Documenti," Appendix VIII.a, pp. 95-96 has published the text of an account of the same event, from the archives of Foligno.

this time the Observance was either "moderate" or "literal," and moderate reformers wanted to extend some measure of reform to the Conventual lifestyle, which was seen as "lax" according to Observant standards. To this end, the Chapter worked toward creating constitutional directives that would be acceptable to both Conventuals and Observants. The result was the "Martinian Constitutions," which, in the view of Duncan Nimmo, "embodied the Church's moderate position—the *via media* between two extremes, the strict and the lax, [as] defined by the thirteenth century papal declarations."[50]

Internally, however, the Martinian Constitutions were not really a compromise. Written by a committee led by John Capistran, who could have been perceived by the Conventuals as a moderate only with great difficulty, the Constitutions favored an Observant interpretation of Franciscan life.[51] The newly-elected minister general, William of Casale, took an oath to accept the Constitutions and to conduct visitations to see that their standards were implemented throughout the provinces of the Order. Furthermore, he would be accompanied on the visitations by Capistran. The delegate-friars to the Chapter also took an oath, binding themselves and those whom they represented to accept and obey the Constitutions.[52] Between June and August great turmoil disturbed the Order of Friars Minor. The delegates reneged on their oath; William appealed to Martin V to be excused from the task of visitation and from the promise of enforcing the Constitutions. To counter the Chapter enactments, a campaign was launched to restore the Conventual style of Franciscan life, culminating in a decree dated 23 August 1430 that granted friars the right to possess and administer landed property and permanent incomes, directly violating the *Rule of 1223*.[53] Such a decree certainly indicated that

[50]Nimmo, 606. Nimmo writes from the perspective of Capuchin history, that is, the Capuchin reform movement of strict observance in the sixteenth century.

[51]Moorman, 447, says that Wadding called the Martinian Constitutions "Capistran's shears." See *AM* X, 161-62.

[52]Nimmo, 610. See Moorman, 447-50 and Iriarte, 71-73 for two remarkably different perspectives.

[53]Ibid., 611.

the attempt to assert an Observant reform was at the very least ill-timed; the reform came close to total failure.

With respect to Angelina and her federation, the fundamental issue, as extracted from Jacobilli's text, seems to be that the tertiaries had promised obedience to others instead of to the Friars Minor, in apparent attempts to circumvent *Licet inter coetera*. With additional background information from the Friars' Chapter, it seems probable that the over–riding motive in 1430 was the Conventual attempt to reassert authority over any form of Observance, including what might be called "Tertiary Observance." Such information places the forced promise of obedience made by Angelina in an entirely different light than that provided by Jacobilli. In addition, the simplicity and immediacy of obedience which Jacobilli ascribes to Angelina in this part of his narrative remains open to question. It is certainly not the same picture of Angelina he gave in either the struggle with her father over the question of marriage or the staunch self-defense advanced at the court of Ladislas. It stretches credibility too far to expect such a complete reversal of personality in Angelina. Once again, Jacobilli has omitted a significant portion of the real story because it did not serve his hagiographic intention.

In another vein, Jacobilli presented his material without understanding that if Angelina had in reality founded a way of life for *monache claustrali* of the Third Order, visits to other monasteries and the travel thus required would have violated the principle of enclosure he so strongly advocated. Part of his text acknowledges that there were journeys even up to the time of Pope Pius II (1461). He writes:

> But as time passed, the long and dangerous pilgrimages were judged not suitable to women: so that Father Louis of Vicaenza, Vicar General of the Observants in 1430, (sic) sought from Pope Pius II that the renewal of the privileges of the Mothers [ministers] should be prohibited, that the ministers could no longer elect the minister general and no longer visit the monasteries; but that for the future they must live in their own convents and conform to the usages of all other enclosed nuns. . . .[54]

---

[54] *Vita* IV, 52.

A major error must be pointed out: Pius II was not in office in 1430, Martin V was. The year is obviously incorrect. The correct date for abolishing the office of minister general is 1461.[55] Two insights may be garnered here concerning Jacobilli's material: "no longer visit the monasteries" does not fit the picture of a community that from its inception had been "enclosed"; also, it is very important to note that in writing about the necessity of itinerant movement for pilgrimages, Jacobilli did not use the phrases "enclosed women" or *monache claustrali* in the second line of the excerpt above, but merely "women." Jacobilli evidences in this section the cultural imperative of the larger Italian medieval society, not just an ecclesial agenda. In a narrower perspective, it appears that the cause of the quarrel was connected to the friars' desire, at least within the last several years of Angelina's lifetime, that women who lived communally and appeared to be nuns would follow the prescription of enclosure that governed "real" religious women, in addition to the friars' problems of internal authority discussed above.

Jacobilli does not comment on the immediate reaction of the sisters associated with Angelina in the various monasteries, either to her promise of obedience in 1430 or to the 1461 decree. But he does indicate that the issue continued to be troublesome:

> These good nuns would live a long time under the direction of the Observant Fathers. But in the space of forty years, beginning in 1481, they would give themselves to direction by a new congregation, of the same order of Minors, called the Amadei after Blessed Amadeo Spagnuolo, head and institutor of this reform; these friars had been given in that same year the convent of St. Feliciano in Foligno. . . .[56]

The Amadei, or Amadeiti, were a later manifestation (perhaps even a third generation) of the Observance, inaugurated by Amadeo in 1464. Suppressed between 1470-72, they received canonical approval in the papacy of Sixtus IV, a Franciscan pope. The tertiaries of Angelina turned to the Amadeiti because the so-

---

[55] Pazzelli, *Franciscan Sisters*, 83. See also the text of Mariano of Florence which gives correct date.

[56] *Vita* IV, 53.

called second generation of Observants had obtained authorization to suspend their pastoral care of monasteries unwilling to accept enclosure—including Sant'Anna. The *bizzoche*-tertiary women there were determined to maintain life as an "open" monastery,[57] and so become associated with another reform group within the Franciscan Order.

Finally, Jacobilli reveals historically significant details about the breadth of Angelina's influence. He states that at the time he was writing, (1627) there were 135 monasteries in "twenty-two Provinces throughout the world" associated with the life established at Sant'Anna, comprising 4,323 *monache*. That there was a historical understanding of this "movement" of Angelina's tradition as *Monache del Terz'Ordine Claustrale* is verified not only by the use of that title by Jacobilli and later authors, but also by the representation of such a group in the article of "Costume" in the *Dizionario degli Istituti di Perfezione.*[58]

Among the 135 monasteries referred to by Jacobilli were fifty-three monasteries with 2,185 members in nine provinces of Italy, and twenty-nine monasteries with 479 members in France.[59] This is a tantalizing bit of information which inspires a serious follow-up question: Why does he identify only the data for Italy and France? Where were the other fifty-three monasteries and 1,659 members? Given the information presented in Chapter Three with regard to the spread of the Observants eastward, it might be expected that at least some of the missing groups can be found in Hungary, Bohemia, and Poland.[60]

Approximately 25 years later, Jacobilli's *Vite dell' Umbria* contained a much-reduced summary of the story of Angelina and her monasteries. In it Jacobilli again provided an interesting combination of material from both Mariano of Florence and Mark of Lisbon, without the bitterness of either—and without the story of revoked privileges. Since Jacobilli's focus continued to be the cult of Angelina, it is understandable that he would have carefully selected only the choicest positive elements with regard to her

---

[57] Mattioli, 71-72.

[58] See "Costume," DIP, 1974 ed., p. 242.

[59] *Vita* IV, 51.

[60] This material will be treated in Chapters Five and Six.

history. He set up the positive viewpoint by immediately establishing a papal connection to Angelina: her "foundation" of the monastery of Sant'Anna was approved by both Pope Urban VI in 1385 and Pope Boniface IX in 1395.

In contrast to the 1627 *Vita*, Jacobilli provides in *Vite dell'Umbria* no details of local ecclesial or civil support. He does write of the efficacy of the spreading movement: within Angelina's lifetime fifteen other monasteries were erected in diverse parts of Italy.[61] Jacobilli gives specific dates for each monastery he identifies, and attributes the successful spread of the "reform of the nuns of the Third Order of St. Francis in enclosure with the three essential vows" to "the fruits of the prayers and of the efforts of this Blessed, who was elected the first minister general of all of this her congregation, with many graces and privileges obtained from Pope Martin V. . . ."[62] The concern with edification is both obvious and telling: he attests that Angelina's movement spread because of *her* prayers and efforts; he does not mention the connections to and difficulties with the friars of the Observance, nor does he attribute the growth of her movement to their care and protection. Jacobilli nuances the information about the office of minister general in an interesting fashion: he says only that Angelina was the *first* minister general of her congregation, and does not advert to the abolition of the office within three decades of Angelina's death, as he had in his first *Vita*. Instead, he allows

---

[61] *Vite dell'Umbria*, 34. He identifies them as "in 1387, the monastery of St. Clare in Rieti; in 1390, the monastery of St. Margaret in Ascoli; in 1399, the monastery of St. Agnes . . . in 1400 the monastery of St. John in Todi . . . .In 1420 the monastery of St. Onofrio in Florence was erected by four of her disciples, nuns of the monastery of Foligno;. . .in 1422 the monastery of S. Cecelia of Città del Castello was erected, and that of S. Quirico in Assisi. In 1426 the monastery of St. Agnes (later called St. Bernardine) in Viterbo was established; in 1427, that of St. Anthony of Padua in Perugia; in 1429, the monastery of S. Appollonia and of St. Margaret in Rome; in 1431, S. Catharine of Pusterno in Spoleto; in 1433, S. Elisabeth in L'Aquila, a new S. Mary in Ancona and S. Mary Magdalen in Piacenza; and other monasteries were established after the death of Angelina by her disciples. . . ." In the years between 1627 and 1652 Jacobilli has changed some of these details, but the discrepancies are too complex to be discussed here. See Filannino, "Fondazioni," 451-57, for a corrective on dates and actual affiliation of these monasteries.

[62] Ibid.

readers to assume that the custom of electing the minister general had continued to the time he was writing *Vite dell'Umbria*.

Jacobilli does add a remarkable phrase to this portion of his narration. He writes: "We have found at the present time under this *Tertiary Institute of St. Francis of the Observance* (italics mine) 135 monasteries in twenty-two separate Provinces of Europe, totalling 4,323 nuns."[63] By the time *Vite dell'Umbria* was published, Jacobilli felt secure enough to classify the institute of Angelina as "Tertiaries of St. Francis of the Observance." Does this mean the institute was called by the same name in some one or another of the sources Jacobilli used, including the archives at Sant'Anna, or that Jacobilli was inventing a name for the phenomenon? It is possible that he used a variety of descriptive terminologies precisely because he kept revising his work; in any event, by the 1650s there were many houses of "Tertiaries of the Observance of St. Francis" present not only in Italy but all across Europe as well.

At this point, it is worthwhile to examine the earliest historiographic information, that found in Ughelli. What does the corrector of Jacobilli's genealogy say about Sant'Anna and its governance? He is very brief. Angelina is said to have "abandoned the world with its vain pomps, retiring to Foligno, taking the attire of St. Francis, giving herself to works of piety and of charity." Ughelli recognizes life at Sant'Anna as "the beginning of the Congregation of the Tertiaries of St. Francis" but does not associate the life in any way with Jacobilli's term, *monache claustrali*. As Mark of Lisbon and Jacobilli had done, Ughelli likewise credits Angelina with the establishment of many other monasteries in diverse parts of Italy, "of which she was the Head, or Superior, or we ought to say General."[64] There is no reference to the conflicts between the sisters and friars, nor are there any statistics about the number of monasteries or sisters living in them. Ughelli did include several documentary items from archives in Foligno and Todi; in these documents Angelina is variously referred to as *religiosam dominam* (religious Lady), *abbatissam monasterii*

[63] Ibid. These are the same numbers cited in the re-published *Vita* I in spite of the passage of twenty-five years between the two works.

[64] *Albero et Istoria*, 63-64.

(abbess of the monastery), and *ministra* (minister) of the monastery in Foligno.[65] One item from 1400 refers to the "Third Order of Saint Francis under the Institute of Lady Angelina."[66] The latter point is important in that Ughelli differentiates Angelina's group as one institute among many belonging to the Third Order of St. Francis, a point some of the historians who follow him fail to make.

Tertiary Responses to the Earliest Sources

Thus far, the material from Mariano of Florence, Mark of Lisbon, and Ludovico Jacobilli has provided essentially parallel interpretations of Angelina's life at Foligno and the growth of a number of what can be called "federated houses." However, it must be said that none of the cited sources gives an internal view of events. What is missing is a response emanating from predominantly internal records, or from members of Angelina's congregation itself. However, recent examination of both internal and external historical records by members of the congregation provides a dimension for the history of interpretation that has heretofore been lacking. Such an examination and interpretation is now possible thanks to the work of Sisters M. Clotilde Filannino and Lorella Mattioli, both of whom have already been cited in this present work. Their contribution is especially important with respect to those events between 1428-1484, the years in which the struggle of the Foligno tertiaries to maintain the original lifestyle established by Angelina became more and more difficult.

A key point that must be made is that Sant'Anna pre-dated Angelina's arrival; it was a *bizzocaggio*, a house of *bizzoche*, founded by Trinci. Both Filannino and Mattioli work from this particular understanding of the "founding moment." Filannino holds that the original project was a monastery of *bizzoche* who wanted to remain faithful to the original design and who resisted assimilation into the Second Order.[67] Mattioli describes the

---

[65] Ibid., 63-65.

[66] Ibid., 66. This is a testament of Margherita of Salimbene, related by marriage to Angelina's family. It names Angelina as an heir.

[67] Anna Filannino, "Il monastero di S. Anna nell'etá moderna e contemporanea," in *La Beata Angelina da Montegiove e il movimento del Terz'Ordine regolare francescano femminile*, ed. R. Pazzelli and M. Sensi (Rome: Analecta TOR, 1984), 222-23. The essay is

original entity as Franciscan tertiary women living in community rather than in their own homes, neither Damianites nor monastically vowed, whose "profession" was promise of obedience to the *Rule of Nicholas IV*.[68] A text used within the congregation for a continuing formation program in 1993 contains an arresting claim that Trinci wanted to establish a women's branch of the Observance, by means of instituting a community that would adopt the same lifestyle as Paoluccio's groups, i.e., contemplative prayer, poverty, intimate fraternity, eremitical life in a monastery at the margins of the city, without enclosure, under the spiritual direction of Trinci's disciples.[69] It is not without importance that the current congregation descendant from Angelina accepts this particular construct of their historical foundation.

Archival documents from the civil archives of Foligno, cited by Mattioli, identify Angelina under various terms: she is "professed," *gubernatrix*, "abbess of the monasteries," or "minister of the order of continents," while papal documents refer to her as "minister" and "minister general."[70] According to internal interpretive understanding, the office of "minister" was more like that of a *maestra* of the beguinages of northern Europe than it was to an enclosed abbess.[71] Since the *Rule of Nicholas IV* contained no prescriptions for common life or internal administration of a house following a common life, it may be proposed that an important aspect of Angelina's role involved the establishment of guidelines to fill in what was missing in the *Rule of Nicholas IV*. This is probably why Mariano of Florence, Mark of Lisbon, and Jacobilli all refer to "privileges and concessions" granted to Angelina by

---

based upon study of archival records in the Monastery of Sant'Anna, the civil records of Foligno, and the archives associated with the history of the Observants at the Portiuncola in Assisi. She also affirmed the *bizzoche* nature of Sant'Anna in an interview given on 27 May 1994, in Rome, Italy.

[68] Mattioli, 44-47.

[69] Lazaro Iriarte, "Evoluzione storica del francescanesimo: secoli XIII-XV," *Anno V di formazione permanente*, unpublished manuscript, 11. Iriarte claims that Angelina's presence at Foligno is first attested to in a recently discovered notarial document dated 4 December 1399, in which she is referred to as "'Angelina de Montiovis' who stays in the monastery of friar 'Paoluti of Foligno.'" See "Evoluzione," 12.

[70] Mattioli 45, citing Sensi's "Documenti," 82-83 and BF VII, n. 1826, pp. 206-07.

[71] Mattioli, 46.

Boniface IX, Martin V, and Eugene IV. In fact, the 1403 letter *Provenit ex vestrae* is considered the official recognition of the *bizzocaggio*-monastery's way of life, one characterized as providing "a space of freedom, in order to devise a style of community life in conformity with the semi-religious state they had chosen."[72] Canonically, it allowed the tertiaries of Sant'Anna to choose a confessor who would absolve them from the penalty of excommunication that had been imposed upon tertiaries living in common under the umbrella of the *Rule of Nicholas IV*, an excommunication imposed with *Sancta Romana* in 1317.[73]

It should be remembered that when the Friars Minor held the 1430 Chapter part of the agenda was to formulate a response to the 1428 decree that had granted the federated tertiary houses the right to elect one of their own as minister general, with the right to accept profession and to visit each house.[74] The obedience promised by Angelina to Galasso of Naples in November 1430 is presented in the earliest sources in a rather matter-of-fact manner, with no reference to the internal problems it caused for the congregation, and for Angelina herself. If implemented, the promise would have had dire consequences. Knowing this, the tertiaries reconvened in Chapter themselves a week after Angelina's promise. The community decided to defend the privileges and concessions on which their life had been based and selected a Third Order friar, Stephen of Como, as a legal representative before the Holy See. Angelina's name is not contained on the list of sisters present and voting at this Chapter—an anomaly in the long list of documents in which her name does appear. In contemporary terms, what this means is that Angelina was temporarily removed from office.[75] However, she was almost immediately returned to her leadership role and remained in office until her death.

The sisters of Angelina's federation and the friars of the Province of Umbria would return many times to the disagreement about enclosure. On one side were the *bizzoche*-tertiaries, some civil authorities, and some members of the Roman Curia; on the

---

[72] Ibid.

[73] See pp. 72–73 above. I am indebted to Sr. Clotilde Filannino for this insight.

[74] See above, p. 82 ff.

[75] Mattioli, 50-51; see also Sensi, "Documenti," 70-71.

other, Friars Minor.[76] In May, 1440, the federated houses of the congregation received from Pope Eugene IV a reconfirmation of the privileges granted to Angelina by earlier popes. In explicit language, the document reaffirmed the legality of the local and general ministers, provided for an alteration in the "habit," for dispensation from [making] the vow of poverty, for the choice of confessors other than Friars Minor, and it gave canonical recognition again to the election of a minister general.[77] For a time, at least, the way of life established by Angelina was restored: tertiary-*bizzoche* women lived a common life under the *Rule of Nicholas IV* without enclosure or solemn vows. And, for a while, they were "loosened from the jurisdiction of the Friars Minor."[78]

In 1446, however, the same pope was induced by the friars to place all monasteries of Third Order women under the jurisdiction of the Vicar General of the Observants (John Capistran, a staunch defender of the Third Order); this did not attenuate their autonomy.[79] But between the 1440s and 1461 the conflict kept reappearing. In 1461 the friars succeeded in dismantling the federation by reason of the abolition of the office of minister general, as presented earlier. In 1480 the Holy See expressly approved the merit of the vows made by both men and women tertiaries of St. Francis; according to Filannino, they "without doubt must have been considered solemn vows"[80]—at least by the Holy See, if not by the tertiaries.

By 1482 the friars had also received papal approval for withholding pastoral care from unenclosed monasteries; at this

---

[76] Mattioli 52; Filannino, "La storia," 225. See also Sensi, "Documenti," 110-11. These are not the Friars Minor of the Observant tradition of Paoluccio, but those of the mindset of the friars who reneged on their promise to obey the Martinian Constitutions of 1430.

[77] BF n.s. I, n. 466, pp. 222-23; Mattioli, 64. The specific monasteries named in the bull are Sant'Anna in Foligno, St. Onofrio in Florence, St. John in Todi, S. Quirico in Assisi, and St. Margaret in Ascoli; there is also the umbrella of "other sisters elsewhere under the rule and observance of the Third Order, which Bl. Francis instituted, and who are called by the name 'of penance'."

[78] Mattioli, 64-65.

[79] Filannino, "La storia," page 222, note 6. The papal bull can be found in BF n.s. I, n. 1045.

[80] Filannino, "La storia," 222, note 6.

time the tertiaries appealed to local civil authorities and to the Roman Curia for assistance. In November of that year Pope Sixtus IV sent a letter to the guardian of St. Bartholomew, a house of Observant friars in Foligno, "inviting" the friars to restore to the monasteries appropriate pastoral care and *not* to try to place them under enclosure.[81] In December Sixtus issued a document in favor of two houses of *bizzoche*-tertiaries in Perugia, St. Anthony (said by Mariano of Florence and Jacobilli to have been founded by Angelina) and St. Agnes. Sixtus was responding to what must have been a detailed letter,

> the tenor of which is clear from the response. The friars believed that strict enclosure would be beneficial to their souls, but the [tertiaries] were not of the same mind. Enclosed, they would hardly be able to hear one Mass a day, but going out they would be better able to nurture themselves spiritually, listening every day to the preaching of the Word of God. Because they lived on alms and could not get aid from relatives, enclosed they would encounter serious difficulties in providing for their needs.[82]

The pope again exhorted the friars to resume their pastoral ministry to the tertiaries and not impose strict enclosure. Although the issues above were presented by houses in Perugia, they are, no doubt, equally relevant to Foligno.

In June 1483 the conflict overflowed into the civil arena. The communal council meeting of Foligno voted to choose three or four citizens, acceptable to the tertiaries, who would have authority to intervene in the case. By September the Pope had written to the Vicar General of the Observants of Umbria; in December the Bishop of Ostia, as Cardinal Protector of the Franciscan Order, wrote a threatening letter to the friars, as did the apostolic chancellor, a native Folignese.[83] The friars did not back down, and

---

[81] Ibid., 225, citing the Archives of the Monastery of St. Anna, ms. "Regola e Costituzioni," 28 r.

[82] Ibid., citing BF n.s. III, n. 1677. The introductory material indicates that the "Minor Observants are to abstain from imposing enclosure on the monasteries of St. Anthony and St. Agnes in Perugia."

[83] Ibid., 226.

in January 1484 the Vicar General called a Chapter at Perugia, trying to get the inflexible friars to assume responsibility for the difficulties, but no agreement could be reached, even after three days' discussion. The Vicar General consulted with the Cardinal Protector; ultimately, in early February, he sent a letter to the entire province, recommending prudence and patience—virtues conducive to peace and harmony. Late in February the communal council of Foligno said that they understood the difficulties of the monastery and would like to see the matter settled. It is not clear if the council knew of the Vicar General's letter or not; but they proposed to send a letter to him requiring that if they did not receive an affirmative response (apparently to the request that the friars resume appropriate relations with the monastery) within fifteen days, the citizens would look for another group of religious to provide pastoral care "for the Countesses." The final result, after more skirmishing, was the connection of the monastery with the Amadeiti.[84] None of these details are found in Jacobilli's work.

Certainly, the material available through the work of Filannino and Mattioli offers a much sharper insight into the work of Mariano, Mark, and Jacobilli. As troubled as the relationship between tertiaries and the friars was, it must nevertheless be measured in the context of the self-understanding of the participants: both sides were convinced of the correctness of their position. History, however, has presented only one side of the story. It is only in the latter half of the current century that the Tertiary Franciscans of Blessed Angelina have been able to publicly reaffirm their own interpretation of their history and identity.

Nineteenth and Early Twentieth Century Sources

As in the second chapter, one source furnishes a Franciscan interpretation of the material found in Jacobilli, *L'Aureola Serafica*. Even though the work relies extensively on Jacobilli, the material found therein is particularly important in light of the difficulties and inconsistencies surrounding the story of Angelina and the Observant friars' care and protection.

---

[84] Filannino, "La storia," 227-28.

L'Aureola presents Angelina's "commission" as being sent by God to Foligno to found a *monastero di clausura* subject to the Rule of the Third Order of St. Francis.[85] She arrives there in 1395 with seven companions, visits the bishop, who then requests and receives papal approval for the project. Ugolino di Trinci is identified as the donor of land for the construction of the new monastery, which is completed two years later. In all of this, there is no difference from Jacobilli. However, the description of the life is, if possible, even more monastic than that found in Jacobilli: deClary says that Angelina is named abbess at age 20 and a year after moving into Sant'Anna, she and her companions "were allowed to make the solemn vows of religion, to which they added the vow of enclosure."[86]

L'Aureola follows Jacobilli with reference to the widespread fame of the way of life at Foligno, the establishment of St. Agnes in 1399 "at the request of the people," and the desire of other towns to have similar monasteries established. In dealing with the 1421 document[87] of Martin V which permitted the "Franciscans of Foligno" to leave Foligno to accede to the requests for new houses, *L'Aureola* specifically names St. Quirico in Assisi, 1421; St. Bernardine (originally St. Agnes) in Viterbo, 1427; St. Onofrio in Florence, 1429, and St. Elisabeth in L'Aquila, 1433.[88] There is no mention at all of the influence of the Friars Minor of the Observance in the establishment of these houses, nor of the Conventuals, a truly amazing omission, since *L'Aureola* is a Franciscan source. Instead, *L'Aureola* shifts the focus to papal involvement: "In 1428 Pope Martin V joined together all the monasteries founded by Blessed Angelina into a single congregation, under the governance of a Superior General."[89] Credit for the formation of a unified congregation is given to the pope, and the language of leadership becomes "superior general," clearly a post-Tridentine and a nineteenth-century term which gives no suggestion

---

[85] *L'Aureola*, 84.

[86] Ibid., 85.

[87] See note 38, this chapter.

[88] Ibid., 86-87.

[89] Ibid., 87.

of the concept of "minister" so widespread in the origins of the Franciscan tradition.

Moreover, there is no acknowledgement of strained relations between Angelina's communities and the First Order; the complicated and continuing difficulties are ignored, and the relationship is reduced to a very simple statement that in 1430 Martin V placed Angelina's "Institute" and its diverse communities under the jurisdiction of the Friars Minor. Additionally, the matter of who empowers Angelina as leader of the congregation is obscured; *L'Aureola* says that Angelina was "called to the office of Superior General, which she occupied until her death on 14 July 1435," with the implication that it was either the pope or the Friars Minor who called her to leadership rather than her own sisters.[90]

Finally, *L'Aureola* reports that "in life" Angelina had established 16 monasteries, a number taken directly from Jacobilli's first *Vita*, but *L'Aureola* does not identify all of them. As to houses outside of Italy, *L'Aureola* once again echoes Jacobilli, commenting that at the time he wrote, he counted 54 houses in Italy and 29 in France, but rounds off the number of members, stating that in Italy there were over 2,000 "religious" and in France, 500.

L'Aureola states that Angelina had given her daughters the Third Order *Rule of Nicholas IV* as well as constitutions "suitable for religious life,"[91] thus affirming the role of Angelina at the "founding moment" even while imposing the construct of "religious life" on the picture. *L'Aureola* also uses the term "regular tertiaries" in describing Angelina's descendants as they would have looked approximately a century after the most flourishing years of Angelina's federation: "Leo X modified the Rule of the Third Order in favor of Regular Tertiaries" on 15 January 1521 by adding prescriptions for Third Order members living in enclosure and removing parts of the 1289 Rule pertinent to Third Order

---

[90] Ibid. In *LSB*, 502, one reads that the insititute of Angelina "owed to" the "four pillars of the Observance" (Bernardine of Siena, James of the Marches, Albert of Sarteano, and John Capistran) "in great part its rapid diffusion throughout Italy and the rest of Europe."

[91] Ibid., 90.

secular life.[92] Although the *Rule of Nicholas IV* continued to be the guideline for Third Order Secular men and women living in the world as ordinary laity, after 1521 a legal and practical separation of the Third Order into two branches took place, and the original expression of a reformed *bizzoche* way of life took another step toward monasticization. *L'Aureola* seems to be the first source to clearly address this major development.

As for other sources analyzed in Chapter Two, the material they offer concerning the development of Angelina's movement is limited. In G. M. Romano's entry in the *Dizionario di Erudizione Storico-Ecclesiastica*, we have already seen the following report on Angelina and the foundation of her movement: "Exercising the higher virtues for some years, she thought to reform the *monache* of the Third Order of St. Francis, and in 1385, backed by pontifical authority, erected the first monastery in Foligno."[93] Romano holds that "to the merit of her surprising activity there soon were erected in Italy twenty other monasteries that she herself comforted with visits and words of life." The number of monasteries attributed to Angelina differs from other sources, but the nuance of "surprising activity" and "comforted with visits and words of life" open an interesting interpretive avenue. One wonders why Romano would use the phrase "surprising activity," unless it refers to his surprise at external activity rather than enclosed inactivity. Similarly, why include the phrase "comforted with visits" unless there is an underlying recognition of disturbances and conflicts which Romano considered inappropriate to name specifically? Why was there need for Angelina to comfort her sisters?

The last pre-World War II entry to be cited is the "encyclopedic" entry by L. Oliger, taken from the *Dictionnaire d'Histoire et de Géographie Ecclésiastiques*. Published in 1924, it contains an interesting rendering of Angelina's history. He writes of her as taking up a "retired life with other noble women" and working for the poor. Sant'Anna is once again represented as having been from the beginning a monastery of Third Order

---

[92] Ibid. This is the interpretation of *L'Aureola*. The prescription was requiring the vow of poverty for *all* tertiaries living in community without enclosure. See Chapter Six, page 132–33 and following for a more complete discussion.

[93] Romano, 78.

cloistered sisters and the first of several founded by Angelina. Oliger names only the earliest monasteries associated with Foligno, and follows earlier writers who say that "many Italian towns, including Assisi, Florence, Viterbo, L'Aquila, would ask to establish monasteries of the same institute."[94] Regarding governance, Oliger says that Angelina "consented" to the requests, and "governed as superior general of the new foundations."[95] Unfortunately, Oliger's language removes any sense of leadership from the portrait of Angelina, once more offering a misleading view which supports (perhaps unconsciously) an early twentieth-century Catholic hierarchical view of governance; or, perhaps he echoes the original controversy of the fifteenth century.

In spite of the misleading view of Angelina's role as leader, Oliger recognized, as had *L'Aureola*, the structural and ideological change that had occurred with the promulgation of the *Rule of 1521* by Leo X. He states that the "order of Regular tertiaries, approved by the Church" (meaning Angelina's way of life) proliferated more and more, and cites Jacobilli's seventeenth century figures of 135 monasteries, 53 in Italy and 29 in France. Use of "approved by the Church" carries connotations of both seventeenth and nineteenth century ecclesial concerns, yet Oliger again seems uninterested in the location of the other 53 monasteries counted by Jacobilli. Why had the other monasteries, those not in Italy and France, not been identified by this time?

As far as the relationship between the houses federated with Angelina and the Friars Minor is concerned, there is no treatment of their troubles. Oliger omits that part of the story completely, passing over the period between 1428-1461 in a way that allows what happened to be summarized in one sentence: "But already under Pius II each monastery, with an abbess at its head, became independent."[96]

In evaluating the nineteenth century treatments of the story of Angelina's movement, the sources cited above furnish a severely limited view. They likewise offer a restricted treatment of the

[94] Oliger, 54.

[95] Ibid. These are taken form Mariano of Florence, who is cited in Oliger's sources.

[96] Ibid.

discordant relationship between the tertiary women living a common life according to the *Rule of Nicholas IV* and friars, preferring to exclude almost completely that portion of the biographical materials. Reasons for this omission can only be surmised, but among them one would have to include the complexity of the larger issues in Franciscan history, especially the Spiritual-Observant connection; the division of the First Order into three branches (Conventuals, Observants, and Capuchins) by the late seventeenth century; and the division of the Third Order into Regular and Secular branches.

Post World War II Works

With regard to the first three sources, that is, Cerafogli, Alessandrini, and D'Alatri, only a brief commentary is needed which is related specifically to new information or specific corrections. In addition, there are other appropriate materials to be cited because they offer significant insight into the history of interpretation. For the most part they consist of revisions or corrections by D'Alatri and works emanating from the internal life of the Tertiaries of Foligno, important because they reveal how the story has been told in internal sources—revealing the on-going self-understanding of the descendants of Angelina.

Cerafogli's entry in the *Biblioteca Sanctorum* of 1961 seems to follow the path of "selective history" established by other writers cited in the preceding two sections of this chapter. In his article, Cerafogli retains the detail of a 1397 profession of three vows, but calls them "evangelical" rather than solemn vows, placing a late-twentieth-century understanding of vows on his interpretation.[97] He names the monasteries in Assisi, Viterbo, Florence, and Rieti, following no specific earlier writer but mixing together information from a variety of sources.

Cerafogli cites Oliger, and implicitly, deClary, in crediting Martin V with the unification of Angelina's monasteries and with placing them under the jurisdiction of the Friars Minor. He does add one meaningful detail, often ignored by other writers, probably because it did not fit the "enclosed life" model within Angelina's

---

[97] Cerafogli, 1231.

story. Cerafogli writes that Martin V had also "assigned as their specific scope the education of young women."[98] This detail is both correct and incorrect; many of the houses associated with Angelina did engage in the education of young women—but they had done so well before Martin V "assigned" them the task.

A major corrective piece, as indicated in Chapter Two, is the work by Alessandrini in the *Enciclopedia Italiana*. He presents three dates for Angelina's arrival at Foligno, citing Jacobilli (1395), Wadding (1397), and Simoni (1385); he calls Sant'Anna the "first convent of regular tertiaries" and he is the first modern writer to retrieve the significance of Sant'Anna as the "monastery of the countesses." Alessandrini indicates that the other monasteries were of the same kind, i.e., almost exclusively women from noble families. He lists the monasteries named by Jacobilli, but corrects the foundation story about St. Onofrio, saying it had been founded a century earlier by Angela of Foligno and was reformed by Angelina.[99]

Alessandrini's interpretation of the issue of governance disagrees with the traditional one. He writes:

> The monasteries of the regular tertiaries were all linked among themselves and were administered by the sisters in a practically autonomous manner, according to precise constitutions and privileges obtained from Pope Boniface IX, Martin V, and Eugene IV, through the enterprising initiative of Angelina. The "minister" of each house, together with her discreets, met every three years in order to celebrate a Chapter and to elect a "minister general," who, accompanied by her more expert and capable sisters, periodically visited the various communities, in order to be able to maintain. . . discipline and to select the local leaders.[100]

For the first time, Angelina is called a leader of "enterprising initiative." For the first time in modern historiography, Angelina is recognized as the one who *obtained* constitutions, rather than as

---

[98] Ibid., 1232.

[99] Alessandrini, 209; based on Ughelli.

[100] Ibid.

a passive recipient of imposed law. Alessandrini appreciates Angelina's charismatic nature and leadership ability, as well as the autonomous self-governance of the women of the houses "linked among themselves." He demonstrates positive regard for the difficulties involved in the roles of minister and minister general without criticizing the itinerant lifestyle that the task of visitation required. Such attitudes differ greatly from the attitudes found in Mariano or Mark.

With reference to the spread of the "regular tertiary" movement and to the disagreements with the Friars Minor, Alessandrini continues his corrective:

> There were numerous disciples of Angelina, whose direction belonged in theory to the Observant friars; but in practice the sisters tended toward self-governance. From this situation will arise conflicts and resentments, especially after the vicar of the Order, Louis of Vicenza, succeeded in 1461 in obtaining from Pius II the abrogation of the privileges conceded to Angelina: the calling of the Chapter and the naming of the minister general (AFH XIV, 30).[101]

Alessandrini states openly the difference between theory and practice, and reports without comment the success of Louis of Vicenza in having the pope revoke privileges related to self-governance. In light of the language Alessandrini has used above, it seems that silence in this case is not so much positive agreement with what was done as much as implicit disapproval.

As in Chapter Two, the last post-World War II entry is the work of Mariano d'Alatri found in the *Dizionario degli Istituti di Perfezione*. In the sequence of interpretive material, it holds minimal value, other than reinforcing a connection to the eremitical aspect of Franciscan life which had reappeared with Paoluccio Trinci and his generation of the Observance. Angelina and the tertiaries live *ritiramente* (hidden) while devoting themselves to works of piety and mercy toward the poor. Enclosure in not alluded to at all in spite of the fact that every source listed

---

[101] Ibid.

in D'Alatri's bibliography treated that issue as part of the movement since its foundation.

Some three years later another entry written by D'Alatri appeared in the *Dizionario degli Istituti di Perfezione*, covering the "Franciscans of Blessed Angelina."[102] After summarizing the events and describing the foundation as one of women leading a common life according the *Rule of the Third Order of St. Francis*, Angelina's foundation is clearly described as non-monastic and un-enclosed:

> In the exercise of apostolic activity the early sisters did not impose self-limitations: they accepted work in all fields open to women's action in the 15th and 16th centuries. After the death of blessed Angelina, the forms of apostolate remained unchanged: even the abolition of the office of minister general imposed by the Pope, recognizing a kind of autonomy of individual houses, did not reduce the actions in local situations. These actions were carried on until 1617, when in consequence of the Council of Trent, the religious were forced by animosity to accept enclosure.[103]

After Trent's imposition of enclosure, according to D'Alatri, the Franciscans of Blessed Angelina did not renounce all apostolic works but "continued to exercise those that were compatible with the new kind of life: education and religious, cultural, and social formation of young women who lived in the monastery and from which they went out prepared for life."[104] It seems apparent that D'Alatri had consulted the internal sources of the community in order to prepare this piece.

Conclusion

As with Angelina's life before Foligno, so, too, in her life after 1395 a number of historically verifiable elements might be

---

[102] Mariano D'Alatri, "Francescane della beata Angelina," DIP, 1977 ed. In depicting the growth of the Institute D'Alatri cites incorrectly the figures found in Jacobilli, transposing 135 houses to 305. This is most likely an error due to the Italian language similarities for the numerals involved.

[103] Ibid.

[104] Ibid., 270.

expanded upon. Based upon the sources used in this chapter, the following series of conclusions can be drawn: (1) Angelina arrived in Foligno and chose to associate herself with the monastery of Sant'Anna, founded by Paoluccio Trinci for *bizzoche*-tertiaries; (2) Sant'Anna was an "open monastery" of noble women who chose to follow the *Rule of Nicholas IV* and lead a common life; (3) the spirit of the house was that of "regular observance," i.e., literal observance of the *Rule* for tertiaries;[105] (4) the tertiary-*bizzoche* boundaries were fluid because the women did not envision for themselves the enclosed life of nuns with solemn vows; (5) Angelina was by 1415 the leader not only of Sant'Anna but also of a group of houses affiliated with Sant'Anna; (6) self-governance was of singular importance to this group; (7) the Friars Minor were, at best, inconsistent in their attitudes toward such tertiary-*bizzoche* women; (8) the internal problems of the friars played a major role in several stages of the process of monasticization, a process that took until 1617 to complete; (9) Angelina's form of life was dynamic enough to spread throughout Europe by the seventeenth century.

If one removes the enclosure agenda from the source materials, what surfaces is a picture remarkably similar to that found in Chapter Two. Angelina is once again recognizable as a leader of women in various places, faithful to the inspiration of her own vocation. She helped shape a more specific model of tertiary common life based on Franciscan ideals. In an interesting reversal of the first part of her life, at Foligno Angelina enjoyed civil as well as papal support. It was not the secular world that troubled Angelina after 1395; rather, the struggle of the last thirty years of Angelina's life emanated from internal Franciscan roots. It also seems that the issue of "decentralized individuals" and boundary maintenance appertains, especially within the Franciscan context. The Friars Minor replaced the feudal nobles and the King of Naples as the disgruntled power-brokers and "authority" which stood against Angelina.

---

[105] "Regular observance" appears often in papal bulls directed to houses connected to Sant'Anna. See BF n.s. II, n. 437, addressed to St. Anthony in Perugia: "sub regulari observantia vestri tertii ordinis S. Francisci de Poenitentia"; BF n.s. II, n. 241; BF VII, n. 1826, addressed to "Angelinam de Marscianam Fulgin."

But something must have been good and "right" for the women, because numerous houses flourished in spite of the troubles with the question of supervision or self-governance. Many similar monasteries were part of Angelina's institute at the time of her death, and the number increased under the continuing watchfulness of her "disciples." Monasteries in twenty-two provinces of Europe followed the *forma vitae* of tertiary common life without solemn vows, especially without the vow of poverty. Angelina refined the parameters of that life and set up guidelines for those areas not covered by the *Rule of Nicholas IV*. What follows in the next chapter turns to the missing houses of Angelina's Institute, recovered in connection to the spread of the Observance eastward.

CHAPTER FIVE

Establishing the Observance in Poland

Even as the tertiary women associated with Angelina of Montegiove and her federated monasteries struggled to maintain their identity as unenclosed ecclesial women in the second half of the fifteenth century, their form of life moved beyond the borders of Italy. Material presented in the last chapter revealed, via the sixteenth-century work of Mariano of Florence and Mark of Lisbon, a polemical attitude within the Order of Friars Minor toward the communities led by Angelina. But later historical records show that two of the major figures in the "second generation" of Italian Observance, Bernardine of Siena and John Capistran, knew of and encouraged the extension of Angelina's tradition in Italy (Bernardine) and Poland (Capistran). Foundational material taken from fifteenth- and sixteenth-century civil and conventual archives substantiates the eventual migration to Poland of Tertiary Observance in the style of Sant'Anna and Angelina of Montegiove. Examination of some of these sources will offer an entry into additional material (to be treated in the next chapter) through which it is possible to identify a significant number of Polish houses related to Angelina's Institute.

Bernardine of Siena and John Capistran

The Italian Observance reborn through the efforts of Paoluccio Trinci in the late fourteenth century had been characterized by an eremitical life, its hermitages usually located separately from the large houses of the urban, "conventual" friars. Its members were, for the most part, plain and simple men, more often lay brothers than clerics.[1] But no single form of Franciscan life is permanent, and as new members entered Observant houses—including men desiring ordination—the perennial Franciscan quandary concerning a choice between an active life or a life of solitude resurfaced. When in 1405 Bernardine of Siena was appointed as one of the Order's official

[1] Cf. Nimmo, 587.

preachers the transformation of Paoluccio's tradition began in earnest.[2] As for the women of Angelina's monasteries, the "urban recluse" model remained in place, and remained, as well, an integral aspect of Tertiary Observance.[3]

Due to his preaching ministry, Bernardine ran into opposition at once from his confreres in the hermitage at Il Colombaio:

> they did not have the books which were a necessary preliminary to effective preaching; the devotion of one of their fairly small number to study and preaching meant that the life of the community would be upset, both spiritually and materially (by his absence from . . . divine service and the necessary collection of alms).[4]

The friars who lived with Bernardine considered the active life "inimical to the properly eremitical spirit of prayer and solitude which was their own highest aim," and thought that an apostolic life was "incompatible with that [life] bequeathed them" by Trinci."[5] In spite of these difficulties, perhaps with Bernardine as example, more friars came out of Observant novitiates committed to preaching, evangelization and itinerancy. Among them was John Capistran, who fell into Bernardine's sphere of influence and became his most fervent disciple. Trained as a civil lawyer, Capistran served at the court of Ladislaus, King of Naples, before entering the Friars Minor of the Observance in 1415.[6] In addition to his work on the Martinian Constitutions discussed in Chapter Four, one of the significant areas of endeavor undertaken by Capistran was the defense of the Third Order. He claimed that after the

---

[2]Ibid., 588.

[3]Mario Sensi writes of the "hermits" of the Third Order, a "penitential movement that was allied to the reform of the regular observance promoted by Paoluccio Trinci and that later found its charismatic guide" in Angelina of Montegiove. See M. Sensi, "La Regola di Niccoló IV dalla costituzione 'Periculoso' alla bolla 'Pastoralis Officii' (1298-1447)," in *La "Supra Montem" di Niccoló IV (1289): Genesi e diffusione di una regola*, ed. R. Pazzelli and L. Temperini (Rome: Analecta TOR, 1988), 178.

[4]Nimmo, 588.

[5]Ibid.

[6]Ibid., 457. This is the same Ladislaus of Naples so prominent in the story of Angelina.

Council of Constance he had obtained "about a hundred bulls" for the Third Order.[7] In the 1450s and '60s his work with the Third Order in eastern Europe involved both establishment of the Observant branch of the Friars Minor and the reception of women tertiaries into penitential, "observant" life.

Both Bernardine of Siena and John Capistran had connections with the tertiary form of life established at Sant'Anna. In 1426 Bernardine preached a series of Lenten sermons in the city of Viterbo; one result of his preaching was the foundation of a monastery for Third Order women. The names of the sisters sent from Foligno to Viterbo as a result of Bernardine's request are found in the Archives of the Monastery of Sant'Anna: Chiara of San Venanzo, Letitia of Santi da Capodacqua, Santa, and Orifica of Foligno.[8] As indicated in Chapter Four, Jacobilli included St. Agnes monastery in Viterbo as part of the federation associated with Angelina of Montegiove.[9] When Bernardine was canonized in 1450, the sisters of St. Agnes in Viterbo began to identify themselves communally as "*bizzoche* of S. Veradino."[10]

In addition, Capistran undoubtedly knew of Angelina's houses: he had instructed a group of tertiary women from Parma to contact sisters from Piacenza who lived "the way, form, institutions and regulations of the monastery of Foligno"—so that the sisters from Piacenza would come to Parma to instruct the tertiaries there in that way of life.[11]

Such cases demonstrate that, if women tertiaries desired to live a more perfect life without entering the enclosed life of the Poor Clares, both Bernardine and Capistran were willing to direct

---

[7] John Hofer, *St. John Capistran, Reformer*, trans. Patrick Cummins (St. Louis: B. Herder, 1943), 100. Also, see Matanic, "San Giovanni da Capestrano," 81-90 for an examination of four specific texts in which Capistran's influence is presumed present.

[8] AMSA, Ms. "Regola e Costituzioni," f. 33r, cited in Filannino, *Studi sulla B. Angelina*, 101, note 64.

[9] See note 61, chapter four above.

[10] Act of 1454, "Margarita Cleri," 123; cited in *S. Bernardino - S. Giacinta 1426-1807 Notizie Historiche*, ed. G. Regis (Viterbo: Tipografia Cionfi, 1907), 9, note 16. It is unclear why "V" is used rather than "B."

[11] See BF n.s. I 509-10, n. 1021 and BF n.s I, 299, n. 632. This material is cited by Filannino in "Fondazioni," page 5, notes 15 and 16.

at least some of them toward the form of life of Angelina's "Institute." One of Capistran's letters indicates that he considered himself to some extent responsible for what he called "religious of the Order of penance," an important point to remember as the discussion below unfolds.[12]

Eventually, Bernardine of Siena became one of the first Observants to serve as Vicar General of the Friars Minor. After forty years of preaching throughout Italy, he died in L'Aquila on 20 May 1444; he was canonized in 1450. Capistran outlived his mentor by some eleven years, also served as Vicar General of the Observants, and became the leader of the Cismontane Observant houses, as well as a famous opponent of the Hussites.

Capistran Establishes the Observance in Poland

In the last years of his life (1451-56) John Capistran left Italy to confront heretical groups in Silesia, Hungary, Bohemia, and Poland. Along the way he "planted" the Observance in those regions.[13] In 1452 Pope Nicholas V "erected into a Province all the convents [male] founded by" Capistran. In Poland the Observant Friars Minor were called "Bernardine Fathers" and by 1467 the number of Observant houses was large enough to warrant the establishment of three separate provinces in Austria, Bohemia and Poland.[14] So it is historically correct to speak of expansion of the Observant movement into eastern Europe in connection with the journeys of John Capistran.

---

[12] Capistran wrote in a letter: "I have the general care of devout professed brothers of the Order of Minors of the Observance, and the professed Sisters Minoresses, and Clares or Damianites of the Observance, and of those religious of the Order of Penance, in Cismontane parts." From D. Fabianich, *Storia dei Frati Minori dai primordi della loro istituzione in Dalmatia e Bosnia fino ai giorni nostri* (Zara, 1864), 47; quoted by Matanic in "Defense," p. 48, note 4. *Lives of the Saints and Blesseds of the Third Order of St. Francis*, IV (Taunton, England: 1886), 224, note 28, explains that "*The Cismontane family* comprised Italy, the adjacent islands, Austria, Poland, Turkey, etc. *The Ultramontane family* (that is, situated with regard to the Italians, *beyond the Alps*) extended over France, Spain, Belgium, Rhenish Prussia, the British Isles, and later on the New World." Hereafter cited as *LSB*.

[13] BF n.s. I, n. 1658 (4 May 1453): the bull grants Capistran the right to receive candidates for the Friars Minor of the Observance in "every place" he visits in Bohemia, Austria and Moravia.

[14] *LSB*, 394, note 62.

But what of Third Order Observance? In the preceding chapter, information provided by Jacobilli and cited by later writers indicated that in 1626-27, when Jacobilli was writing and publishing his first version of a *Vita* for Angelina, there were 135 houses of the "institute" located in twenty-two provinces of Europe. The question was raised: if Jacobilli counted among them fifty-four in Italy and twenty-nine in France, where were the others? Since Capistran preached in and established houses of friars of the Observant Tradition in the cities of Moravia, Silesia, Bohemia, and Poland, could houses of women of the Tertiary Observance also have been established in those places? For Poland, the answer is definitely "yes."

From 28 August 1453 to May 15th of the following year, Capistran lived in Cracow as the guest of both King Casimir IV and Cardinal Sbigniew Olesnicki. He was present at the marriage of Casimir to Elizabeth, sister of King Ladislaus of Bohemia.[15] His biographers indicate that he preached daily, in Latin; that he propagated devotion to his recently canonized friend, St. Bernardine of Siena; and that he ultimately invested 130 teachers and students from the University of Cracow as Friars Minor.[16] Cardinal Olesnicki donated to Capistran a newly built church, which Capistran asked to be called the Church of St. Bernardine in honor of Bernardine of Siena.[17] Therefore, the friars associated with that church and with the Observant tradition in Poland were called "Bernardine Fathers" by the people.[18] While at Cracow Capistran acceded to the request of one of the noblewomen of Warsaw who wanted the Observant friars to come to her city; in

---

[15] Hofer, 292.

[16] *LSB* IV, 392, 394, 401. Hofer indicates that by early February, 1454, the "Observants of St. Bernardine" were 80 in number; see *Capistran*, 299-300.

[17] Hofer, 431.

[18] Romuald Gustaw, *Klasztor i Kociólw. Józefa: SS. Bernardynek w Krakowie 1646-1946*, Biblioteka Krakowska 105 (Cracow: 1947), 30. Gustaw was a "Bernardine Father" who served as Chaplain at the Convent of St. Joseph in 1945-46. Founded in 1646, St. Joseph Convent ultimately absorbed the convents of St. Agnes and St. Colette--the first Third Order houses of women in Poland. Hofer, 431, indicates that in Poland during the years Capistran was there a number of convents and churches were founded bearing the name of St. Bernardine, as throughout the entire Province.

1454 Capistran sent seven friars to establish a foundation there.[19] Both in Cracow and Warsaw women asked to be received into the Third Order almost immediately.[20]

When Capistran died in 1456, less than three years after leaving Cracow, "convents" of Bernardine Fathers were well established in several places in Poland. In various places, usually in conjunction with the foundation of a convent of friars in a particular place, groups of women joined the Third Order for the enrichment of their spiritual lives. The Tertiary Observance moved into Poland through these women.

The Origins of the "Bernardine Sisters"

The preaching of John Capistran affected a large segment of the population in Cracow beyond those at the university who joined the Friars Minor. According to Gustaw:

> . . . not only young men under the influence of the firey sermons of St. John Capistran begged for the habit of St. Francis; the women came, too, and begged to be received. The Saint could not accept them into the Second Order of St. Francis, that is, the Poor Clares, who at the time had in Cracow their own convent under the name of St. Andrew; it was under the jurisdiction of another branch of the Order of St. Francis, that is, the Friars Minor, later called Conventuals, and here in Poland "Franciscans." Desiring nevertheless to defer to the request of the devout women, St. John accepted them into the Third Order, meant by St. Francis for people "living in the world," and even in marriage, and not connected in any way with a monastery.[21]

---

[19] Kamil Kantak, *Bernardyni Polscy 1453-1572*, Vol. I (Lwow: Nakladem Prowincji Polskiej OO. Bernardynów, 1933), 11 and *LSB*, IV, 402. Kantak used the records of the Province as his source for his work, and may have found this information in a number of manuscripts; however, he gives no specific references concerning these records.

[20] Bogumil Migdal, "Bernardynki," *Zakony w. Franciszka w Polsce w Latach 1772-1970*, I, ed. Joachim Bar (Warsaw: Akademia Teologii Katolickiej, 1978), 27 (hereafter cited as Migdal); and H. E. Wyczawski, "Krakow," *Klastory Bernardyksie w Polsce e Jej Granicach Historyczynych* (Kalwaria Zebzydowska, 1985), 544 (hereafter cited as *KBP*). Neither of these sources gives footnotes or citations; instead, they provide only bibliographic titles for each section of their work.

[21] Gustaw, 30. He summarizes Holzapfel's "Tertius ordo regularis feminarum," in *Manuale historiae Ordinis Fratrum Minorum* (Fribourg, 1909), 612-17. Obviously, the

As Gustaw continues, he notes that the history of tertiary women connected to the preaching of John Capistran belongs to three groups in Cracow: two in an area called Stradom, and one in an area called Kazimierz (see figure 5, p. 114).[22] Gustaw, other secondary literature and hitherto unnoted documentary sources clarify their affiliations: one group in Stradom is identified as the sisters of the convent and church of St. Agnes, and the other group is known as the "Koletki," or Colettes, a group with a house but no church.[23] The Kazimierz tertiaries are usually identified only by the geographic location, although they may be the group which lived near the "St. Nicholas Gate."[24] The sequence of "foundation," i. e., the order in which the women gathered together to live a common life according to the *Rule of Nicholas IV*, is impossible to ascertain. Most twentieth-century histories mention all three groups, but without agreement on which group was comprised of those received by Capistran himself. Material on Capistran in the *Dizionario degli Istituti di Perfezione* specifically identifies him as the founder of St. Agnes Convent in Cracow.[25] In addition, the histories are complicated by the use of multiple terms of identification in Poland, just as in Italy. Sources use "kletki," "tercianki," "Koletanki," and "bernardynki," but all of them refer to the women leading a communal life according to the "Third Rule of St. Francis."[26]

---

internal problems of division between the Observants and Conventuals were experienced in Poland just as in other places and influenced Capistran's attitude in directing women to the Third Order.

[22] Gustaw, 31-32; and Wyczawski, "Krakow," *KBP*, 517, 522, and 524 for each group, treated separately. The Kazimierz group is the most difficult to treat, because of the absence of any internal records that clearly pertain to them.

[23] Gustaw, 29-30. The designation "Colettes" is related to the name given by the women to the house in which they resided: St. Colette. It does not mean that they were connected to the reform of the Poor Clare convents in France, led by Colette of Corbie (+1447). It may, however, have something to do with the fact that Colette was a member of the Third Order before she reformed the Poor Clares.

[24] Gustaw, 31, n. 3 cites the Archiwum Aktów Danwych m. Krakowa, ms. Ambrozego Grabowskiego, no. 23, p. 1037, r. 1456.

[25] O. Bonmann, "Giovanni, da Capestrano, santo," *DIP*, 1977 ed. The same article credits Capistran with awareness of the problems of Angelina and her tertiaries, and states that his "Defense of the Third Order" was at least in part related to achieving positive ecclesial recognition for groups such as hers.

[26] See Kantak, 256; Gustaw, 29; Wyczawski, "Krakow-w. Koleta," *KBP*, 522.

The map below reveals the basic location of the first houses of tertiaries in Cracow in the 1450s. The large area is the Kazimierz area (spelled Casimiria). The area marked by the [X] is the location of the church and convent of St. Agnes and the house of the Colettes. Today there remain two intersecting streets, Agnieszka and Koletek, marking the area; the buildings are used for care of the elderly.

Two testaments recorded in the Acts of the city of Cracow from the 1450s provide the earliest civil references to these women. The first is a testament dated 14 May 1454, which is a bequest to "the young women of the Third Order of St. Francis."[27] It is worth noting that the date of the bequest is one day before Capistran left Cracow. The second document dates from 1458 and mentions a home by the Mikolajski (St. Nicholas) Gate.[28]

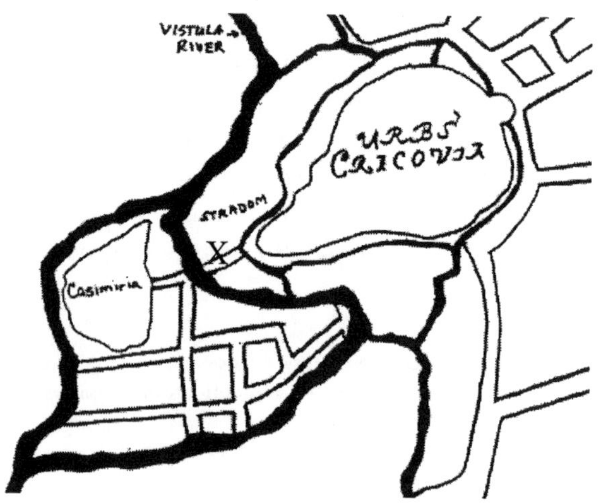

Fig. 5: Map adapted from photo of display at St. Agnes Church, Cracow. Original display said to have been provided to the Church by Jagellonian University.

[27] Kantak supplies a date of 14 May 1454 for Test 33 1454 f. 3, but does not specifically state that the document is from the Archiwum Akt Dawnych w Krakowie; see Kantak, I, 256, note 2.

[28] Archwum Aktów Dawnych w Krakowie, Test 52; cited by Kantak, 256, note 3. Gustaw, 31, also mentions two archival documents, but gives dates of 1456 and 1458; note 23 above gives full citation for the 1456 document. There is no note referring to the 1458 item.

Internal archival records from the community which descended from the "Third Order of St. Francis" mentioned in the 1454 document can be found in the Archives of the Bernardine Sisters who have resided at St. Joseph Convent in Cracow since 1646. These archives supplement the city records. A diploma dated 28 June 1462 names the members of a civil commission and confirms that Stanislaw Dzywczak gave his house on Stradom to the "ladies in the convent of St. Bernardine on Stradom" and that this house was received by their guardian, Dwchon of Cracow. Attached to the document is the official seal of the city of Cracow (see figure 6, p. 116).[29] Because the document uses neither "St. Agnes" nor "Colettes," it is uncertain which group received this house. Later documents suggest it may have been the latter since St. Agnes is specified clearly when it was the recipient. Thus, in another diploma, dated 21 November 1463, the same commission confirmed that Blaszko and his wife Swietochna gave their house on Stradom built near the river to Marusza, the superior, and to the ladies of the convent near the church of St. Agnes of the congregation of St. Bernardine in Stradom and that this house was received by the sisters' guardian, Marcin Belse (see figure 7, p. 116).[30] The expansion of the group at St. Agnes is indicated clearly in a third internal document, dated 30 April 1464: the same commission confirmed that Zofia of Cracow gave up through the mediation of her husband, John, the blacksmith of Cracow, half of her house next to the church of St. Agnes in Stradom, to Dorota Wanczykowna, a "sister [religious] of St. Bernardine."[31] Given the different dates of donation, the different guardians, and the fact that diplomas of 1463 and 1464 name "the church of St. Agnes," it is possible, and perhaps probable, that the earliest donation (1462) is connected to the "Colettes."

---

[29] Archiwum klasztoru SS. Bernardynek przy kosciele w. Józefa w Krakowie (hereafter ACSJ), diploma 3. There are sixty-four such diplomas in the archives, covering the years 1434-1872. Each document is listed only as "diploma" with a number. The diplomas are the original documents, not copies, kept in separate envelopes. There are also 232 manuscript items in the archives, several of which contain multiple documents.

[30] ACSJ, diploma 4. The official seal is missing.

[31] ACSJ, diploma 5. Seal is missing.

Fig. 6: Diploma 3 from the Archives of St. Joseph Convent, Cracow (Photo by author)

Fig. 7: Diploma 4 from the Archives of St. Joseph Convent, Cracow (Photo by author)

In attempting to establish specific identities for the group at St. Agnes and for the "Colettes," other internal documents are helpful. In a collection of documents at St. Joseph Convent which covers the years from 1461 to approximately 1850, the very first text states that St. Agnes Convent was the "first in Poland among all the convents of the Ladies of the Third Rule of St. Francis" and says they were not cloistered, just as the "kletki"—a possible corruption of *Koletki* or Colettes—were not.[32] A later version of the foundation story contained in a manuscript written in 1735 in St. Agnes Convent tells the story in a somewhat different manner; it makes no mention of John Capistran and refers instead to John Hincza as the "saintly founder."[33]

Yet another early modern text (date unknown) claims a direct link with John Capistran: "The beginning of the order of sisters of the Third Rule of St. Francis in this place" stems from the fact that:

> King Casimir III of Hungary imported St. John Capistran, and also with him came tertiaries [female plural ending] where now is the church and convent of St. Agnes . . . where there was first a small chapel . . . [and] the sisters of the Third Rule of St. Francis lived without cloister up to the year 1461.[34]

---

[32] ACSJ ms. 206 (1461 - ca. 1850), "Documents pertaining to the Convent of St. Agnes," document 1, in Polish. The date on the document is "146_"; the discussion of enclosure suggests a post-enclosure point of view, and likely dates from after 1461, since that is the year in which the first move toward enclosure took place. The history of this convent will be more fully presented in Chapter Six.

[33] ACSJ ms. 207, "Description of the founding of the very famous convent of the virtuous lady and martyr, St. Agnes," p. 6. The text focuses on Hincza and Gabriel of Verona, and presents a version of the founding story that emphasizes the vows and enclosure, much as did Jacobilli's work on Angelina. The historical and cultural realities of early eighteenth-century Poland undoubtedly shaped the telling of the story.

[34] ACSJ ms. 206 (1461-ca. 1850), 2-5. There is a pencilled-in date of 1461-1709 on this section of the manuscript. It is probably a copy made later rather than earlier, due to the incorrect identification of Casimir as "III" rather than IV--likely a scribal error. The DHGE lists no Casimir III, and gives 1456 as the date of the marriage of Casimir IV (see DHGE, 1949 ed.).

"Imported" is a deliberately considered translation, consciously used here, (even though it could also be translated "invited") because it implies being brought in for a specific purpose. The choice of "imported" reflects the presence of Capistran in Cracow as the result of repeated, insistent requests of King Casimir, who intended that Capistran establish the Observant friars in the kingdom.[35]

A most important piece of data is hidden within this text: Capistran is said to have *brought women tertiaries into Poland.* This is the only reference in internal documents to this kind of interpretation, but it offers intriguing opportunites for speculation, especially with regard to the Tertiary Observant communities associated with Angelina of Montegiove. There has been a long-standing discussion over the possibility that some of Angelina's "disciples" came to Cracow to model the communal Third Order Observant life. Given the connection of Capistran to the tertiaries of Angelina at Piacenza and his advice to the tertiaries of Parma about learning that way of life, he could conceivably have brought some tertiaries east. Honorat Kozminski's work published in Poland at the beginning of the twentieth century summarizes the discussion about such a possibility:

> What nationality were they, since they were called Koletki? Through whose efforts were they invited to the Polish capital? The chronicles of the congregation have not preserved the details from those times. We presume only that probably one of the Italian convents . . . sent them to Cracow around 1453 at the same time as the Bernardines [men] arrived there with St. John Capistran. From various manuscript excerpts from the convents, we can find out only this, that Koletanki in Cracow from the beginning lived not far from the Bernardine Fathers, and lived by the work of their hands and from alms.[36]

Raising the question of nationality and a possible connection to an unidentified Italian group of convents in conjunction with the

---

[35] Hofer, *Capistran*, 295. Hofer and *LSB* both identify the King as Casimir IV.

[36] Honorat [Kozminski] Kapucyna, "Koletanki Polskie," *Swiety Francizek Seraficki i nasladowcy jego II* (Warsaw: Druk Piotra Laskauera i Spólki, 1902), 290.

arrival of Capistran in Poland under an entry dealing with the "Koletanki" provides food for thought, to say the least. Whether "invited" or "imported," some of the Koletki were not Polish. Kozminski echoes the material from the archives of the Bernardine Sisters convent, cited above, even if his excerpt does not mention St. Agnes Convent by name.[37]

A more recent source, one which deals with the history of St. Agnes Church itself, clearly affirms the "foreign origin" construct:

> Historical records permit us to cite the first accurate date for the church of St. Agnes as late as the fifteenth century. "Behold, in the year 1459 Hincza from Rogow, the administrator of the salt mines in Wieliecka, and an official of Sandomierz, builds a wooden convent and church, by the name of St. Agnes, and gives them to the *zakonnicem* of the Rule of St. Francis of Assisi, brought over by St. John Capistran, so-called Bernardines."[38]

The rest of the Kozminski passage where he suggests that his sources were in convents, presumably of Colettes, requires additional comment. The records of the congregation called the "Koletanki" have been divided between the Archives of the Convent of St. Joseph and the Archives of the Bernardine Fathers, both in Cracow, but Kozminski chose not to acknowledge this (perhaps because the Bernardines of his era had distanced themselves from the Koletanki, perhaps because of his own agenda). Some of the records of the Colettes are located in the archives of

---

[37] Rev. K. S. Gruczynski, a Polish scholar and historian who is currently writing a study of St. Agnes Church in Cracow stated in an interview in Cracow that there is no historical proof that Capistran brought women tertiaries with him into Poland. Either he is unaware of ms. 206 in the Archives at St. Joseph Convent which mentions "tertiaries" —in the female plural—who came to Poland with Capistran (see p. 117), or he has some reason to consider it insufficient as "historical proof." The content of the text clearly contradicts Father Gruczynski's point of view. Interview by author, written notes, Cracow, Poland, 30 September 1995.

[38] Henryk Werynski, *Ku Czci w. Agnieski* (Cracow: N. P. Garnizona, 1958). This is a small pamphlet found in the library of the Bernardine Fathers in Cracow, in which a sub-section is titled "History of the Military Church of Cracow"; it is on p. 9 of this section that the cited material is found. *Zakonnicem* would mean religious women, the "so-called Bernardines." Unfortunately, there is no citation of primary source material by Werynski.

the Bernardine Sisters because the last Colettes were absorbed into the St. Joseph Convent group in 1823 (as were the sisters from St. Agnes in 1788). In "Koletanki Polskie" Kozminski identified by name the last two Colettes, and those same names appear in the registry of the sisters at St. Joseph.[39] His separation of the history of the Koletanki and the Bernardine Sisters, in spite of documentary resources cited above indicating they are connected, is problematic; in reality the history of the Koletanki/Colettes constitutes a major part of the history of the Bernardine Sisters.[40]

Another source indicates that there was apparently a property dispute between the sisters at St. Agnes and the Colettes (another indication of troubled relations); an archival record at St. Joseph Convent indicates that part of a property with buildings next to the bishop's palace belongs to the "sisters of the Third Rule of Saint Francis" and not to the convent of St. Agnes. The location next to the bishop's property evokes two considerations: it echoes the protection and assistance given by the bishop of Foligno to Angelina when she arrived there, and it provides a strong link between the Colettes, Capistran and the "imported tertiaries," since Capistran had been the guest of Bishop Olesnicki.[41] The archival category in which this document is located is "Convent of St. Colette."[42] From the sources other than Kozminski it is possible to identify the Colettes as one of the early groups treated in the

---

[39] Kozminski, 291, and Gustaw, Table 5, p. 189. The sisters were Nepomucena Walewska and Apolonia Smagalska.

[40] In the same interview cited in note 37, Rev. Gruczynski stated that some of the original group of tertiaries gathered at St. Agnes left in a disagreement over enclosure, and opened a new house—St. Colette—but he did not provide historically verifiable sources to support his statement. Other viewpoints on the Colette foundation will be treated in greater detail in the next chapter. It is noteworthy that Sr. Zygmunta Froncek included the "Sisters at St. Coleta (sic) convent" as Bernardines. See p. 4 of "Historical Sketch of the Bernardine Sisters, O.S.F. 1457-1957," from the Archives of the Bernardine Franciscan Sisters (hereafter ABFS), n. p., a monograph published by the community for the 500th anniversary of foundation.

[41] See p. 77, Chapter Four and p. 111 above for information about respective bishops.

[42] See Gustaw, 10, for a list of the manuscripts of ACSJ under the heading "Konwent w. Kolety." See also the description of ms. 222.1 in the *Katalog Archiwum Bernardynek w Krakowie*, Biblioteki i Muzea Kóscielne, Tom. 20, ed. Romuald Gustaw and Kazimierz Kaczmarczyk (Lublin: Nadbitka z Czasopisma Archiwa, 1970).

documented history of the Bernardine Sisters—and the history implies an originally "foreign" influence.

Conclusion

What can be said with assurance about the establishment of the tradition of Tertiary Observance in Poland? First, the Third Order phenomenon of women in Italy living a common life under the *Rule of Nicholas IV* and support of that life by Bernardine of Siena and John Capistran has been documented. Second, the arrival of this form of life in Poland coincided with the arrival of John Capistran and the Friars Minor of the Observance in Cracow, Warsaw, and other places. Third, historians refer to three distinct groups of unenclosed women tertiaries present in Cracow in the second half of the 1450s, groups which soon enough were confronted with questions of enclosure and obedience to the guardians of the Observant Friars Minor. Finally, the possibility exists that at least one of the Cracovian groups was taught Tertiary Observance as it had been lived in Italy in the houses associated with Angelina of Montegiove, either during the federation period of the 1420s-30s or in the subsequent struggles over governance in the 1450s or 60s; it would, in either form, have had as basic elements an "open monastery" and *bizzoche* (support yourselves by the work of your hands) model.

What happened to Tertiary Observance as it developed in Poland requires a more detailed examination. How many groups of tertiaries can be identified in addition to Cracow's groups? What kind of parallels were there to the Italian Tertiary Observant experience especially with regard to enclosure? Did the Friars Minor provide and sustain a relationship of loving care and special solicitude? Did the tertiary sisters promise obedience in return—and more importantly, was the promise freely given or coerced? Some clarity on these questions will emerge from the material in the following chapter.

CHAPTER SIX

Angelina's Presence

— Bernardine Life and History

Chapter Five documented the migration of the Observant Tradition into Poland and identified Cracow and Warsaw as two cities in which Third Order women's groups were begun while John Capistran was in Poland. But that barely introduces the scope of Third Order presence there, or the historical ramifications with respect to Angelina's movement. Chapter Five proposed that perhaps two or three houses known to Jacobilli were in Cracow. Were there others, tertiary women related to the St. Agnes and St. Colette groups of Cracow, and did they constitute a spread of Angelina's Institute? After Tertiary Observance came to Poland, how did it survive? What kind of life did the women live, enclosed or not? Did they observe the *Rule of Nicholas IV* (or of Leo X after 1521)? How did they support themselves? What relationship did they have to the Friars Minor known as Bernardine Fathers?

The answers are found within an examination of the first one hundred to 150 years after the arrival of Capistran in Poland, when the rapidly-spreading Observance there flourished. It can be established that by 1590 groups of tertiary women living according to the Third Rule of St. Francis had emerged in at least sixteen different towns or cities. The information about each house varies, but certain common characteristics link them to what has been called thus far Tertiary Observance. The characteristics of these early groups include: (1) living a common life; (2) adherence to the *Rule of Nicholas IV*, and later the 1521 revision by Leo X; (3) association with the parish church of the Bernardine Fathers in a given place; (4) living without enclosure at the time of foundation; (5) making private vows of obedience and chastity, but not of poverty; and (6) certain basic elements of what later came to be called "apostolic life," but which were related to Third Order life of the fifteenth century.

To establish such conclusions, documentation internal to the tradition will be used to supplement material from histories compiled by the Friars Minor. Additional historical resources brought forward for the first time provide new insight in two areas: (1) the long-term significance of Angelina within Third Order history, and (2) the transmission of her story into the twentieth century within the Bernardine Sisters' congregation. And an appeal will be made to another source not used in preceding chapters: reference to and analysis of pieces of material history, that is, of representations of Angelina in iconography, art, and stained glass present in Poland and the United States which support the identification of the Bernardine Sisters as part of the extended tradition of Angelina.[1]

Foundations at Cracow: 1454-1594

The standard against which all of the Polish tertiary groups are to be measured is that set in the convents of St. Agnes and St. Colette in Cracow, discussed in the previous chapter. Because Cracow stands as the place of foundation, it is important to delineate more thoroughly the history of the original groups. In 1453-54, as indicated above, John Capistran had received an unspecified number of "devout women" as tertiaries, undoubtedly with the understanding that they would live a common life according to the *Rule of Nicholas IV*. According to historiographic sources about the Cracow communities, the "original" form of life joined personal vows of obedience and chastity to common life and the *Rule of Nicholas IV*.[2] The tertiaries "led a frugal life, supporting themselves by the work of their hands and by donations. For liturgical functions they went to the Bernardine Fathers and were under their supervision."[3] As tertiaries they were involved in charitable works such as care of the sick or of the poor

---

[1] The Bernardine Franciscan Sisters, present in the United States since 1894, were founded by a group sent from Sacred Heart Convent in Zakliczyn, Poland. Zakliczyn had been founded in 1882, by two sisters from St. Joseph Convent in Cracow, itself founded in 1646 from St. Agnes, founded in 1459 or earlier. There is, then, a direct and uninterrupted connection back to the 1450s.

[2] Gustaw, 30; Wyczawski, "Krakowsw. Koleta," 522.

[3] Gustaw, 31.

and supported these charitable works from their own financial resources.[4]

Within a short time some, but not all, of the St. Agnes group desired to live a "true" religious life, that is, with statutes and enclosure.[5] The house became the enclosed "St. Agnes Convent" referred to in a number of documents and historical summaries. One of the more significant internal documents indicates that St. Agnes Convent was the "first in Poland among all the convents of the Ladies of the Third Rule of St. Francis." The same text also states that the tertiaries of St. Agnes Convent were not cloistered at first, but soon "made efforts to become enclosed" (even though six members of the group did not want to accept the cloister).[6]

The effort to become enclosed involved making requests for "statutes" or "constitutions," which were received some two years after John Hincza's donation of the convent and church (see p. 117 above). The requested statutes still exist, in an eighteenth-century Polish translation; the text is addressed to the "dear daughters in the Lord Christ, the Mother or Elder and the Sisters of the Third Rule of St. Francis, known as the Penitents, who live together in

---

[4] Froncek, "Historical Sketch of the Bernardine Sisters, O.S.F. 1457-1957," page 1. She seems to be compiling material from Czeslaw Bogdalski, *Bernardyni w Polsce 1453-1530* (Cracow: Rudolfa Butryma, 1933). Bogdalski wrote a two-volume history of the Bernardine Fathers which includes voluminous but widely scattered references to the various foundations of Bernardine Sisters.

[5] ACSJ ms. 207, page 6: "Description of the founding of the very famous convent of the virtuous lady and martyr, St. Agnes." The early eighteenth-century book in which it is contained is, in its own words, "accurately copied from the archives of the Observant Fathers." Page 4 indicates that it was necessary to retell the founding story in the early eighteenth century because of the loss of records and older manuscripts as a result of the destruction of the convent during the Swedish invasion in the 1650s.

[6] ACSJ ms. 206 (1461-ca. 1850). The document is identified with a page number added in pencil (1); it also has an incomplete date: 146_. It is difficult to tell if there once had been a numeral in the last place which was later removed, or if it had never been filled in. The indication that the women had lived without enclosure is found in the same ACSJ manuscript, and on page 6, the year of enclosure is given as 1461. The same year for enclosure is indicated in ACSJ ms. 206 (1461-1709), 18. There is nothing in the foundation story that would preclude what can be called the "Angelina influence" of an open monastery/ convent, because between 1453-1461 none of the Cracow groups lived within enclosure.

community in Cracow, by the Vistula."[7] It affirms that the women insistently requested "statutes through which you would offer yourselves more peacefully and in a secure way as a pleasing sacrifice to God," living in community in an enclosed convent.[8]

The "Statutes of Rangoni" are the work of Gabriel of Verona (later, Cardinal Rangoni), who had accompanied John Capistran to Poland in 1453; he would, therefore, have known the tertiaries' origins. Rangoni was the Vicar General for the Cismontane Observant Province between 1460-62.[9] In the introduction to the text, Gabriel of Verona indicates that he had spoken with Pope Pius II about the tertiaries' request for enclosure, and had received a mandate to "undertake to do all, as I may deem necessary, for your holy demeanor, that is, to enclose, establish, order, decree and protect . . . such things that in your Order and condition be strongly kept and retained for all time."[10] In effect, he had been granted "carte blanche" with respect to the community.

Two comments must be made concerning the "Statutes of Rangoni." First, that they date from either 1461 or 1462 is noteworthy because of Pius II's role in the dissolution of the office

---

[7] ACSJ ms. 151, 8r, hereafter referred to as "Statutes of Rangoni." This book is a hand-written copy from approximately 1735. The full text covers fol. 8r-14v, or pp. 17-30. The latter numbers derive from the inclusion of the "Statutes of Rangoni" between two other texts in the manuscript. The date on the Rangoni text is 146?; historical works such as Migdal and Gustaw claim that the date was 1461. The last numeral seems to have been erased, but a photocopy partially brings out the missing number as a 2. This text has yet to be published or studied, since up until the present it has been held as an interior manuscript of the Bernardine Sisters. A Latin version, presumed to be the original language, does not exist in the Archives of St. Joseph Convent. The *AM* XIII, 438, identifies three houses of "Sisters of the Third Order" in Cracow, two without enclosure and St. Agnes with enclosure, in year 1465.

[8] ACSJ ms. 151, "Statutes of Rangoni," 8v.

[9] J. Komorowski, "Kronika Komoroski," *Monumenta Poloniae Historica* V, 195; *AM* XIII, pp. 49-50 refers to the work of Gabriel of Verona in Poland in 1457; p. 169 of the same volume of *AM* refers to "many and beneficial constitutions published [decreed]" in the Chapter of the friars held in Lublin in 1459, which Gabriel gave to the rest of the Order and Provinces. See also Gustaw, 32; Kantak I, 16, 256; Migdal, 27.

[10] ACSJ ms. 151, "Statutes of Rangoni," 9r. The BF II, n.s., n. 864 affirms that Gabriel of Verona had been given a papal commission, dated 23 December 1460. The text of the commission, however, is not printed in the *Bullarium;* a note refers to the Reg. Vat. t. 504, f. 37—that is, the Vatican Archives. At this time, the text remains unrecovered.

of minister general for Angelina's tertiary houses in 1461.[11] It is also meaningful that while Rangoni speaks of the "Order" to which the sisters belong, clearly linking them to the Third Order of St. Francis intended for those "living in the world," he does not see a contradiction in linking Third Order women and enclosure. With the acceptance of the "Statutes of Rangoni" approximately eight years after the arrival of Capistran in Poland, a canonically erected convent of tertiary sisters had been established in Cracow. It remained the only such "canonical" convent for over a century.

At St. Agnes Convent, how long the "Statutes of Rangoni" were adhered to is uncertain, as is the extent of the enclosure observed there.[12] At some point the sisters "kept an educational institution, wherein many noble and aristocratic families placed their daughters," but this may have begun in the seventeenth century.[13] As for the religious life of the community, the Divine Office was sung in Latin, and the women devoted themselves to a "contemplative" life, although there is little detailed information about what the term "contemplative" meant at the time. Handwork, especially the embroidery of vestments, was also part of the tradition and a source of income. The "work of your hands" as the source of one's livelihood connects these women to the Italian *bizzoche* tradition in a very concrete way. Governance involved the election of a superior and discreets every three years, and the Chapters were under the supervision of the Provincial of the Observant Friars, although it is not clear when that supervision began.[14] After the "Statutes of Rangoni" were promulgated, some of the tertiaries remained outside the enclosure of St. Agnes. They

---

[11] See Chapter Four.

[12] There is an interesting bull from 1472 that indicates the strictness of the life at St. Agnes. It grants the request for a transfer of a Poor Clare from a monastery in Theuz, in the diocese of Prague, to a "coenobium" of the "Third Order of St. Francis with enclosed nuns" in Cracow. This must be St. Agnes Convent. See BF n.s. III, n. 146.

[13] Migdal, 34.

[14] Wyczawski, "Krakow-sw. Koleta," *KBP*, 518. It could have begun as early as 1461, with the Statutes of Rangoni, since their provisions referred to the role of the "Guardian of St. Bernardine" in selecting the "mother" (superior) in case the previous one should die before her term of office was complete. See "Statutes of Rangoni," 14r. The three-year cycle of elections duplicated the practice of Sant'Anna and of the Friars Minor.

more than likely moved to the house of the Colettes, or perhaps to the Kazimierz group, although this is less tenable historically.[15]

But the convent of St. Agnes is not the only Third Order Observant group in Cracow for which significant information exists. The convent called St. Colette probably dates from 1458; at least, this is the date the Bernardine Sisters' history has used.[16] Other sources say the Colettes sprang up simultaneously with the 1454 group that became St. Agnes Convent.[17] At the beginning they, too, lived a common life, followed the *Rule of Nicholas IV*, and professed vows, that is, simple and private vows of chastity and obedience. The people called them tertiaries, Colettes, and "klepti" or "klepki," an untranslatable colloquial expression.[18] The membership of this house came "principally from common ordinary women" who were unenclosed and who earned their livelihood "from the work of their hands." They worshipped at the church of

---

[15] The latter possibility may be considered, based on two sources. First, in the ABFS, ms. 501.1.A-1-3 there is a typescript translation of parts of the work of Czelaw Bogdalski on the history of the Bernardine Fathers in Poland (Polish title not given), published in Cracow in 1933. Bogdalski (Vol. II, p. 179) identifies a convent "on the Casimir called the convent of St. Colette." This view does not fit the perspective outlined in Chapter Five, it conflates two locations. The two Bogdalski volumes are now in the library of Alvernia College, Reading, Pa. Secondly, the connection may be considered if one relies upon the internal but undocumented version of foundation dates of the Bernardine Sisters' houses. On 25 September 1995 Sr. Kinga Josefowicz, the present superior at Sacred Heart Convent in Zakliczyn, Poland, gave the author a typed list of convents with a date of opening and a date of closing. There is no provenance given for the list, which is titled "Bernardine Sisters' Convents in Poland—Dates of Foundation." Although it differs in some significant respects from other sources, it agrees on most of the dates of foundation found in Gustaw, Wyczawski, and Migdal. The "Zakliczyn list" gives 1458 as the foundation year for Cracow-St. Casimir. However, there is a problem in that "St. Casimir" is anachronistic: the person born in 1458 who became "St. Casimir" is not the person for whom the location was named; other sources use "Kazimierz" in a geographical sense.

[16] Zakliczyn list. The same date is given for the group in Kazimierz. At least one published history of the Bernardines gives the same date; see H. E. Wyczawski, "Klastory bernardynek wedlug dat fundacji," *KBP*, 571, table 2.

[17] Gustaw, 31; Migdal, 34.

[18] Wyczawski, "Krakow-sw. Koleta," *KBP*, 522; Gustaw 29. "Colettes" is a name found in descriptions of other tertiary groups in Poland, also connected to locations in which the Bernardine Fathers resided: Kobylin and Tarnow. Parallel lifestyles are found in many more places, as will be evident in what follows.

the Bernardine Fathers and had an assigned place there.[19] Similarly, histories of the Bernardines mention the group at Kazimierz as contemporaries of the Colettes, stating that they followed the same style of life, and in some cases, call them the "Colettes at Kazimierz."[20] Both the house of St. Colette and the Kazimierz group lived an open and active life until the 1590s, when the issue of enclosure could no longer be avoided. Both Wyczawski and Gustaw refer to "abuses" present in the unenclosed houses, but do not specify what the problems or "abuses" were.[21]

Sixteenth Century

The Transition to Enclosed Communities in Cracow

The situation in Cracow—two houses of unenclosed tertiaries and one enclosed house—lasted for more than 140 years, until the attempts to enforce the decrees of the Council of Trent began. In 1560 the Council had ordered strict enclosure and solemn vows for all religious,[22] including tertiaries leading a common life, but the decrees were not immediately implemented in Poland.[23] Ultimately, however, by 1592 the Provincial of the Bernardine Fathers was ordered by the papal nuncio to carry out the reforms of Trent "without compromise."[24] In Cracow, the first tertiary community to be "reformed" was the Kazimierz group, supposedly because of "abuses and lack of discipline prevalent among the sisters."[25] In effect the house was summarily closed and the sisters transferred to the Colettes on Stradom.[26] Some of the Kazimierz

---

[19] Wyczawski, "Krakow sw. Koleta," *KBP*, 522. Migdal, 34, says that the sisters had their own chapel, but no church. He does not mention their going to the church of the Bernardine Fathers.

[20] Wyczawski, "Krakow sw. Koleta," *KBP*, 522 for calling them the "Colettes in Stradom and Kazimierz"; see same author, "Krakow-Kazimierz," *KBP*, 524, for a virtually identical description of life as given in the section on the Colette house.

[21] See next page.

[22] See Pazzelli, *Franciscan Sisters*, 99, which refers to the decree "De regularibus et monialibus," chapter v, and to *Conciliorum Oecumenicorum Decreta* (Herder, 1962), 753-54.

[23] ACSJ, ms. 207, p. 6.

[24] Kantak II, 358, cited in Gustaw, 32-33.

[25] Gustaw, 33.

[26] Ibid.; see also Wyczawski, "Krakow-Kazimierz," 524.

tertiaries vehemently resisted this move, and the Provincial, Gabriel of Czerniejew, called in civil authorities. Those sisters who would not go to Stradom were "dissolved" and the community at Kazimierz ceased to exist. Gabriel then turned his attention to the enlarged group at St. Colette, where he met additional opposition.[27] One of the problems was that with thirty women residing there the house had become too crowded, and the Colettes complained. In 1593 the guardian of the Bernardine Fathers bought half of a neighboring piece of land; the other half was donated, and the guardian built a stone convent for the community.[28]

According to historical interpretations given by both Gustaw and Wyczawski, the sisters at St. Colette tried to frustrate the "reform" in every way, even appealing to civil and ecclesial authorities. The Cardinal at the time, Jerzy Radziwill, requested the 1594 Chapter of the friars not to impose any further reforms on them. The response of the Chapter was to remove the "stubborn" Colettes from the house and prohibit the remainder from accepting novices until the next (1597) Chapter of the friars.[29] The 1594 Chapter also had elected a new Provincial, Benedict Gasciorek, who quickly persuaded the Cardinal of the need to enforce the decrees of Trent.

One point needs emphasis with respect to the Colettes. Even though Honorat Kozminski treated the "Koletki"—what he calls "Koletanki"—as a different entity than Bernardines, internal tradition of the Bernardines at Zakliczyn embraces the Colette heritage as its own. A letter sent in May 1971 from the superior at Zakliczyn to the Bernardines in the United States in response to a request for information on Bernardine history gives the name of a Polish source, Sergius Skalniak, which cannot be further identified. The summary in the letter includes the statement that "The female component called the 'Colettes' were the nucleus of the present Bernardine Congregation of the Third Order Regular of St. Francis." The summary reports the enclosure of the group at St.

---

[27] Gustaw, 33.

[28] Wyczawski, "Krakow-sw. Koleta," *KBP*, 522. A Latin text for the donation exists in Cracow, ACSJ ms. 222, with "7" pencilled in on the upper right corner of the page.

[29] Gustaw, 33; Wyczawski, "Krakow-sw. Koleta," 522.

Agnes in 1459 and says that the "remaining convents continued for about the next century as "Colettes" living a common life without the enclosure while attending services at the Bernardine Fathers Monastery (sic)."[30] Among the places Skalniak listed as part of Gasciorek's reform of "Colettes" are Cracow, Poznan, Warsaw, and Lvov (Lwow); and "in other towns, the 'Colette' houses were partially dissolved. Others lost the right to accept Novices (sic), a strategy aimed at extinction."[31] The source (Skalniak) cannot be checked, but it is a first tantalizing indication of an alternative tradition within the community. If one accepts the internal understanding and very much unadorned and apolitical interpretation contained in this document, a greatly altered picture of Third Order history in Poland ensues; in the latter view, the Colette life undoubtedly contained the seeds of what evolved eventually into the "Bernardine Sisters."

In Cracow, Gasciorek followed through on the work of the previous Provincial, Gabriel of Czerniejew, both at St. Colette and St. Agnes. On 4 November 1594 the thirty Colettes in Stradom heard the order that all tertiaries living communally be enclosed.[32] Because the Colettes did not have their own church or a stable source of income (since they primarily consisted of women who were not nobility), Gasciorek decided to dissolve the convent. He forbade the sisters to accept new candidates and advised the sisters already living at St. Colette to transfer to St. Agnes Convent.[33] However, St. Agnes already had its own church, and enclosure had been in place to some extent since 1461-62; to transfer there meant acceptance of a different form of life. The Colettes decided to

---

[30] The date of 1459 more accurately refers to the year in which the convent was donated by John of Hincza. ABFS ms. 501.1.A -1-7-2a, dated May, 1971; translated from Polish in January, 1985 by Sr. Victorine [Cieslukowski], the late Vicar General. The author/source is identified as "Father Sergius Skalniak, OFM, Bernardine." It is unclear if this text is a direct quote of Skalniak's work, or is the work of "Mother M. Kinga" [Josefowicz], the superior who sent it to the U.S. In September, 1995 Sr. Kinga referred to a Skalniak "book" several times in conversation with the present author, but could not find the book in the community library or archives at Zakliczyn.

[31] Ibid.

[32] Gustaw, 34.

[33] Wyczawski, "Krakow-sw. Koleta," *KBP*, 523. Gustaw, 34-35. Gustaw softens his description of the event, claiming that only the prohibition against novices was enforced, not the transfer to St. Agnes.

remain where they were. For many years they obeyed the prohibition against new members, but in 1638 the last survivor, rather than allow the community to die, accepted three novices (defying the long-standing prohibition), thus ensuring the survival of the house. By 1649 there were so many sisters that the Chapter of the Bernardine Fathers decided to limit their number to 33.[34] The community survived all the way into the nineteenth century, finally closing under duress from civil and church authorities in 1823.[35]

With respect to the group at St. Agnes, when attempts were made in 1594 to implement the "reform" of papal enclosure and solemn vows at St. Agnes Convent, sources indicate that Gasciorek met much resistance: "The tertiaries residing there made to that point only simple vows, excluding the vow of poverty, and lived according to the *Rule of Nicholas IV*. They did not want to accept the new *Rule of Leo X* or the edict of Pius V."[36] The "new" *Rule of Leo X* was not new; it had been promulgated in 1521 with the precise intention of adapting the *Rule of 1289* for tertiaries living a common life. Immense diversity existed among groups that had formed in the fifteenth century, since the 1289 *Rule* had not provided for regulating common life or for internal government. Many groups, including the tertiaries of Angelina, had fashioned their own "constitutions." Because of such diversity, in 1521 Leo X addressed the problems of communities living by a *Rule* unsuited to their needs (i.e., a rule containing articles pertinent to married couples but lacking material for those "who serve the Lord . . . in virginity and celibacy").[37]

---

[34] Wyczawski, "Krakow-sw. Koleta," *KBP*, 523, and Gustaw, 36.

[35] Gustaw, pp. 74-77; Migdal 34; Wyczawski, "Krakow-w. Koleta," 523.

[36] Gustaw, 33. The papal decree pointedly mentioned "women who are called tertiary sisters or Penitents . . . who live a common life"—clearly inclusive of Third Order Franciscan women of the tradition of both the Polish tertiary communities and Angelina's tertiaries. See *Bullarum, Diplomatum et Privlegiorum Santorum Romanorum Pontificium Tauriensis editio*, 1862, t. VII, pages 447-52, (cited in Pazzelli, *Franciscan Studies*, note 13, page 101).

[37] "Rule of the Brothers and Sisters of the Third Order of St. Francis as Contained in the Bull of Leo X," in *Rule and General Constitutions of the Brothers of the Third Order of St. Francis* (Dublin, 1910), 22 (hereafter, *Leo X*). For the Latin text, see Wadding, *AM* XVI, 1933 ed., 147-50.

Analysis of the *Rule of Leo X* suggests that the resistance at St. Agnes and other tertiary houses to the 1594 reform was both a response to the *Rule* and to its post-Tridentine re-interpretation and enforcement. First, Leo X's text was addressed specifically to "Brothers and Sisters of the Third Order of Blessed Francis, living in congregation under the three essential vows."[38] The text does not refer Third Order communities which did not make the third vow, to live "without property," so it appears to be based upon an inaccurate assumption that all Third Order groups at the time of its promulgation made the vow of poverty. At St. Agnes in Cracow, for example, the "Statutes of Rangoni" made mention neither of the "three essential vows" nor of any individual vows; as to "poverty," Rangoni prescribed only that the community "possess all things in common."[39] Any tertiary group with *bizzoche* roots could, with some justification, say that the 1521 text did not apply to them since they had never intended as part of their vocation to renounce property, nor was it their practice. Secondly, the *Rule of Leo X* did not require enclosure for every tertiary community. It did command a *continuation* of enclosure wherever it had already been vowed: "The Sisters, also, are bound to keep enclosure, who have already vowed to keep it . . . ." However, it *granted* the right to choose enclosure *"provided that the hospitality and charity which they are wont to exercise towards the infirm . . . suffer no detriment"* (emphasis added).[40] According to the text of 1521, enclosure and a vow of poverty were required only where they had previously been in place, and it is clear that the *Rule* in no way intended to impose them or to change the tertiary custom of charitable work. The struggle and resistance not only at St. Agnes but also in many other tertiary houses must be considered in light of the internal understanding of the original form of life and the sisters' desire to preserve the vocational charism as they understood it.

At St. Agnes, issues of property and ownership were at least as significant as the enclosure question. The members of the community received numerous donations, which often were invested in prop-

---

[38] *Leo X*, 21.

[39] ACSJ ms. 151, "Statutes of Rangoni," 10r. This is significant, especially as a connective thread between Cracow and the Angelina tradition.

[40] *Leo X*, 30.

erty; the dowries of new members were also substantial, because many of the women came from nobility or were from families of "city patricians."[41] By the closing years of the fifteenth century the community had been able to lend money, even to the King of Poland.[42] The 1521 *Rule of the Third Order*, as presented to them in the 1594 reform, would have altered the very foundation of their way of life. The poverty question from the interpretation of Observant friars once again distorted the Third Order interpretation.

At St. Agnes Convent in Cracow the issue of poverty versus the right to maintain ownership of property and management of income stands out most clearly at the time of Gasciorek's reform: only eight sisters and one novice agreed to accept the changes, while fifteen others refused. Although the majority did not accept the reform, Gasciorek decreed that they were no longer permitted to hold any office in the community, i.e., superior, vicar, portress, etc., and they were not to vote in any election. Only the nine who made solemn vows (and placed their personal monies in a communal fund) were eligible to vote or hold office. The fifteen sisters who were thereby made a second-class group asked to leave the cloister; the conditions under which this would be permitted were very harsh, so they remained.[43] In effect, then, two different communities with different standards for the implementation of Third Order life lived under the same roof.

At the end of the sixteenth century there remained a diversity of lifestyles for the tertiary groups in Cracow: the Colettes lived according to the prescriptions of the *Rule of Nicholas IV* and without enclosure, and were comprised of women who had lived at Kazimierz as well as the core group; at St. Agnes, some of the group lived according to the same lifestyle as the Colettes, and a smaller part of the group lived according to the rules of the Tridentine

---

41 Wyczawski, "Krakow-sw. Agnieszka," 518.

42 ACSJ diploma 8, dated 8 March 1474 indicates that John of Hincza has acted as a sort of broker for the community: "money had been loaned to the king, and king is now responsible for annual payment of interest to the Convent of St. Agnes."

43 Gustaw, 34-35. The conditions for transfer included being allowed to go only to some enclosed group with solemn vows, finding a group to accept them, and making a new novitiate.

reform given them by Benedict Gasciorek. The multi-tiered community at St. Agnes was deeply divided, and in 1646 the superior of St. Agnes moved with some sisters who wanted a new reform, to a new convent, St. Joseph. At that point, three separate groups of "Bernardines" lived widely varied lifestyles in three different convents in Cracow.

The drive of Benedict Gasciorek to impose solemn vows and papal enclosure on the Third Order sisters in Cracow and the attempts of many of the women to remain faithful to the original form of life mirror, albeit 160 years later, the struggles of Angelina of Montegiove and the Italian Observant Tertiaries. Gasciorek spent 1594-95 traveling across Poland, visiting most of the tertiary groups associated in some way with the Bernardine Fathers, and ordering that the sisters make profession of solemn vows, including poverty and enclosure. Two conditions accompanied the order: the sisters had to have their own church, and they had to have a stable source of income, since they would no longer be permitted to leave the convent to seek alms or to work outside the enclosure. In the places where these conditions could be met, there was no deliverance from the new laws. The *option* of not being enclosed which had been permitted by the *Rule of Leo X* was abolished. It mattered little that enclosure would end many of the works of charity which had always been part of Third Order life. The reaction of Trent to the Reformation swept away the interpretive freedoms that had existed for tertiaries for centuries.

Houses Open in Jacobilli's Era

As the Bernardine Fathers moved across Poland into Lithuania and the Ukraine, so did the Tertiary Observance. Between 1454-1627 over twenty groups of tertiary women were established in conjunction with the friars' foundations or were founded by means of the transfer of some members of an existing house to a new location.[44] The places and dates of foundations outside of Cracow which follow are divided into two classifications. The first

---

[44] For information concerning these houses, see Appendix C. Additional information can be found in my doctoral disseration, "Retrieving a Living Tradition: The Recovery of the Historical Significance of Angelina of Montegiove: Franciscan, Italian Beguine, and Leader of Women (UMI, 1996).

consists of houses clearly founded as part of the extension of tertiary life that was unenclosed and involved in some form of semi-active religious life, following the *Rule of Nicholas IV*. The second, smaller group consists of houses founded after 1590 either as enclosed houses in which the members were required to make the three vows or as new houses for the unenclosed when the original foundation accepted enclosure.

Based on available sources, none of the Polish tertiary communities established before 1590 and ultimately called "Bernardine Sisters" was *originally* founded on a monastic, solemn vows-and-enclosure model of religious life. All but one of the groups attended the churches of the Observant Tradition friars (that is, the Bernardine Fathers), at least in the beginning. Classic signs of tertiary-*bizzoche* life adhere to every group to some degree: dependency on alms and donations from benefactors; self-support from the "work of their hands"; some form of charitable service, such as caring for the sick, praying for the sick or the dead, attending funerals, or even some form of educational activity. Most groups are referred to at some point in the early history as tertiaries; they often are described as retaining ownership of property and use of income. In a few cases there are examples of exemption from taxation, and resultant conflicts with the pastor of a church. The vows of chastity and obedience are present—but no indication is given as to who received the obedience. (That any particular group was under the jurisdiction of the Bernardine Fathers, it may be said, does not automatically insure the promise of obedience was made to the friars' guardian or provincial, although it is likely that this is what happened, at least in some places.) Perhaps the most accurate descriptive statement that can be offered about the early foundations is that there were many commonalities among the groups, but there was also room for diversity: before the 1590s there does not seem to have been a uniform code for the form of life. However, after the Council of Trent, that changed radically, as shown above.

The unenclosed houses consist of the following foundations: Warsaw (1454), Wschowa (1456), Kobylin (1456), Poznan, 1457, Lwow (1460+), Kalisz and Przeworsk (1465+), Radom (1468),

PLACE	DATE OF FOUNDATION	DATE OF CLOSING
CRACOW (SC)	1453	1823
CRACOW (SA)	1453	1788
CRACOW (KAZ)*	1458	ca. 1595
WARSAW (SC)	1454	1655
WSCHOWA*	1456	1538/58
KOBYLIN*	1456/91	1600
POZNAN	1457	1655
LWOW	1460+	1782
KALISZ	1465+	1804
PRZEWORSK*	1465+	ca. 1600
RADOM*	1468	ca. 1595-1600
KOWNO	1468+	1885
KOSCIAN	1472	ca. 1630
WILNO (Zar)	1495	1655/1864
BYDGOSZCZ	ca. 1500	1615
LUBLIN	1535	1864
WARTA	1538	1898
TARNOW	1550	1783
WILNO (SM)	1594	1886
WARSAW (2)	1594	1656
PRZANYSZ	1605	1871
WIELUN	1613	EXTANT
GRODNO	1617	1853
BRESC-LITEWSKI	1622	1656/1831
DRZEWICA	1626	1814

Fig. 8: Chart of Bernardine convents 1454-1626. Based upon Zakliczyn List, Migdal, and *KBP.* The five locations not included by Jacobilli are noted with an asterix (*).

Another house could have been included in the list, a third house in Warsaw known as Warsaw-Praga. The inclusion of Warsaw Praga is tentative, at best. Migdal dates the foundation as 1622, and the Zakliczyn list and *KBP* as 1666. So it has not been listed.

Kowno (1468+), Koscian (1472), Wilno-Zarzesce (1495), Bydgoszcz (ca. 1500), Lublin (1535), Warta (1538), and Tarnow (1550). Of these, Kobylin, Przeworsk, and Radom disappeared before 1626. In Cracow the group at Kazimierz was suppressed (1594) for refusing to accept enclosure.

The convents founded as enclosed communities were in Przanysz (1605), Wielun (1613), Grodno (1617), Bresc-Litewski (1622), and Drzewica (1626). In Wilno a second convent—enclosed—was established (St. Michael-1594) while the first Wilno group remained unenclosed. When the original Warsaw group accepted enclosure, women not willing to lose their original form of life opened a new unenclosed house (1594), also in Warsaw.

Examination of this material leads to the conclusion that Jacobilli could have had information on as many as twenty houses of Tertiary Observance founded in Poland between 1454-1626 to include in his work on Angelina in 1627 (see figure 8, p. 138).[45]

Common Threads in Tertiary Life: Italy-Poland

Specific internal parallels exist suggesting that the broad concepts of Polish Tertiary Observance emanated from the tertiaries of Blessed Angelina. If life at Sant'Anna and other monasteries associated with her federation was unenclosed and marked by works of charity, it likewise had a distinctive communal and spiritual design. A brief overview of what Tertiary Observance meant with respect to common life, spiritual praxis, and the role of work both in Italy and Poland provides additional grounds for linking the communities in Poland to the tradition of Angelina.

Regarding the common life of tertiary houses in Angelina's tradition, it is possible to deduce what some of the administrative decisions made by Angelina might have been, or at least what the tradition had allowed to evolve by the end of the fifteenth century. The inferences which follow are drawn from the text of early "constitutions" of Santa'Anna in Foligno, which can be dated

---

[45]The list has been compiled from the secondary sources used in this chapter and in Appendix C, even though there are some differences in those sources about given houses.

at just after 1476 and are conserved in a sixteenth-century copy from the monastery of St. Onofrio in Florence.[46] The guardian of common life was the minister; she had authority to dispense any sister from any item in constitutions as well as to exact obedience; she accepted confession of faults of the sisters; she visited the cells of the sisters to see that they observed the prescriptions of the community, and where there was need, provided for the comfort of the sisters.[47] But the office was not so authoritarian as it may first seem. The final disposition in the text of the constitution provides that "the minister must hold a chapter with all the sisters once a week" to administer the "good order of the house, [aimed first at] the honor of God, the health of the heart, and the peace of the house."[48] In addition, part of the mechanics of ensuring good administration of the community was provided by means of an article outlining the structure of administration (if not exactly governance): the minister, in consultation with a few of the older sisters, every All Saints Day would assign the offices of sacristan, *corista* [choir person/director of Divine Office], *chanovaia* [equivalent to steward, the one in charge of the pantry or larder], infirmarian, portress, mistress of novices, and other offices to whoever seemed proper. The sisters to whom the offices were given were to humbly accept them, not excuse themselves and do them with patience.[49]

Specific areas of spirituality likewise warrant attention. One of the most significant areas pertains to the Divine Office. The *Rule of Nicholas IV* had provided for private recitation of the Office (for those who were able), and participation at the funerals of confreres. It had also provided that every brother and every

---

[46]The manuscript is currently at Oxford, Bodleian Library, Canon. Liturg. 347 (cat. 19433): *Manual of Offices and Constitutions*. The text of the "Ancient Constitutions of Foligno" has been published as the Appendix to Marco Bartoli's "Le antiche costituzioni delle monache di Foligno," in *La Beata Angelina da Montegiove e il movimento del terz'Ordine regolare francescano femminile*, ed. R. Pazzelli and M. Sensi (Rome: Analecta TOR, 1984), 135-38. Citations from the text of the constitution will be documented as "1476," with a page reference in Bartoli's Appendix.

[47]"1476," 137.

[48]"1476," 138.

[49]"1476," 137-38. One senses here the remnants of the guidelines of Angelina, since all the early sources mention her right as minister general to visit houses and remove from office incompetent administrators. See Chapter Four, above.

sister should hear Mass daily in his/her parish; but it prescribed meetings for common prayer only once a month.[50] For Angelina's community there was a major change; instead of minimal significance, the Divine Office was given a "particular importance and was quite regulated."[51] The center of the house was the church, and the choir was the locus of common prayer. It was expected that every sister would be present for the recitation of the hours of the Office, day and night, unless prevented by infirmity or age, or excused for a specific purpose approved by the minister.[52] The penitential psalms were always to be said in the choir; and the Office of the Dead was always to be said in choir except on solemn feasts or their octaves. Specific qualities of saying the Office were prescribed: a submissive voice, pausing always at prescribed places, behavior which did not lead to distraction or errors in recitation, etc.[53] Beyond the prescriptions for common prayer, Angelina's Observance also provided for a rich experience of private prayer, primarily in terms of "reclusion" and "contemplation." Chapter Four provided several instances in which authors recognized Angelina's desire and choice to live *ritiramente.* Evidence of how that was put into practice also emerges from the 1476 Constitutions. Between Prime and Terce each sister was to remain in her cell "in prayer." In summer, after the midday meal, "a bell rang and all went to their cells and stayed there in contemplation. . ."[54]; during the time of silence, the sisters engaged in whatever aspect of solitude suited them. So an alternating set of requirements guided *bizzoche*-tertiary spiritual life: common prayer in the choir and private prayer in one's cell marked the spiritual rhythm of Tertiary Observance.

A third element found in the 1476 constitution is the community's understanding of work. By the time of this document, work had become, according to Bartoli, one of the cornerstones of common life. The constitution prescribes that: "No sister must do work other than that which is granted her and entrusted by the minister or

[50] Bartoli, 124.
[51] Ibid., 128.
[52] "1476," 135.
[53] "1476," 135.
[54] "1476," 136.

whoever she appoints." And, as the work, so must the product of work serve the common life: "No sister must work to have her comforts or desires met, but everything is for the use of the house, always with the permission of the minister."[55] According to Bartoli, the "new" concept here is that of common usefulness: the work (probably weaving or embroidering, the "work of one's hands") had to serve the common sustenance of the sisters.[56] In effect, all income was "common" and had to support the life of the group.

None of the above prescriptions of the 1476 constitutions are particularly startling, nor would they have contributed to the difficulties with the friars. Their importance lies in the similarity to materials relevant to the tertiary groups in Poland. According to the index found in Appendix C, part III, the role of the Divine Office or the Office of the Blessed Virgin is mentioned in the descriptive material about the Bernardine houses in Cracow, Warsaw, and Tarnow; the penitential psalms or Office of the Dead are mentioned in reference to Warsaw and Poznan. Manual work or the "work of their hands" is mentioned for Cracow, Warsaw, Lwow, Kalisz, Przeworsk, and Warta, and may be presumed for any houses founded in relationship to them—Kobylin, Tarnow, Przanysz, and Wielun—or for any house to which the label "Colettes" was attached.[57]

In addition, an examination of the text of the "Statutes of Rangoni" from 1461 produces a number of remarkably close parallels with the 1476 constitutions of Angelina, as the texts on the next page illustrates.

Because Rangoni's text pre-dates the 1476 text by fifteen years, there are no verbatim matches; it is probable that Rangoni was not literally copying a text from Italy and that the 1461 Statutes reflect to some degree an outsider's understanding of the tertiary life. Nevertheless, when the essence of the cited texts is combined with the historical perspective already presented, the similarities in the guidelines increase the sense of a strong relatedness

---

[55] Bartoli, 129.

[56] Ibid., 130.

[57] See Appendix B.

1476 Text	Rangoni text
The minister must hold a chapter with all the sisters once a week [to administer the] good order of the house, the honor of God, the health of the soul, and the peace of the house.	I order and decree that every Friday after Compline . . each sister is to humbly and devoutly confess her faults concerning public failures, omissions and faults committed.
Every sister must be present for the recitation of the Hours of the Office, day and night, unless prevented by infirmity age, or excused for a specific purpose assigned by the minister.	I order and decree that the educated of similar sisters celebrate the major canonical Hours or the Office of the Blessed of Virgin Mary according to the customs of the Roman church in Latin.
[Penitential psalms were] "always to be said in the choir; from the feast of Cross in September until Easter, [they were to be said during the night]	. . . and also the vigils for the dead after Vespers and the penitential psalms after Lauds, from the feast of St. Francis until Easter.
[In summer, after the midday meal] a bell rings and all go to their cells and stay there in prayer	And in the summer, when the sisters rest after lunch, no one is to speak to another without any need or a just cause.
No sister must do work other than that which is granted her and entrusted to her by the minister or whomever she appoints.	I order and decree that . . . you are to live from your work and from the goods that will be given to you.
No sister should work to have her comforts or desires met, but all for the use of the house, with the permission of the minister.	You are to possess all things in common, whether moveable goods or landed properties. No one is to possess anything without the permission of the Mother or Elder.

between the tradition of Angelina and Tertiary Observant life in Poland. This seems particularly true in three areas: the use of income for the common good, praying the hours of Divine Office in common, and time reserved in the privacy of one's room for individual prayer.

In summation, based on the texts of the archives of both congregations, on the developmental process and the similarities of conflicts presented thus far, it is clear that a relationship existed between the Tertiary Franciscans of Blessed Angelina and the Bernardine Sisters of the fifteenth and sixteenth centuries, both in terms of the founding moment and in terms of the effective history of the relationship between the tertiaries and the friars.

Historical Transmission of the Angelina Story

The connection of the tradition of Angelina of Montegiove to the history of the Bernardine Sisters in Poland has been recognized not only within the latter community itself, but also by historians who have published material which confirms the connection. Further, the connection has been passed on through the narrative history and spiritual tradition of the Bernardine Sisters in the United States, although in a sometimes fragmented manner. The final section of the present chapter will introduce some of the ways in which the transmission of the story has been accomplished.

The comments of Kozminski and Werynski cited in Chapter Five indicate the kinds of external reference made to the possible importation of Third Order women into Poland by Capistran.[58] In addition, there are other more reliable resources which attest to the Angelina influence as part of the foundation story of the Bernardine Sisters. The entry describing the community in the *Dictionnaire d'Histoire et de Géographie Ecclésiastiques* contains the following information:

> *Bernardine Sisters of the Third Order of St. Francis,* American Congregation of pontifical right of regular tertiaries of St. Francis, of Polish origin.
>
> In 1457, in Cracow, a group of noble women of Cracow belonging to the Third Order of Saint Francis desiring to

---

[58] See pp. 117–19 above.

> live a common life in the manner of the daughters of Blessed Angelina of Marsciano established a community under the influence of the Friars Minor, established in the city by St. John Capistran; since they [the women] assisted at Divine Office in a church dedicated to St. Bernardine of Siena, they were designated under the name of Bernardines.[59]

The entry continues with a brief comment on the foundations of St. Joseph Convent in 1646 and Sacred Heart Convent in Zakliczyn in 1883 and concludes with a longer summary of the history of the American foundation.[60]

Another source, Bogumil Migdal's history of religious orders in Poland, gives a more detailed summary of the presence of the Angelina tradition in Bernardine history. Migdal has been cited frequently with respect to the foundation of specific houses in Poland; and in the general introduction which precedes the treatment of the history of each house, Migdal provided a section on "The Genesis of the Order." In the introductory section he connects a number of Third Order historical threads:

> The Franciscan women's order known in Poland as the Bernardine Sisters was formed from the Third Order (secular) provided in 1221 by St. Francis of Assisi for lay people. Toward the end of the fourteenth century the Third Order Regular grew out of it. This was the work of Blessed Angelina Corbara of Marsciano. . . .[61]

Migdal proceeds through a detailed history of Angelina's foundation, including the approval given by Pope Martin V to the practice of choosing a "Mother General" (although he gives date as

---

[59] R. Aubert, "Franciscaines Bernardines" *DHGE*, 1977 ed.

[60] The bibliographic references provided by Aubert include articles in the *New Catholic Encyclopedia*, 1967 ed., on the Bernardines and Alvernia College, which is sponsored by the congregation. The material in those articles is based upon information provided primarily by the American community and its archives, although the archives in Zakliczyn and Cracow are also listed. The article on the community was written by Sr. Zygmunta Froncek and the article on the college was written by Sr. M. Accursia Pezynska. They held the offices of President and Academic Dean at the time.

[61] Migdal, 26.

1438 rather than 1428); triennial chapters; the suppression of the chapter and elections by Pius II; he also follows the traditional Friar Minor interpretation that the cause for the suppression was "relaxed discipline" and a "lack of higher supervision and guidance."[62]

Sources such as Migdal rely, of course, on the internal souces of the communities involved and not solely on the literature. It ought not be overlooked that none of the archival materials cited in either Chapter Five or the preceding sections of this chapter mention Angelina in any way: not as Angela of Civitella nor as Angelina of Marsciano, Corbara, or Montegiove. How then, did the material about Angelina enter into the external historians' accounts? The recent journey to Poland undertaken by the author had as one of its objectives a search for precisely those types of sources. However, none were brought forward. In the absence of a manuscript tradition in Poland naming Angelina, an alternative form of historical material has provided some assistance in tracing Angelina's presence in the tradition.

St. Joseph Convent was founded from St. Agnes Convent in 1646; for the most part, the sisters currenty living there acknowledge most strongly historical details that occur after that date. Earlier historical information holds a much less important place for them. Nevertheless, they responded to requests about Angelina by directing the author to an oil-on-cloth portrait of Angelina dating from the early eighteenth century.[63] The artist's name is unknown, as is the date of the painting.[64] The sisters definitively identified

---

[62] Ibid. Migdal refers to the reform of "similar convents" in Burgundy by St. Colette of Corbie and attributes to this reform "a new name for the congregation: Collettines or Colettes." This is an inaccurate conflation of ideas, apparently in an attempt to explain the references in Bernardine history to the "Koletki" or "Koletanki."

[63] The painting is in oval frame, attached in 1972 to a large altarpiece of what appears to be black walnut, now located in a second floor corridor of St. Joseph Convent. Before 1972, the painting of Angelina was located in the convent's sacristy; in that year, it was affixed to the corridor altarpiece. Information provided by Sr. Benigna, archivist at St. Joseph Convent, Cracow, 2 October 1995; notes of author. Reproduction in text based on photograph taken by author 26 September 1995.

[64] ACSJ, ms. 4, p. 15 contains the following entry: "All the paintings in the choir as well as the wooden grill were completed at my expense." The entry is attributed to Sr. Apollinaria Brzechwanka (+1714). It is uncertain if the Angelina portrait was

the figure in the work as Angelina and suggested that it dated from 1714 (see figure 9, p. 147). It is possible that information about Angelina had by this time entered the consciousness of the sisters at St. Joseph through the literaure, i.e., some form of Jacobilli or other writers, but this is far from certain, and is not part of the record of the sisters.

A second painting that may represent Angelina is found in the sisters' choir, although the name assigned to the image is "S. Aniela" or S. Angela. Several concerns arise, however, in conjunction with this choir painting. The first is the name ascribed to the figure it portrays: S. Aniela. It is possible that the conflated name of Angela of Foligno had been substituted, or that the sisters at that time knew Angelina as "Angela" from early Franciscan sources that identified her as Angela of Civitella.[65] A second consideration lies in the location of the painting, next to one of "S. Mary Francis" [of the Five Wounds], a Third Order Franciscan, reproduced as figures 10 a & b below.

Chronologically, it is probable that neither choir painting (nor most likely the others) can date from 1714, because St. Mary Francis was born in 1715 and was canonized in 1867. Thus, although the St. Joseph Convent archivist thinks that the 1714 entry in the manuscript cited above (note 66) refers to these choir paintings, it seems likely that they should be dated later than 1714, and the oil of Angelina in figure 9 is part of the material referred to in manuscript four at St. Joseph Convent.

There is no intrinsic connection between the two figures of Mary Francis and Aniela, but within the context of the narrative history of the American Bernardines, their side-by-side location may be quite meaningful because an American tradition naming Angelina

---

among those referred to in this entry; however, when Mario Sensi was shown a photograph of the Angelina painting he immediately identified it as "early eighteenth century" without knowing the provenance of the photo. Interview by author in Spello, Italy, 14 October 1995.

[65] See Mariano of Florence, "Tertii Ordinis," 142v, and Mark of Lisbon, *Chroniche*, 27, cited in chapter 2. When the sisters at St. Joseph were asked if the painting in the choir could be Angelina, they said they had no way of knowing. Even modern scholars sometimes use "Angela of Marsciano" as the identification of Angelina; see Anna Benvenuti-Papi, *"In castro poenitentiae" Santità e società femminile nell'Italia medievale* (Rome: Herder Editrice e Libreria, 1990), 538.

Fig. 9: Angelina at St. Joseph Convent, Cracow (From photograph by author)

Fig. 10 a & b: Mary Francis and Aniela at Cracow (From photos by author).

"Angela" does exist, and it is found in connection with the name of S. Mary Francis. Throughout the sequence of Constitutions found in the archives of the Bernardine Sisters in the United States, the names of Mary Francis and "Blessed Angela of Marsciano" are contained as the final Third Order Franciscan women's names listed in the article identifying the "special patrons" of the community. The text of the 1962 document reads:

> Our Congregation venerates as special patrons: the Blessed Virgin Mary under the title of her Immaculate Conception; Saint Joseph, Spouse of Mary; the Seraphic Saint Francis; Saint Clare; Saint Bernardine of Siena; Saint Anthony of Padua; Saint Elizabeth of Hungary; Saint **Mary Frances**; Saint Theresa of the Infant Jesus; Blessed **Angela of Marsciano**. The feast of the Immaculate Conception shall be celebrated with special solemnity and devotion.[66]

Up to the Second Vatican Council, the short form of Angelina's name combined with the family name of Marsciano has been part of the manuscript tradition of the constitutions of the American Bernardines, and most likely stems from the oral narrative tradition at St. Joseph Convent and from its art.

From at least 1933 onward, a sequence of other documents reveals how the story of Angelina was transmitted within the American congregation. In 1933, the American sisters published an article which reveals their understanding of their origins. The material appeared in *Przeglad Katolicki* (for which a draft typescript exists); Angelina is identified as "blessed Angela of Foligno." In an archival typescript, however, Foligno is crossed out and "Marsciano" is printed in as the correction. It is impossible to

---

[66] *Rule and Constitutions of the Franciscan Sisters of Saint Bernardine of Siena*, Villanova, Pennsylvania (General Motherhouse, 1962), article 9, p. 27. Similar references are found in the constitutions from the Brazilian province in 1951 (ABFS ms. 301.1.4.9, p. 30); a Polish-English language 1948 constitution published in Reading by the General Motherhouse (ABFS ms. 301. 1.4.8, pp. 40-41); a Latin text of the constitutions sent to Brazil with the first Bernardines who went there in 1936 (ABFS ms. 310.1. 3.6, p. 6); the first bound copy of a Constitution found in the archives, dated 1935, in Polish (ABFS ms. 301.1.4.1, p. 23); and several Latin typescripts from 1933, indicating a process of preparation for the submission of the Constitution to Rome. The bound copy is found in a red hard-cover edition, ABFS, ms. 301.1.3.4; "Angelam de Marsciano" is found on p. 6.

know when the pencilled-in correction was made but the error in the published text was apparently brought to the attention of the community, because a corrected manuscript dates from just a few months later.[67]

In 1934 Mother Ladislaus Liponska, the superior at Cracow, wrote a brief history of the foundation of the community in which she referred to the influence of "Beata Angelina de Marsciano /+1435/ in Italia."[68] Material dated 1934 in the Reading archives contains both Polish language and English language texts of similar information; the Polish text refers to "Blessed Angela . . . in Italy" and the English text refers to "Bl. Angela."[69] Another document from 1934 states specifically that the "The Convent (sic) of St. Agnes . . . was an outgrowth of a Community (sic) based on the Third Order of St. Francis, organized in Italy in 1395 by Blessed Angela."[70] "Angela" continued to be used in spite of the material sent from Poland in 1933. By 1939 the narrative had changed: "In 1395 Bl. Angela of Marsciano founded a cloistered congregation of women with the Rule of St. Francis."[71] A few years later, in "A Sketch of the Origins of the Bernardine Sisters," the account reads: "The community was modelled on a Community based on the Third Rule of St. Francis organized in Italy in 1397 by Blessed Angela de

---

[67] The article is found in a photocopied excerpt of *Przeglad Katolicki*, (May, 1933): 11-15, located in ABFS ms 501.4.3.37A. The typescript is found in ABFS ms. 501.4.3. 37-2, dated 1933 and identified as "for Przegala Kat." The 1934 typescript (ABFS ms. 501.4.3.38a) intended for a parish in Stamford, Connecticut, used only "Blessed Angela" without a place-association.

[68] ACSJ ms. 131 (1645-1943). Latin text, with the official seal of the convent, dated 30 August 1933. A Polish text with the same date but without an official seal is found in the same manuscript.

[69] ABFS mss. 501.4.3.38a and 501.4.3.40b respectively. It is possible that the text of Mother Ladislaus may have been sent to Sister M. Edmund [Loyes], a member of the General Council in the United States at the time, or it may have been brought back by two American Bernardines who travelled to Poland in 1934.

[70] ABFS ms. 501.4.3.40b, an English-language typescript titled "A Sketch of the Origin and Development of the Bernardine Sisters of St. Francis of Reading, Pennsylvania." At some point, someone added "1934, S. Edmund" to the top page.

[71] ABFS ms. 501.4.3.42a. A typescript titled "The Franciscan Sisters of Saint Bernardine commonly called the Bernardine Sisters," on the letterhead paper of Little Flower Catholic High School for Girls, Philadelphia, Pennsylvania. A pencilled addenda reads "by S. Edmund?" and gives the 1939 date.

Marsciano."[72] This statement is the earliest reference in American Bernardine texts which acknowledges that Bernardine life in Poland at the time of foundation was "modelled on" Third Order life "organized by" Angelina.

The archival texts cited above indicate that someone in the American congregation was attempting to interpret the information contained in Mother Ladislaus' documents, and perhaps had added to her own knowledge from some unknown sources (or perhaps confused herself at times.) If nothing else, there is clear evidence here of the kind of struggle involved in establishing an identity—evidence found both in the community's Polish history and in the American congregation's attempt to articulate its full heritage. One constant in the struggle, nonetheless, was repeated reference to the identity of a foundational figure called "Angela of Marsciano" who is in fact Angelina of Montegiove.

One of the more intriguing documents in the American archives is a text dated 1940, written by Mother Angela [Wojtkowiak], the Superior General at the time.[73] In a circular letter to the community, in place of the ordinary spiritual exhortation for the month, Mother Angela presented a lengthy document rather revelatory of the identity question. The text is a survey of the Franciscan heritage of the community and consists of twenty-one questions and answers. Some of the Franciscan figures discussed are St. Francis, St. Bernardine of Siena, St. Elizabeth of Hungary, and "Blessed Angela of Marsciano." Items thirteen through fifteen deal with Angelina/Angela. Question thirteen asks why "honor Bl. Angela or Angelina Marsciano as our special patron?" The response indicates the standard hagiographic understanding of Angelina as foundress of a

> regular Third Order congregation of St. Francis with a cloister. She, therefore is the Mother and Patron of the

---

[72] ABFS ms. 501.4.4.46-2a; the typescript identifies Mother M. Edmund as author. An undated item from about the same time states that "Bl. Angela de Marsciano in Italy formed an active community." See ms. 501.4.3.47-1a.

[73] ABFS ms. 103.3.4.3 b through n. This text has only recently been translated into English. The English material about Angelina is the work of Sr. Florence Kruczek and Sr. Marie Cecile Pokorski, both Bernardine Sisters; the rest of the manuscript was translated by a small team of Felician Sisters of Lodi, New Jersey, December, 1995.

> Bernardine Sisters in Poland who follow the Third Order Rule but live like the St. Clares (sic) in enclosure. Honor for Bl. (sic) Angelina came to us, even though we are not cloistered, in memory of our coming from the cloistered Bernardines.[74]

Question fourteen asks "What are the most important facts from the life of Bl. Angelina Marsciano?" The answer offers major insight into the state of confusion over Angelina's names: it identifies the family names of Marsciano and Corbara, and then states that Angelina of Marsciano is "sometimes Angelina of Civittella (sic) from her husband's name or Angelina Foligno because her tomb is found in this place," but she is not to be confused with Angela of Foligno, the penitent mystic who lived "a few decades" before her.[75] The remainder of the reply relies heavily upon Jacobilli-based information, giving a date of birth of 1377, mentioning the vow of virginity at age twelve, the wedding-night apparition, the trial before Ladislaus of Naples, and so on. The final paragraph includes a reference to the Viterbo convent founded at the request of St. Bernardine, "which still exists to this day." The last paragraph also states: "Within 100 years of the death of Angelina there were about 130 such convents, among these the convent of St. Agnes of the Bernardine Sisters, on the banks of the Stradom in Cracow."[76] It seems unlikely that a copy of Jacobilli was the direct source of this information; more probably, some version of *L'Aureola Serafica* was available to Mother Angela. However, the inclusion of the Bernardine Sisters in Cracow within the context of Angelina's "convents" was a very significant statement based upon internal tradition, even if Mother Angela most likely did not recognize the importance of the connection.

Question fifteen asks "What kind of administration was in these cloisters?" The response covers the basic information about self-governance in each house connected to Angelina and the 1428 decree of Martin V approving the election of a minister general from within the associated houses; it also mentions the 1436 decree

---

[74] ABFS ms. 103.3.4.3e.

[75] Ibid.

[76] ABFS ms. 103.3.4g.

of Eugene IV allowing an assistant general to substitute in the visitation of the houses. And, significantly, it states that "All the sisters were subject to the Friars Minor of the Observance."[77] Once again, there is no way to identify the source of this information. The last part of the response to question fifteen raises some additional questions about the source. Citing the traditional point of view that weaknesses or abuses crept in, Mother Angela then states that "the superiors general and their assistants often found themselves behind cloistered walls; again they did not want to give them control."[78] It may be presumed that "they" refers to the Friars Minor of the Observance and "them" refers to the general and her assistants. Mother Angela did not see the implicit contradiction between the material in item thirteen in which she told the Bernardines that Angelina founded an enclosed Third Order way of life. The final part of the answer in question fifteen indicates enclosure was imposed on the community.

By 1945, a somewhat standardized version of the history was published in *Polish-American Studies* after the community in the United States celebrated its fiftieth anniversary. Unfortunately, the tradition of inaccuracy continued: the founding date associated with "Blessed Angela of Marsciano' is given as 1335, and the date of foundation in Cracow is doubly-flawed in that it uses the year 1459 and implies that John Capistran was still alive.[79] In 1950 the community published a biography of the American foundress, Mother Veronica Grzedowska. Within this text, the foundation of the original Bernardines in Cracow is connected to John Capistran; while the work makes no mention of Angelina or the Italian "model," it does repeat the information that the first Bernardines were "engaged in social activities, nursing the sick and taking care of the poor, using for this purpose funds which they gained from

---

[77] ABFS ms. 103.3.4g.

[78] Ibid.

[79] Sr. M. Zygmunta Froncek, "A Half-Century on American Soil," *Polish-American Studies* (January-June, 1945), 24. The 1335 date may simply have been a misreading of 1385; the second error conflates the date of foundation of the canonical convent with the "initiative" of St. John Capistran. A note written in an unknown hand on the last page of the archive copy reads "Delivered at Orchard Lake College, October, 1944 at a meeting of the Polish American Historical Association." The text is uncatalogued in the ABFS collection, and no ms. number has been assigned.

the labor of their hands, like sewing, embroidery, or work in the church."[80]

More powerful pieces of the historical transmission of the presence of Angelina in the Bernardine tradition remain. All of the manuscript items cited above from the archives date from 1933 or later, but they are not the earliest manifestations of Angelina in the American foundation. In 1906 the American foundress and the earliest sisters moved to what became the motherhouse of the congregation, Sacred Heart Convent at Mount Alvernia, just outside the city of Reading, Pennsylvania. In 1912-13 the original building and the main chapel were expanded; the chapel expansion led to the presence of the oldest Angelina material—in the form of a fresco and eventually a stained glass window. The chapel nave was lengthened and two side aisles were added. Above the main altar a panoramic fresco of important figures in Franciscan history and spirituality was added in 1916-17 (see figure 11 a & b, p. 155).[81] In addition to Saints Francis of Assisi, Bernardine of Siena, John Capistran, Bonaventure and Anthony of Padua, a significant number of women saints were included: Saints Clare, Elizabeth of Hungary, Cunegunda, Colette, and, most important to this work, Angelina of Marsciano.[82] At present the right side of the fresco as one faces the main altar includes St. Bernardine of Siena, St. Anthony of Padua, St. Elizabeth of Hungary, St. John Capistran, and possibly St. Cunegunda, as well as a kneeling figure who might be St. Martin of Tours. The left side of the fresco now includes St.

---

[80] *Under the Shadow of the Almighty*, 31-32. The book was privately published by the community and authored by "a Bernardine Sister."

[81] Based on conversation with Sr. Aurelia Wielgosz, at St. Joseph Villa, Reading, Pennsylvania, March 1993. Sr. Aurelia gave me an index card with the names of some of the figures in the fresco, and indicated that the painting had been done while she was a novice at Reading.

[82] There are no records in the Archives that identify the date, the artist(s), the company, etc. There is no list naming the figures included in the fresco; the list given above is based on the common iconography associated with the figures. The fresco originally portrayed 20 figures on each side of the main altar; in 1960-61 it was "renovated" and today there are only 6 figures on each side of the altar—five men and one woman on the left side, four men and two women on the right. Ironically, Clare of Assisi (who had been on the right side of the altar) was removed, and the sole woman on the left side, who is actually Angelina, was until only three years ago identified as Clare of Assisi instead of Angelina.

Francis, St. Bonaventure, a bishop who might be Louis of Toulouse, Angelina, King St. Louis of France and a kneeling Alphonsus of Ligouri (see figure 12 a & b, p. 156). Angelina is dressed in a long brown habit, a mantle is opened at the right side of her waist, and she wears the typical black veil and white underveil of a late medieval tertiary-*bizzoche*. The distinguishing features of the figure are a book held in the left hand, with the inscription of "III Ordo Regular" on the cover, and burning coals at the opening of the mantle on her right side, just above her right hand. It is the book and the flames from burning coals that clearly and unequivocally identify her as Angelina of Montegiove (see figure 13, p. 156).

The second item of art that substantiates the historical preservation of the Angelina connection is a stained glass window in the left aisle of the chapel. The figure is presently named as "Angelina of Marsciano." She carries in her right hand a book with a cover embossed with a cross; she holds a wooden cross in her left hand, wears a metallic-type of crucifix at her bosom, and wears the white cord and Franciscan Crown (rosary) of the modern era (see figure 14, p. 157). The archives contain no information on the artist, the origin of the window, the date of its installation, etc.[83] At first, since the expansion of the original chapel took place in 1912-13 and the painting occurred some four years later, it was assumed that the windows pre-dated the fresco. Further consideration, however, suggests that the fresco was the first representation of Angelina in the American Bernardine tradition, and the stained glass window dates from a later time, possibly the 1920s or early 1930s.[84] In

[83]The original name under the figure was "B. Angela de Marsciano," according to records from the company that restored the chapel windows in 1976. Fourteen stained glass windows were removed and restored in 1976 by Hiemer and Company from Clifton, New Jersey. A letter dated 25 August 1976 lists the "foreign titles" under eight of the windows and the English version of each name to be used in the renovated window; it was at this time "Angela" was replaced with "Angelina." An earlier letter dated 8 April 1976, the estimate for the project, stated that the "stained glass [from different windows] was made and installed over a period of years" and that the best proposal for preservation was complete removal, disassembly, cleaning, repair and reassembly with new lead between the pieces. Copies of the letters were furnished to the author, 20 November 1995.

[84]This judgment is based upon conversations with stained-glass artisan Gerhard Hiemer, of Hiemer and Company, Clifton NJ. Mr. Hiemer's father worked on the 1976 restoration of the windows. The company was established in the United States

reality, she wears the Bernardine habit of that era—white cord, Franciscan Crown, metal crucifix. Ironically, the white underveil of a tertiary woman is absent.

Fig. 11 a,b: fresco above main altar, Sacred Heart Convent Reading, Pennsylvania (Copy from photo taken for the fiftieth anniversary celebration (1944); archives of Bernardine Sisters, Reading, Pennsylvania).

---

in 1932, but the family had a studio in Munich, Germany for much longer. Mr. Hiemer examined his files, and based on the photographs they contained concluded that the windows may have been made in the later 20s or early 30s. He could not tell from the black-and-white photos if the windows were made in Europe or the United States.

Fig. 12 a,b: altered fresco above main altar, Sacred Heart Convent, Reading, Pennsylvania (Photos by author).

Fig. 13: Enlargement of Angelina of Montegiove from fresco in fig. 12 b (Photo by Centennial Committee, 1993).

Fig. 14: Stained glass window, Sacred Heart Convent Reading, Pennsylvania (Photo by author).

Conclusion

The Observant Tradition within the Franciscan family was brought to Poland 1453-54 through the preaching of John Capistran. Where there were friars, there were women seeking to live a more perfect Christian life. Observant friars typically directed them to the Third Order secular way of life. Often, some of the tertiary women would begin living a common life, following the prescripts of the *Rule of 1289*. In Cracow, as a result of the preaching of Capistran and the presence of the Observant friars, by the 1460s three groups of Third Order women had been established. As the Observant friars moved into new locations, the Third Order women also appeared, although some of the groups emerged without any connection to the so-called Bernardine Fathers.

The majority of the houses of Tertiary Observant women established between 1454-1626 were unenclosed, open houses with women living a common life, praying or attending liturgical devotions at a church connected to the Bernardine Fathers, retaining ownership of goods and income, and *not* making a vow of poverty. The *practice* of poverty was not uniform; St. Agnes in Cracow received a directive to "possess all things in common" in 1461 but in other houses the sisters retained the income of property and administered their own goods. It was only after the implementation of the Tridentine reform that full monasticization (enclosure) occurred. But the move toward a uniform practice of poverty had not been fully accomplished even by 1646, since one factor in the foundation of that house was the diversity of opinion about poverty at St. Agnes at the time. Full Tridentine reform did not occur in all places at the same time.

Ludovico Jacobilli may have had knowledge of the Polish houses of Observant Tertiaries. As many as twenty houses existed in 1626, and at least fifteen of them had originated as unenclosed houses. The convents of St. Agnes and St. Colette in Cracow, and numerous houses emanating from them, had originally had some awareness of the way of life of the Tertiaries of Blessed Angelina, although St. Agnes Convent had chosen to accept enclosure in 1461. Other women, called Colettes at the time, were located in many areas of Poland: two places in Cracow, others in Poznan, Warsaw, Lwow, and Vilno. A tradition that the form of life they followed was modelled on Angelina's community endured not only in Poland in the first several centuries after foundation, but was transmitted to the American community by the early part of the twentieth century. Evidence for the connection of the way of life of the Tertiaries of Blessed Angelina and the Bernardine Sisters rests in an oral tradition, a spiritual tradition, a manuscript tradition, and in an art history tradition.

Acceptance of the connection between the Bernardines and the Tertiaries of Blessed Angelina has implications for the present-day communities. In the course of research in preparation of this present work, different pieces of the author's understanding of the connection were offered to Sr. Clotilde Filannino and to the communities of Angelina's congregation at Foligno, Pasano, and Rome. In June 1994 the author explained to the Generalate community in Rome the conclusions she had drawn as of that time, and presented to Angelina's tertiaries several copies of the Angelina figure found in the fresco in the chapel at Sacred Heart Convent in Reading,

Pennsylvania.[85] The Tertiaries of Blessed Angelina responded with the statement, "We did not know we had so many sisters!" As a result of the shared information, the Mother General of the Tertiaries of Blessed Angelina presented a first-class relic of the Blessed to be given to the Minister General of the Bernardine Sisters. The latter presentation was made at the General Chapter of 1994.[86] Although this is not necessarily a "scientific proof," it does affirm in the strongest possible way that the discovery of the bond that exists has been life-giving for both congregations.

---

[85] The copies have been placed in the generalate convent, the monastery of Sant'Anna in Foligno, the recently-restored hermitage nearby, and the convent in Assisi.

[86] 12 July 1994. The relic is kept at the Bernardine Sisters' generalate in King of Prussia, Pennsylvania.

CHAPTER SEVEN

Retrieving the Living Tradition:

Historical and Theological Implications

The present work has engaged in a rediscovery of one area of early Franciscan history and explored the evolutionary process Franciscan Third Order life and praxis underwent as conflicts over vocational ideals developed. In part, the rediscovery responds to that historical elitism which elevates the First Order to a preeminent place in the Franciscan world. Therefore, this work strives to generate a deeper appreciation for Third Order history and to encourage a more complete inclusion of the stories of Franciscan women in that history. On the other hand, it also responds to a radical feminism that interprets the past exclusively in terms of the oppression of women and completely rejects any possibility of remaining within the Christian or Franciscan traditions.[1] As a result, a tension between Franciscan ideals and feminist interpretation permeates this final chapter.

The received tradition concerning Angelina of Montegiove and the *absence* of a received tradition about Tertiary Observance support the stance taken by feminist history and theology: women's history is incomplete, and the integrity of the Christian tradition requires recovery of the missing pieces. Emanating from the position that feminist historical theology is itself a method, the present work recovered and reinterpreted ancient texts relevant to Angelina; discovered new texts which support the thesis that she was indeed a woman whose leadership promoted an identifiable women's movement; and demonstrated that a use of internal sources has a major impact on the re-telling of the story. Support of the thesis required both exegetical and admittedly eisegetical work; the latter is unavoidable when dealing with the recovery of a lost

[1]Mary Daly, especially in *Gyn/Ecology The Radical Metaethics of Radical Feminism* (Boston: Beacon Press, 1978, 1990 is the most representative figure in this group.

tradition. Two principles guided the course of research: first, the conviction that an acknowledged relationship to the past is necessary for the creation of a new religious future; and second, a deeply-held belief that historical critique is not disloyalty—rather, it is a critical commitment to the Christian community and its traditions.[2]

Application of these principles led to a third conviction: the living tradition of Angelina's movement offers hope to Third Order Franciscans and to other religious women—indeed to all women—today. With so many levels of diversity present in the Franciscan life, and within the spiritual lives of many women, certainly discussion of the idea of the "living tradition" and its significance ought to continue. An entry into that discussion follows in four areas: the unreconstructed symbol of Angelina, the reconstructed symbol, the feminist critique of the relationship between Franciscan men and women, and the question of committed religious women in a post-Vatican II church. And finally, there will be some probing into "what remains to be done" issues. In each area below the method consists of reinterpretation by means of theological reflection, that is, exploring individual (Angelina) or corporate (Angelina's tertiaries and the Bernardine Sisters) experience in conversation with the religious heritage of Third Order women.[3] Theological reflection has been chosen because it does not require final answers, although it does empower meaningful encounter with areas of struggle: the loss of significant historical models, the search for new symbols and categories, the oppression of women, struggles of identity and evolution, to name a few. Most importantly, however, theological reflection moves individuals and groups toward fidelity and transformation. It is the latter aspect that is most fervently desired.

---

[2]I borrow the first principle from Carol Christ and Judith Plaskow, *Womanspirit Rising*, 11, and the second principle from Elisabeth Schüssler-Fiorenza, *In Memory of Her*, xxii.

[3]Cf. Patricia O'Connell Killen and John de Beer, *The Art of Theological Reflection* (New York: Crossroad, 1995), viii.

Angelina: the Old Symbol

Primary sources written with an uncritical understanding of Angelina of Montegiove illustrate how she became a two-tiered symbol. The first tier portrayed Angelina as a young wife and widow endowed with a love of virginity and devoted to works of charity. After joining the Third Order, Angelina was persecuted when her devotion to virginity led others to the same lifestyle. Her heroic behavior at Naples demonstrated a high degree of holiness, but that holiness did not protect her from additional persecution or from exile. In this first tier of the "old symbol," the value placed on virginity and holiness by Angelina's seventeenth-century biographer shaped the symbol. Other facets of her life—independence, courage, creative leadership—were lost or deliberatley hidden. The significance of Angelina as a lay person in the world is, therefore, the most underdeveloped area of research, and will most likely remain so unless additional material about that part of her life surfaces in civil archives.

The second tier in the old Angelina symbol assigned her responsibility for establishing *enclosed* Franciscan life for Third Order women. It placed her within the Observant Tradition, and therefore identified her as a founder for whom *literal observance of the "Third Rule of St. Francis"* was essential. With respect to her life at Sant'Anna, Angelina herself was never criticized by the chroniclers or biographers; their criticism was reserved for her followers. Jacobilli's biographical works clearly portrayed Angelina as conforming to the expected model of the seventeenth-century church: she was enclosed, obedient, a model of virginity and silence. She was not portrayed as a leader in any specific sense; the lists of the monasteries affiliated with her are attributed by various authors to the influence of the friars or of the Pope.[4] No acknowledgement was made of the "active life" of charitable work continuing after Angelina's move to Sant'Anna. Through the seventeenth and eighteenth centuries, hagiography featured both tiers of the symbol and did nothing to change them. In the nineteenth century the literature returned to awareness of the

---

[4]See chapter four, p. 111.

charitable works of the women who lived at Sant'Anna and to the eremitical aspect of life there, recasting them into a model for a combined "active-contemplative" life. The distorted active-contemplative model matched a viable religious-life model in the nineteenth-century church calling for contemplatives to move into apostolic work.[5] But, in the same era, discussion of the spread of Angelina's influence and example beyond Italy was presented in very limited terms as institutional history, i.e, a number of houses counted—yet only in France and Italy. Writers made no reference to Spain, Belgium, the Germanic regions, Bohemia, Moravia, Hungary, or Poland. Consequently, the "old symbol" proclaimed a very limited sphere of influence for Angelina.

Perhaps the denial of her larger influence is attributable to traditional disavowal of the importance of *bizzoche*-Beguine life even though these and other semi-religious women, penitents, or *conversae* were not entirely absent from any part of Europe.[6] Or perhaps the omission stems from remnants of the conflict with the friars: from the beginning, Angelina's experience as a tertiary woman in conflict with the leadership of the Friars Minor was covered over and misrepresented in various ways.

Once the process of monasticization became a *fait accompli*, there was no need for Angelina's later biographers to refer to the difficulties over enclosure that had marked the history of tertiary women and the Friars Minor in the fifteenth century. The "winners" in the struggle constructed a portrait of Angelina that fit into a patriarchal ecclesial model which did not have room for holy women who were not monastics. Consequently, the story of *bizzoche* women and tertiary women living a common life without enclosure

---

[5]In 1854 Pope Pius IX urged religious [women and men] to "insert themselves in . . . pastoral ministry through association with . . . secular clergy." Cited in Maryann Donovan, *Sisterhood as Power: The Past and Passion of Ecclesial Women* (New York: Crossroad, 1989), 19.

[6]Duane J. Osheim, "The Place of Women in the Late Medieval Italian Church," in *That Gentle Strength: Historical Perspectives on Women in Christianity*, ed. Lynda L. Coon, Katherine J. Haldane, and Elisabeth W. Sommer (Charlottesville and London: University Press of Virginia, 1990), 80. The fact that modern historians have only recently begun to treat this area indicates how deeply the stories of these women are buried.

or solemn vows—women whose search for God and spiritual enlightenment differed from the norm—was not told. How could Jacobilli or the Franciscan chroniclers construct a symbol centered upon a woman whose followers had resisted submission to the friars? They could not, and they did not. The only part of the story that could be told was that which fit the ideals of a post-Reformation Church. It is logical, then, that for several centuries after Angelina's death, hagiography emphasized Angelina's life as that of an enclosed tertiary and profoundly obedient woman. Such a symbol served the purpose of Church reeling from the impact of the Reformation, struggling to synthesize a coherent Catholic identity and to consolidate centralized authority; it also served a post-Vatican I church in its struggle against modernity in the latter part of the nineteenth century and the first half of the twentieth century.

Angelina: the New Symbol

From time to time, symbols can and should be re-examined. This is especially true in light of the sweeping changes intitated with the decrees of the Second Vatican Council some thirty years ago. What would a reconstructed symbol of Angelina look like? Development of a "new symbol" which speaks to Christian women today unfolds many levels of reflection. The first level produces the awareness that Angelina grasped her baptismal consecration as the foundation of her relationship to God, church, and neighbor. One consequence for Angelina: a commitment to God, perhaps even in adolescence or early adulthood, became a *choice* of virginity as fulfillment of her baptismal commitment. In feminist analysis, of course, the issue of virginity is a thorny one. Often, virginity is interpreted as denigrating the full humanity of women or as evidence of patriarchy imposing its will on women in an attempt to achieve greater control over them.[7] In many instances, that was the

[7]For different feminist views on the development of the ideal of virginity, see, for example, Daly's *Beyond God the Father*, 85; Rosemary Radford Ruether, "Misogynism and Virginal Feminism in the Fathers of the Church," in *Religion and Sexism: Images of Woman in the Jewish and Christian Traditions*, ed. Rosemary Radford Ruether (New York: Simon and Schuster, 1974), 150-83; Eleanor C. McLaughlin,

case. But Angelina's *choice* of virginity provides an opportunity for a radical departure from negative feminist interpretation. Although male dominance was certainly part of the culture in which Angelina lived, her promise of virginity and her gathering together other women of similar purpose can be reinterpreted as a stance *against* that patriarchy.

Angelina as a secular woman of the late fourteenth century raised significant questions about the society in which she had been raised, where war and disease were virtually inescapable and where the pursuit of power overshadowed almost all other values, both in civil society and in a church riven by the Avignon schism and preoccupied with protecting the Papal States. In gathering around herself other women who likewise chose virginity as a positive value, Angelina refused to honor the feudal paradigm, provoking the wrath of communal leaders who required women as marriage partners and mothers of new warriors. Too little attention has been given to this Angelina. Tracing the emphases among the Jacobillian biographies shows that Angelina recognized the difference between valuing virginity and condemning marriage—even though her accusers did not. She seems not to have been trapped by dualistic thinking that marked the patriarchal culture in which she lived. In voicing her consciousness (at the trial in Naples) that choosing virginity and condemning marriage constitute different issues, Angelina became a transgressor: a public, speaking, informed, moral leader.[8] Put another way, Angelina knew how to choose "enduring truths."[9] She also knew how to differentiate those truths or values from limited particulars conditioned by social or cultural expectations. Such informed and courageous leadership was not the norm for late medieval Italy, nor is it always the norm today.

"Equality of Souls, Inequality of Sexes: Woman in Medieval Theology," 213-66 in the same volume; and Kari Vogt, "'Becoming Male:' One Aspect of Early Christian Anthropology," in *Women: Invisible in Church and Theology*, ed. Elisabeth Schüssler-Fiorenza and Mary Collins (Edinburgh: T & T Clark, 1986), 72-83.

[8]Elizabeth Alvida Petroff, *Body and Soul: Essays on Medieval Women and Mysticism* (New York/Oxford: Oxford University Press, 1994), 161, 176.

[9]Philip Sheldrake, *Spirituality and History: Questions of Interpretation and Method* (New York: Crossroad, 1992), 84.

The reconstructed symbol of Angelina—a woman making a free choice for virginity, proclaiming its value and calling others to join her—offers immense food for thought to modern religious women who struggle with voicing self-understanding and vocational awareness. It seems clear that Angelina's intention in joining the Third Order was to enter tertiary life because it offered a recognized category through which she could devote herself more fully to the gospel and move into deeper discipleship even while remaining "in the world," with emphasis on being in the world and not inside the enclosure. These same questions of deeper discipleship and devoted gospel life beset women in the church today.

A second level of reflection with respect to the "new symbol" concentrates on Angelina in her communal life (1395-1435). A revised interpretation of the mature Angelina reads her as a symbol of a transformed church, albeit an idealized one. This Angelina does not operate from the dualism that divides sacred and profane, nor does she fit the imposed "canonical model" that prescribed religious life for women between the sixteenth and mid-twentieth centuries, the model imposed upon her by the post-Tridentine mentality of her first biographer. In one respect, a reconstructed symbol represents all women who live in ways which call forth a church not limited by patriarchy, elitism, or insistence that women's lifestyles be identical.

Angelina, reconstructed as unenclosed and mobile yet committed to communal life, symbolizes a church appreciative of charismatic women who by preaching and by courageous example contribute to the living tradition of Christianity and to the continuing development of women's spirituality in spite of cultural, political, or ecclesial barriers.[10] Assuredly, the retrieved Angelina is a woman who worked collaboratively not only with her own sisters, she also used contacts with the friars of Paoluccio's movement, with the bishop of Foligno, and with at least three popes to ensure that the semi-religious eremitical-active life of Sant'Anna and the other houses affiliated with it preserved their vocational integrity.

[10]See chapter five in Sheldrake for an excellent analysis of the "development of religious life" issues. For Angelina, the ecclesial resistance I refer to alludes to the leadership of the Friars Minor between 1428-1435.

Asking for and receiving papal approbation, she used the power of the church to break through a number of cultural restrictions. For example, women choosing their own "superiors" and investing them with authority certainly did not fit the socio-cultural paradigm of the time. In addition, as itinerant minister general conducting visitation of various houses Angelina embodied values of practicality and flexibility that contradicted prevailing cultural views of women as weak and dependent upon male authority.[11]

In one sense then, the "new symbol" of Angelina allows her to be considered a *prototype*, that is, an original model which is not forever static and which is open to the possibility of change and development.[12] The monastery at Sant'Anna was not founded by Angelina, and to say she reformed it (as some historians have said) seems inadequate. Rather, life at Sant'Anna was *transformed* so that it combined elements of *bizzoche* independence and Franciscan common life in imitation of the poor Christ. During her own life at Sant'Anna, Angelina assumed different roles at different times, and successfully modelled for her sisters ways to blend independence and accountability. Tertiary women led by Angelina were free to promise obedience to another woman, to retain ownership and administration of their own goods, and to pursue their spiritual lives in an atmosphere which respected individuality and personal responsibility. Such a form of life required each member of the group to grow in respect for her own vocation without imposing her individual choices on another. The community at Sant'Anna as a corporate entity unequivocally demonstrated these values: we need only recall the results of Angelina's unauthorized promise of obedience to the Friar Minor Provincial and the community's immediate repudiation of her right to make such a promise.

---

[11]Sheldrake 121. Sheldrake identifies Angela Merici (d. 1540), Mary Ward (1600s) and the Daughters of Charity of the nineteenth century as models of women's active and mobile religious life. He apparently did not know the story of Angelina.

[12]Schüssler-Fiorenza, 33; Schüssler-Fiorenza states that a prototype *requires* the transformation of its models of faith and community. Given the history of Third Order Franciscan women and the many transformations of the numerous congregations under that title, prototype is a most appropriate label for Angelina.

The Feminist Critique and Franciscan Relationship

A reconstructed story of the relationship between friars and tertiary women requires both a closer examination of early Franciscan writings and reflection on that history. To begin with, the theological reflection must be directed toward what it meant to Angelina to live out the Franciscan core value of brotherhood-sisterhood. "Christology from below" which springs from an understanding of Jesus as our brother informs all Franciscan praxis of the gospel and means that all choices are to be rooted in that Christological position.[13] Chapters four through six above established that the lived experience of Angelina, her Italian companions, and her Polish imitators suffered from the absence of friars who acted as brothers rather than superiors. In looking for a new understanding of Angelina as a Franciscan woman, the problems of relationship with the First Order cannot be ignored.

The area of relationality presents problems. To radical feminists, sisterhood is one thing, but inclusion of males—even as brothers—carries the potential complication of male dominance or misogyny. Modern feminist scholarship tends to present the early friars (including Francis) as no better than reluctant partners or resistant directors of women, or as oppressive of them, and even primary medieval sources about Francis himself reveal what can best be called an inconsistent attitude. Inspection of early sources from an internal Franciscan perspective, however, can provide a less uncomplimentary interpretation, at least with respect to Clare and Francis.

Material in the souces that can be called "positive" deals with Francis' preparation of San Damiano for unidentified "holy women" who would eventually live there (3 Soc 24 b; 2 Cel 204), reveals the profound grief of Clare and the Poor Ladies at the death of Francis (1 Cel 116-17), or demonstrates the deep mutual

---

[13]See Sheldrake, 112-15, for his insight into the Franciscan "Christological choice." The interpretative emphasis of brother-sisterhood is my own, based upon the promise of Francis to Clare, as well as other early sources which indicate that both considered their vocations to have commenced from the time "The Lord gave me brothers" in the case of Francis (Test 14), and in the context of "with a few sisters whom the Lord had given me" for Clare (TestCl, 7) in Armstrong-Brady.

respect Clare and Francis had for each other's vocation (LP 45, LegMaj 12.2). In addition, there are two passages which more clearly indicate an assuredly positive relationship. Both refer to the final portion of Francis' life. One passage describes how two years before his death Francis was staying in a hut near San Damiano and composed a "canticle, words and music, for the consolation of the Poor Ladies of the monastery of San Damiano," which he had one of his companions take to them (LP 42, 45). The second bears full citation:

> Though [Francis] gradually withdrew his bodily presence from them, he nevertheless gave them his affection in the Holy Spirit by caring for them. . . .He firmly promised them and others who would profess poverty in a similar way of life that he would always give them his help and counsel and the help and counsel of his brothers. This he always diligently carried out as long as he lived, and when he was close to death, he emphatically commanded that it should always be so, saying that *one and the same spirit* [1 Cor 12:11] had led the brothers and the poor ladies (sic) out of the world.[14]

These texts validate the words of Clare regarding Francis' promise of loving care and special solicitude frequently cited in this volume. They answer as well those who would deny *any* positive interpretation of the attitudes of Francis toward women: a misogynist would neither send a message of consolation to the Poor Ladies nor acknowledge a common inspiration for their vocations.

The "negative" interpretations generally arise from two sources. The first, interestingly enough, is a section of Thomas of Celano's *Second Life* (2 Cel 205-207). The text reveals a Francis who had a cautionary attitude toward *friars* too eager to associate with the Poor Ladies.[15] In one segment, Francis answers a question as to why he so infrequently visits San Damiano; in another, he is described as rebuking or punishing the brothers who were too eager

[14] 2 Cel 204.

[15] It must be noted, however, that Francis does not condemn the women in any way.

to visit the monasteries. Celano interpolates his own comment that Francis' visits to San Damiano were "forced upon him and rare" (2 Cel 207), but this clearly is a result of some internal struggle within the Friars Minor and is not found anywhere in Francis' own writings. Read superficially, the material has been interpreted as "Francis demeans women." Often overlooked, however, is the comment by Francis (as reported by Celano) that not to have called the Poor Ladies to follow Christ would have been wrong—but "not to care for them once they have been called would be the greatest unkindness" (2 Cel 205). Undoubtedly, this line echoes 2 Cel 204 in its support of a promise of loving care and special solicitude.[16] It may be that Francis as described in these sections has already encountered and is responding to some friar(s) who felt burdened by the responsibility placed upon friar-questors to supply food and beg alms for the Poor Ladies or to provide spiritual care to them.

The second "negative" source, the most likely origin of some misinterpretation of Francis' praxis, comes from 2 Cel 112-114. These passages contain what are probably the most negative expressions about women attributed to Francis. The selection refers to women as "honeyed poison," and "contagion," and indicates that Francis would not look women in the face when he spoke to them. Certainly, this is not the same Francis of 2 Cel 204. It ought not be overlooked that *Second Celano* was written for an already-polarized community, one deeply divided over the poverty question and related issues of adaptation that had fundamentally altered the original movement. The advocates of strict poverty and adherence to the teachings of Francis also were the friars closest to Clare and the women at San Damiano. Perhaps when they became "outsiders" so did anyone associated with them, including Clare and her sisters.

In historical context, the negative material of Celano emerges from a troubled period of Franciscan literature. It is impossible to know how much of the material in these passages is the true Francis and how much Celano is imposing on Francis, but it is reasonable to think that most of the negative material is colored

---

[16]At issue is what agenda was driving Celano. For an astute analysis of the passages in 2 Celano, see Carney, 46-51.

by the internal problems of the Friars Minor from 1230 onward.[17] Under such circumstances, the marked inconsistency of primary sources does not support a radical rejection of all possibilities of collaboration between the friars and women, at least from the perspective of an internal understanding of the material.

This does not eradicate the recognition that one of the profound injustices in Franciscan history was male domination over Angelina's women, both in Italy and in Poland, especially in the era in which full enclosure was imposed. Although Jacobilli claimed that the women of Angelina's tradition were "paternally protected and favored" by Observant friars, he did not consider that for the women paternal protection contibuted to the lose of their autonomy.

Nevertheless, within the painful history of Franciscan men and women, some examples of a praxis of loving care and solicitude do exist. Material reconsidered in the process of research for the present work contains specific instances of brotherhood, care and solicitude for tertiary women. In Italy, decades after the death of Angelina, the Amadeiti worked with her disciples to preserve the tradition from monasticization. In Poland, at Koscian in the 1470s the friar-guardian had a house with a garden built for the tertiaries; at Bydgoszcz the friars intervened on behalf of the sisters in a dispute over taxation with the local pastor.[18] In the closing years of the fifteenth century, during the turmoil of Gasciorek's implementation of enclosure for the tertiaries of Kazimierz and St. Colette convent in Cracow, the guardian (superior) of the Friars Minor of St. Bernardine Church (who was himself subject to the Provincial on crusade, Gasciorek) assisted the women forced together in a too-small St. Colette residence by helping purchase a piece of property on which he built a new convent for the unhappy community. And at Warsaw, when there was obvious confusion over implementation of enclosure and

---

[17]At the time the *Second Life* was written (after 1244), much of the "new" material available to Celano seems to have come from the surviving early companions, who were highly critical of anything that "betrayed" the Francis they had known. Interestingly, there is no cross-reference in the Legend of the Three Companions which contains such negative attitudes toward women.

[18]See original dissertation for the full text (Ann Arbor: UMI, 1996).

enforcement of the *Rule of 1521*, one of the friars returned from the 1603 General Chapter in Rome with an explanation from his Minister General that the order of Pius V for enclosure did not apply to the Warsaw tertiaries because they did not make solemn vows.[19] It is rather striking that some friars would contradict secular clergy and external authorities *on behalf of* the women while other friars enthusiastically moved in the opposite direction, without concern that they were altering the vocations of the unenclosed tertiaries. Unfortuantely, what is not available at the present time is internal resource material such as letters, diaries, community chapter records from the places where friars assisted the women—items that might provide an entirely different perspective from within the Bernardine-Angelina tradition.

Inconsistency marks the whole of Franciscan history; this tension remains unresolved. But to say as some radical feminists do that the friars *never* helped the women and *always* oppressed them is inaccurate.

Commitment in a Post Conciliar Church

In a broader context, the feminist critique challenges modern Third Order women to re-examine the parameters of their lives in light of a commitment to renewed gospel values. Such re-examination does not nullify fidelity to the Second Vatican Council; rather, it enhances it. Nearly thirty years ago women religious of all families—Franciscan, Benedictine, Dominican, and so on—were charged with the task of renewing religious life by means of a "return to the sources." The Counciliar declaration on the renewal of religious life, *Perfectae Caritatis*, contains the following instruction:

> The up-to-date renewal of the religious life comprises both a constant return to the sources of the whole of the Christian life and to the primitive inspiration of the institutes, and their adaptation to the changed conditions of our times. This renewal, under the impulse

[19]Ibid.

of the Holy Spirit and with the guidance of the Church, must be promoted in accord with the following principles:

a) Since the final norm of the religious life is the following of Christ as it is put before us in the Gospel, this must be taken by all institutes as the supreme rule;

b) the spirit and aims of each founder should be accepted and retained, as indeed should each institute's sound traditions, for all these constitute the patrimony of the institute.

(*Perfectae Caritatis* 2)[20]

Many questions emerge with regard to the issues of "founder," "adaptation," following the "impulse of the Holy Spirit," and the recovery of the living tradition of Angelina of Montegiove. Although Angelina was not in a literal sense the "founder" of Third Order Regular life, she is, as has been proposed above, a *prototype*.[21] Angelina's leadership and the way of life established at Sant'Anna as an original model may be profitably examined—especially since it was not static at the time of establishment and is open even now to the possibility of change and development under the impulse of the Holy Spirit. Feminist historical theology can now acknowledge that Angelina of Montegiove and the women who shared her way of life—whether at Sant'Anna, throughout Italy, or in Poland—were inspired by the Holy Spirit in the fulfillment of their vocations. They developed a common life according to the spirit of a Rule meant for people living in the world, praying together and praying in solitude, dedicating their financial resources to service of the group and of their marginalized

---

[20]See Austin Flannery, ed., *Vatican Council II: The Conciliar and Post Conciliar Documents*, 2nd edition (New York: Costello Pub. Co., 1977), 612.

[21]John Lozano, in *Foundresses, Founders and Their Religious Families*, trans. Joseph Daries (Chicago: Claret Center for Spirituality, 1983), 3, indicates that there are "different ways of being a founder." I substitute prototype for founder in light of that statement and of the following criteria clearly applicable to Angelina: "founders" feel called by God to create a new religious family or a "new family of evangelical life"; they assign goals, set up guidelines, or give a rule or constitutions to the family; and they often come to a "gradual discovery" of their own vocation (see Lozano, 3, 44).

neighbors. These are the "sound traditions" of tertiary observance that *Perfectae Caritatis* calls our patrimony.

The continuation of *ressourcement* in the last three decades has not only helped Third Order women recover the original vision, it also helped them learn how the process of de-monasticization occurred and changed their self-understanding.[22] The *bizzoche*-tertiary women of the Observant tradition made private "simple" vows until early in the seventeenth century, when enclosure and solemn vows were imposed. It was only in 1900 that the institutional church finally recognized religious who made "simple vows"—those not papally enclosed because of apostolic ministry—as "true religious."[23] But a 1917 revision of canon law helped obscure individual community characteristics, because from that time forward all constitutions were written to meet the prescriptions of canon law. This legalistic way of defining a congregation had widespread impact, especially as diocesan congregations moved to regain pontifical status—including the Bernardine Sisters in the United States. A kind of "generic religious life" overshadowed founders' legacies and spiritualities within specific traditions. For women of the Third Order traditions, one consequence of the generic understanding of religious life was the loss of any deep sense of Franciscan heritage.

Although enclosure had been ameliorated, other monastic practices had not. Structure and symbols remained essentially

---

[22]*Ressourcement* or "resourced theology" according to the late Yves Congar is "a theology recentered and reoriented upon the Christian mystery which is identical with the paschal and parousial mystery." Yves Congar, "Le Purgatoire," *Le Mysterie de la mort et sa celebration*, Lex Orandi 12 (Paris: Les Editions du Cerf, 1951): 326, cited in Charles R. Meredith, "Themes of Thomistic Eschatology in the Ecumenical Theology of Yves Congar," dissertation for The Catholic University of America, 1993, 19. It is this principle that inspired the "return to the sources" directive found in *Perfectae Caritatis*.

[23]The recognition is contained in "Condite a Christo," by Pope Leo XIII. See Donovan, 49. Within three years the Tertiary Franciscans of Blessed Angelina had successfully overcome the nearly four-hundred-year-old obligation of papal enclosure and once again became an active community. The Bernardines in the U.S. were already not observing papal enclosure, although they remained under the jurisdiction of the Reformed Friars Minor in Poland, a long-distance connection that had sporadic repercussions until the first World War.

unchanged until Vatican II.[24] When *Perfectae Caritatis* called for a return to the sources, a major clash over ecclesial identity resulted, especially in American communities with European backgrounds. As the renewal process unfolded it became important to be "Franciscan"—but often values of Franciscanism conflicted with traditions and values of a specific community. For example, Bernardines in America were challenged to less rigid adherence to Polish identity, to serve in more parishes that were not ethnically Polish, and to begin examining how to live out the Council's "preferential option for the poor."[25] Mission—a Franciscan value—began to challenge ministry—a canonical apostolic model. When the question of studying the founder's heritage arose, the problem of *which* founder should be considered followed: Mother Veronica Grzedowska, Mother Hedwig Jurkiewicz (founder at Zakliczyn), Mother Teresa Zadzik (founder of St. Joseph Convent), St. John Capistran, or St. Francis?

John Lozano writes that each founder—Clare, Francis, Veronica Grzedowska—had a unique charism which the Holy Spirit transmitted to their disciples, and I would propose that this is likewise true of each prototype such as Angelina of Montegiove.[26] Lozano also asserts that it is the mission of the

---

[24]For specifically American analysis of the changes in American religious life, see, among others, Joan Chittister, *Winds of Change Women Challenge Church* (Kansas City: Sheed and Ward, 1986; Patricia Wittberg, *Creating a Future for Religious Life* (New York/Mahwah: Paulist Press, 1991); and Mary Ewens, "Women in the Convent,"in *American Catholic Women A Historical Perspective*, ed. Karen Kennelly (New York: Macmillan, 1989), 17-47.

[25]A fruitful area of study would be the Americanization of European-origin communities and the strength of ethnic background. Some work has been done: see Mary Ewens, *The Role of the Nun in Nineteenth Century America* (New York: Arno, 1971, 1978, 1984; Grace Donovan, "Immigrant Nuns: Their Participation in the Process of Americanization: Massachusetts and Rhode Island, 1880-1920," *The Catholic Historical Review*, LXXVII (April 1991): 194-208; and Patricia Byrne, "Sisters of St. Joseph: The Americanization of a French Tradition," *U.S. Catholic Historian* 5 (Summer/ Fall 1986): 241-72, for the Pre-Vatican II era. Much remains unexplored, especially in terms of analysis of the post-conciliar era. "Preferential option for the poor" was not the language of the Council, but its genesis can be found in *Gaudium et Spes*, the Pastoral Constitution on the Church in the Modern World, 69. See Donal Dorr, *Option for the Poor A Hundred Years of Vatican Social Teaching* (Maryknoll, NY: Orbis Books, 1983), 122.

[26]"Charism" was first used by Pope Paul VI in *Evangelica Testificatio*, 11, in 1971; with respect to founders' charism, it was first used by the Congregation of Bishops

descendants of a given religious family to live, safeguard, deepen, and constantly develop the charism and provide for its growth.[27] In light of the recovery of the living tradition of tertiary observance and the complex history of Third Order women, what must now be discerned is the possible meanings Angelina and her contemporaries offer us for this era and for our future. The challenge is to re-examine what we *thought* the sources said, and to apply to our lives the lessons embodied in the reconstructed symbol.

If Third Order Regular women peel away centuries of cultural accretions—customs, habits, security in apostolic work which we once thought defined us and religious life—what is left? What would it mean if every Third Order congregation were to look at Angelina and learn from her courage? What would it mean if Third Order women would deeply internalize the value inherent in a combination of independence and common life so that the female face of patriarchy which exists in our lives could be addressed and erased in our obedience to one another? What if we could muster the courage to embrace Angelina as a prototype of vocational self-understanding and fidelity, and apply what we learn from her to our personal vocational self-understanding?

In the unfolding process which produced this present work, those questions have kept coming back. Especially haunting is the question of fidelity. Religious communities have been (and are) deeply divided and damaged by polarization over "adaptation" and "fidelity." Unfortunately, these terms became ideological battering rams, making post-Conciliar life for women religious painful.[28] At root, the defining question is always fidelity, whether we are looking at Angelina in 1430, the tertiaries of Italy

---

and the Congregation for Religious and Secular Institutes in *Mutuae Relationes*, 11, in 1978. In the broad sense, it means the gift/legacy of the founder for the group of followers and for the church.

[27]Lozano, 29.

[28]See the excellent collection of essays edited by Cassian Yuhaus, *Religious Life The Challenge for the Future* (New York/Mahwah: Paulist Press, 1994) in which post-conciliar difficulties of self-definition and fidelity to charism encountered by women religious are addressed. Of specific relevance to issues of adaptation and fidelity are Barbara Fiand, "Living the Vision: The Present Moment and Future Prospects for Religious life," 35-69; Joan Chittister, "An Amazing Journey: A Road of Twists and Turns," 76-91; and Margaret Brennan, " A White Light Still and Moving," 92-108.

who left the federation because of the troubles with friars demanding obedience in the decades after Angelina's death, or the "Colettes" of Bernardine history whose choice was to stand against enclosure—even when they knew it meant extinction. In these instances, their choices reveal the depth of their vocational self-understanding and fidelity.

I would propose that it is possible to remove the false dichotomy between adaptation and fidelity. In order to do so, we must read "adaptation" as nothing less than learning to understand our vocation as *evangelical*, as a call to bring the gospel alive in the world today just as Angelina, Clare, or Francis did in theirs. Pope Paul VI implied as much in *Evangelica Testificatio*, his *Exhortation on the Renewal of Religious Life* (29 June 1971) when he stated that (1) renewal is the dynamic process due to the action of the Holy Spirit and (2) that it is the *obligation* of religious groups to "be faithful to the spirit of . . . [their] founders, to their *evangelical intentions* and to the example of their sanctity."[29] Franciscan life was not originally monastic. It was itinerant and missionary in intent, and intrinsically person-centered. The earliest "adaptation" of the Franciscan charism was conditioned by the hierarchy's desire to use the friars as missionaries who would bring the effects of Lateran IV to the universal church and to "protect" women, semi-religious or "fully" religious (for whom the "root of evil" was assumed to be going outside the cloister) from heresy and sexual misconduct.[30] Founders' stories throughout the history of religious life unequivocally demonstrate that church culture governed by patriarchal standards and dualistic antagonism toward women radically altered the shape of religious life. Now, however, women religious have an *obligation* (Paul VI's word) to move toward a recovery of original ideals, to study a retrieved history and to embrace evangelical freedom—all of which challenge patriarchal church culture. The result of that fidelity goes beyond external adaptation; it is *internal transforma-*

---

[29]*Evangelica Testificatio*, 11, 6. Emphasis added.

[30]Daichman, 109. Additional material on the misogyny which shaped medieval attitudes on women as the root of evil, see references cited in note 8 above.

tion.[31] In reality, adaptation and transformation for the sake of the gospel *define* fidelity.

Unanswered Questions and Unfinished Business

In spite of all that the present work accomplishes in the retrieval of the living tradition of Third Order history, several areas present partial findings; although many investigative openings have been broached, significant questions remain unanswered.

Beyond Angelina's story, Franciscan history, or the struggles and transformations experienced in the lives of women religious, the present work offers hope in yet another area: renewal of the church through recognition of the gifts of *all* women. Vatican II made the dynamic process of seeking God and living the gospel a renewed theological imperative for the entire church, not just for the hierarchy, clergy, or vowed religious.[32] The Council re-emphasized the call to holiness (what Sandra Schneiders would call the God-quest) for all persons, and paid remarkable attention to the laity and the "action of the Holy Spirit" in their lives.[33] Vowed religious were reminded clearly that they were *members of* the laity, not apart from them.[34] Barriers that had separated vowed women from their sisters "in the world" began to crumble; then the women's movement contributed powerfully to the transformation of a closed convent culture into "an open response to needs on

[31]See Sandra Schneiders, "Contemporary Religious Life: Death or Transformation?" in *Religious Life The Challenge for the Future*, ed. Cassian Yuhaus, 9-34 (New York/Mahwah: Paulist Press, 1994). Schneiders' discussion of the transformation of religious life provoked my interpretation of the sequential relationship of adaptation-transformation.

[32]See *Lumen Gentium*, the Dogmatic Constitution on the Church, 21 November 1964, passim.

[33]Schneiders, 16; *Lumen Gentium* 30-38 deal with the laity; 39-42, with the call to holiness.

[34]*Perfectae Caritatis* 10, speaks of "lay religious life." *Lumen Gentium*, 43d indicates that vowed persons can be either clerics or laity and that religious life is not "a kind of middle way" between those two states. As a result of the Council, baptismal theology assumed a more significant place in church teaching; religious profession is seen as the deepening of the baptismal commitment.

all sides."[35] Women empowered other women, and as the "cloister mentality" receded, other structural changes followed.[36] Women in the convent began to learn what it could mean to be "sisters" instead of "nuns"—sisters to each other and sisters to women outside the convent.[37] In one sense, the transition out of the cloister challenged one small part of the dualistic thinking which has so harmed women throughout history, and advanced a theology of history once proposed by Yves Congar who wrote that the Reign of God "must unite the two realities, now separated, of Church and world, the creational order and the order of redemption."[38]

In a narrower vein, it might be proposed that the process of post-conciliar transformation has led toward something that resembles (at least for Third Order Regular women) a return to the prototype, to the tertiary life of the women in the fifteenth century at Sant'Anna, where women came together to share the God-quest with each other and with all who entered the monastery grounds. One of the fascinating items in the 1476 Constitution of the tertiaries of Angelina is a directive that in the evenings of certain feast days one of the sisters was to "read some devout book to the seculars for a half-hour."[39] The implication seems to be that secular women lived in close proximity to or even inside the monastery; perhaps the reading was a kind of evangelization or spiritual direction or catechesis. It is clear from the context that the "seculars" were not novices or candidates. What, then, was the relationship between these groups of women? This is one of the areas which requires additional investigation. But the implica-

---

[35]Ewens, "Women in the Convent," 42.

[36]See Helen Rose Fuchs Ebaugh, *Women in the Vanishing Cloister* (New Brunswick, NJ: Rutgers University Press, 1993) for an excellent external sociological analysis of the "process of dismantling the traditional cloister" and its impact on religious life as a social institution.

[37]See Marie Augusta Neal, *From Nuns to Sisters An Expanding Vocation* (Mystic, Ct: Twenty-Third Publications, 1990) and Mary Jo Weaver, *New Catholic Women A Contemporary Challenge to Traditional Religious Authority* (San Francisco: Harper and Row, 1985).

[38]Yves Congar, *Jesus Christ* (Paris: Les Editions du Cerf, 1965), trans. Luke O'Neill, *Jesus Christ* (New York: Herder & Herder, 1966), 180. Congar used "Kingdom of God"; feminist theology uses Reign of God.

[39]Bartoli, 132, 136.

tions for the hierarchically structured model of the church are clear: women ministering to and empowering other women can and should be part of the God-quest of the entire church.

Another aspect of the same issue must be addressed, but it is far beyond the scope of the current work. It involves the recovery of the history of relationship between women inside the enclosure (once it was fully imposed) and those outside, or those who lived inside while remaining laity. What motivated the latter to move inside convent walls when they did not claim to have religious vocations? To what extent were early modern houses of religious women places of refuge for other women who suffered physical abuse, economic destitution, or even persecution as witches?[40] Specific-ally, how permeable was the boundary of enclosure during the era of the European witchcraze? What relationship, if any, existed between the resistance of women to total enclosure and the full-scale eruption of the witchcraze of the seventeenth century? This is an area of research which could open entirely new understandings of women-to-women relationships.

Also in need of future study are the missing components of the "Angelia tradition." Tertiary Observance undoubtedly stretched across Europe, branching out westward to Spain and eastward to Poland. Communities other than the Polish tertiaries who were the genesis of the Bernardine Sisters probably have ancient connections to the tertiaries of Blessed Angelina. Over 150 Third Order Regular congregations in Europe can be identified today, but we do not know which ones, or even how many, claim ties to Angelina's tradition. This is an area of recovery that cries out for analysis.

Another area in need of investigation is the modern history of the Polish-American Bernardine Sisters, for whom the role of

---

[40]It is useful to recall the socio-cultural environment in which Angelina was accused of heresy/witchcraft, and the environment of the late sixteenth century during which enclosure was finally imposed. See Quaife, chapters 6 and 7, for discussion of the relationship of misogyny to the witchcraze. Anne Llewellyn Barstow, *Witchcraze: A New History of the European Witch Hunts* (San Francisco: Pandora, 1994) critiques earlier studies of the trials and examines from a feminist perspective issues of gender, geography, economic marginalization, and cultural control.

ethnicity and inherited cultural attitudes toward clerical supervision have yet to be assessed. Ethnicity and a legalistic mindset played a significant part in the gradual Americanization of the congregation and, perhaps even more so in post-conciliar renewal, or resistance to renewal. An analysis of the records of the congregation would furnish rich material for a combined sociological-institutional history, and could offer opportunity for a detailed study of the transmission of the Observant Tradition.

Finally, it is devoutly hoped that Franciscan women and men will benefit from serious consideration of the sometimes troubled history of the Franciscan movement. At the very least, there is something to be said for asking ourselves about re-connecting on a collaborative basis as brothers and sisters, and modelling for the church the freedom of egalitarian male-female relationships based upon the living of the gospel. There are fundamental texts in the Franciscan tradition, beyond those cited in the present work, which can and should lead to more egalitarian and collaborative praxis. There are as-yet-unrecovered stories of important Franciscan women which, if recovered and shared, would enrich the tradition immensely. When additional retrieval and study take place, the collaborative model might once again be the preferred option for the entire movement. And if the Franciscan movement were to teach the larger church, by word and example, the possibilities of full, egalitarian collaboration, it would make a major contribution to the transformation of the church and the demise of patriarchy.

Sources Cited

Archives

Archives of the Bernardine Franciscan Sisters. Sacred Heart Convent, Reading, Pennsylvania.

Archives of the Bernardine Sisters. St. Joseph Convent, Cracow, Poland.

Archives of the Monastery of St. Anna. Foligno, Italy.

Archives of the Province of the Friars Minor. Cracow, Poland.

Library of the Bernardine Sisters. Sacred Heart Convent, Zakliczyn, Poland.

Primary Literature

Armstrong, Regis J., ed. *Clare of Assisi Early Documents*. New York/Mahwah. Paulist Press, 1988. Revised and expanded edition, St. Bonaventure, NY: Franciscan Institute Publications, 1994.

Biografie Antiche della Beata Angelina da Montegiove: Documenti per la storia del monastero di S. Anna di Foligno e del'Terz'Ordine Regolare di S. Francesco. Ed. Anna Filannino and Lorella Mattioli. Spoleto: Centro Italiano di Studi sull'Alto Medioevo, 1996.

Brady, Ignatius and Regis J. Armstrong, ed. *Francis and Clare: The Complete Works*. New York: Paulist Press, 1982.

Bullarium Franciscanum. Volume VII (Rome, 1904).

Bullarium Franciscanum n.s. Volumes I (Quaracchi, 1929), II (Quaracchi, 1939), III (Quaracchi, 1949).

Gonzaga, Francisco. *De Origine Seraphicae Religionis* III. Venice, 1603.

Jacobilli, Ludovico. *Vita della beata Angelina da Corbara, Contessa di Civitella, institutrice delle Monache Claustrali del Terz'Ordine di S. Francesco e Fondatrice in Foligno del Monastero di S. Anna Primo delli Sedici Che Ella Eresse in Diverse Provincie. Foligno: A. Altieri, 1627. Reissued by F. Medina, Vita della Beata Angelina di Marsciano, Contessa di*

Civitella nella Provincia di Abruzzo nel Regno di Napoli, Istitutrice delle Monache Claustrali del terz'Ordine di S. Francesco. Montefiascone, 1737.

—. "Vita della B. Angelina Contessa di Civitella d'Abruzzo, Institutrice delle Terziarie Claustrali di S. Francesco . . . ." *Vite de'Santi e Beati di Foligno, e di Quelli, i Corpi de'Quali Riposano in Essa Città e Sua Diocesi*. Foligno, 1628. 188-208.

—. "Vita della B. Angelina Contessa di Civitella d'Abruzzo, Institutrice delle Terziarie Claustrali di S. Francesco. . . ." *Vite de Santi e Beati dell'Umbria, e di Quelli i Corpi de'Quali Riposano in Essa Provincia, con Le Vite de Molti Servi di Dio dell'Istessa*. II. Foligno, 1652. 33-35.

—. "Vita della B. Angelina Contessa di Civitella d'Abruzzo, Institutrice delle Terziarie Claustrali di S. Francesco. . . ." *Vite de Santi e Beati dell'Umbria, e di Quelli i Corpi de'Quali Riposano in Essa Provincia, con Le Vite de Molti Servi di Dio dell' Istessa. Addition e Corretione alli 3 Tomi de Santi dell'Umbria, Posta al Termine delle Vite de Beati dell'Umbria*. III. Foligno, 1661. 498-99.

Komorowsi, Johannes. "Kronika Komorowski." *MPH*, V. 195.

Marco da Lisbona. *Delle Croniche de'Frati Minori, del Serafico Padre S. Francesco*. Traduzione Horatio Diola. Venice: Erasmo Viotti, 1591. Terza parte. 27-28.

Mariano da Firenze. "Compendium Chronicarum Fratrum Minorum." *AFH* III (1910): 708.

Ughelli, Ferdinand. *Albero et Istoria della Famiglia de'Conti di Marsciano*. Rome, 1667.

Van DenWyngaert, A. "De Sanctis et Beatis Tertii Ordinis iusta codicem Mariani Florentini." *AFH* XIV (1921): 29-31.

Wadding, L. *AM*. Quaracchi, 1932. IX: 1-3, 129-33; IX: 129-33; X: 159-62; 279-80; XI: 123-25; XIII: 49-50, 169; XVI: 147-50.

Secondary Literature

Andreozzi, Gabriele. *La beata Angelina da Montegiove e la Coscienza Unitaria nel Terz'Ordine di San Francesco*. Rome: A. Palombi, 1984.

Barstow, Anne Llewellyn. *Witchcraze: A New History of the European Witch Hunts*. (San Francisco: Pandora, 1994.

Bartoli, Marco. "Le antiche costituzioni delle monache di Foligno." In *La Beata Angelina da Montegiove e Il movimento del Terz 'Ordine Regolare Francescano femminile*, ed. R. Pazzelli and M. Sensi, 123-38. Rome: Analecta TOR, 1984.

Ben-Yehuda, Nachman. "Witchcraft and the Occult as Boundary Maintenance Devices." In *Religion, Science, and Magic In Concert and In Conflict*, ed. Jacob Neusner, Ernest S. Frerichs, and P. V. P. M. Flesher, 229-60. New York/Oxford: Oxford University Press, 1989.

Bigaroni, Marino. "Prime fondazioni di monasteri di terziarie Francescane in Assisi." In *La Beata Angelina da Montegiove e Il movimento del Terz'Ordine Regolare francescano femminile*, ed. R. Pazzelli and M. Sensi, 505-28. Rome: Analecta TOR, 1984.

Bogdalski, Czeslaw. *Bernardyni w Polsce 1453-1530: Zarys Dziejów na tle Wspólczesnych Wydarzen*. Two vols. Cracow: Litodruk, 1933.

Bolton, Brenda. "Daughters of Rome: All One in Christ Jesus." In *Women in the Church*, ed. W.J. Shiels and Diana Wood, 101-116. Cambridge: Basil Blackwell, 1990.

—. "Mulieres Sanctae." In *Women in Medieval Society*, ed. Susan Mosher Stuard, 141-58. Philadelphia: University of Pennsylvania Press, 1976.

—. "Vitae Matrum: A Further Aspect of the Frauenfrage." In *Medieval Women*, ed. Derek Baker, 252-73. Oxford: Basil Blackwell, 1978.

Bowie, Fiona, ed. *Beguine Spirituality*. Trans. Oliver Davies. New York: Crossroads, 1990.

Brennan, Margaret. "A White Light Still and Moving." In *Religious Life The Challenge for the Future*, ed. Cassian Yuhaus, 92-108. New York/Mahwah: Paulist Press, 1994.

Brooke, Rosalind. *Early Franciscan Government*. Cambridge: University Press, 1959.

Bynum, Caroline Walker. "Religious Women in the Later Middle Ages." In *Christian Spirituality II*, ed. Jill Raitt, 121-39. New York: Crossroads, 1987.

—. *Holy Feast and Holy Fast: The Religious Significance of Food to Medieval Women*. Berkeley: University of California Press, 1987.

Byrne, Patricia, C.S.J. "Sisters of St. Joseph: The Americanization of a French Tradition." *U. S. Catholic Historian* 5 (Summer/ Fall 1986): 241-72.

Cambridge Illustrated History of the Middle Ages III: 1250-1520. Ed. Robert Fossier. Cambridge: Cambridge University Press, 1986.

Carney, Margaret. *The First Franciscan Woman Clare of Assisi and Her Form of Life.* Quincy, Illinois: Franciscan Press, 1993.

Carr, Anne. *Transforming Grace: Christian Tradition and Women's Experience.* San Francisco: Harper San Francisco, 1988.

Casagrande, Giovanna. "Forms of Solitary Religious Life for Women in Central Italy." Trans. Nancy Celaschi. In *Franciscan Solitude,* ed. André Cirino and Josef Raischl, 80-116. St. Bonaventure, NY: The Franciscan Institute, 1995.

Chittister, Joan. "An Amazing Journey: A Road of Twists and Turns." In *Religious Life The Challenge for the Future,* ed. Cassian Yuhaus, 76-91. New York/Mahwah: Paulist Press, 1994.

—. *Winds of Change Women Challenge Church.* Kansan City: Sheed and Ward, 1986.

Christ, Carol P. and Judith Plaskow, ed. *Womanspirit Rising: A Feminist Reader in Religion.* San Francisco: Harper San Francisco, 1979, 1992.

Cohn, Samuel K., Jr. *The Cult of Remembrance and the Black Death.* Baltimore and London: Johns Hopkins Uiversity Press, 1992.

Congar, Yves. *Jesus Christ.* Paris: Les Editions du Cerf, 1965. Trans. Luke O'Neill. New York: Herder and Herder, 1966.

Daichman, Graciela. "Misconduct in the Nunnery." In *That Gentle Strength: Historical Perspectives on Women in Christianity,* ed. Lynda L. Coon, Katherine J. Haldane, and Elisabeth W. Sommer, 97-117. Charlottesville andLondon: University Press of Virginia, 1990.

D'Alatri, Mariano. "Leggenda della beata Angelina da Montegiove: Genesi di una Biographia." In *La beata Angelina da Montegiove e Il movimento del Terz'Ordine Regolare francescano femminile,* ed. R. Pazzelli and M. Sensi, 33-46. Rome: 1984. 33-46. Trans. Lori Pieper. "The Legend of Angelina of Montegiove: Genesis of a Biography." *Greyfriars Review* 7 (1993): 95-107.

Daly, Mary. *Beyond God the Father.* Boston: Beacon Press, 1985.

—. *Gyn/Ecology The Metaethics of Radical Feminism.* Boston: Beacon Press, 1978, 1990.

DaMareto, Felice. "L'ordine francescano della penitenza a Parma, Fidenza, Piacenza, e Modena." In *Il movimento francescano della penitenza nella Società Medioevale*, ed. Mariano D' Alatri, 311-21. Rome: Istituto Storico dei Cappuccini, 1980.

DeClary, L. *L'Aureole Seraphique*. III. Paris, 1897. 71-85.

DeClary, L. and G. C. Guzzo. *L'Aureola Serafica: Vite dei santi e beati dei tre ordini di S. Francesco*. Vol 3. Quarrachi: Collegio San Bonaventura, 1899.

Delehaye, Hippolyte. *The Legends of the Saints*. With a Memoir of the author by Paul Peeters. Trans. Donald Attwater. New York: New York University, 1962.

DeRobeck, Nesta. *St. Clare of Assisi*. Chicago: Bruce Publishing Co., 1950.

Donovan, Grace. "Immigrant Nuns: Their Participation in the Process of Americanization: Massachusetts and Rhode Island, 1880-1920." *The Catholic Historical Review*. LXXVII (April 1991): 194-208.

Donovan, Mary Ann. *Sisterhood as Power: The Past and Passion of Ecclesial Women*. New York: Crossroad, 1989.

Dorr, Donal. *Option for the Poor: A Hundred Years of Vatican Social Teaching*. Maryknoll, NY: Orbis Books, 1983.

Ebaugh, Helen Rose Fuchs. *Women in the Vanishing Cloister*. New Brunswick: Rutgers University Press, 1993.

Esser, Kajetan. *Origins of the Franciscan Order*. Trans. Aedan Daly and Irina Lynch. Chicago: Franciscan Herald Press, 1970.

Ewens, Mary. *The Role of the Nun in Nineteenth Century America*. New York: Arno, 1971, 1978, 1984.

—. "Women in the Convent." In *American Catholic Women: A Historical Exploration*, ed. Karen Kennelly, C.S.J., 17-47. New York: Macmillan Publishing Company, 1989.

Fiand, Barbara. "Living the Vison: The Present Moment and Future Prospects for Religious Life." In *Religious Life The Challenge for the Future*, ed. Cassian Yuhaus, 35-69. New York/Mahwah: Paulist Press, 1994.

Fiege, F. M. *The Princess of Poverty*. Evansville, 1909.

Filannino, Anna. "Il monastero di S. Anna nell'età moderna e contemporanea." In *La beata Angelina da Montegiove e Il movimento del Terz'ordine regolare francescano femminile*, ed. R. Pazzelli and M. Sensi, 221-315. Rome: Analecta TOR, 1984.

—. "La beata Angelina dei Conti di Marsciano e le sue fondazioni (communicazione)." In *Prime manifestazioni di vita communitarie maschile e femminile, nel movimento francescano della Penitenza (1215-1447)*, ed. R. Pazzelli and L. Temperini, 451-57. Rome: Analecta TOR, 1982.

—. *Studi sulla Beata Angelina dei Conti di Marsciano, Fondatrice della Congregazione di Foligno.* Master's Thesis for the Catholic University of the Sacred Heart. Milan, 1964.

Flannnery, Austin, ed. *Vatican Council II: The Conciliar and Post Conciliar Documents.* 2nd edition. New York: Costello Publishing Co., 1977.

Flood, David and Thadeé Matura. *The Birth of a Movement.* Paul LaChance and Paul Schwartz. Chicago: Franciscan Herald Press, 1975.

Froncek, Sr. M. Zygmunta, O.S.F. "Half-Century on American Soil." Paper Delivered, Annual Meeting of the Polish-American Historical Association. Orchard Lake, Michigan, October 1944.

—. "Historical Sketch of the Bernardine Sisters, O.S.F." Archives of the Bernardine Franciscan Sisters. Sacred Heart Convent, Reading, PA.

Geary, Patrick. *Living With the Dead in the Middle Ages.* Ithaca: Cornell University Press, 1994.

Gieben, Servus. "L'iconografia di Angelina da Montegiove." In *La beata Angelina da Montegiove e il movimento del terz'ordine regolare francescano femminile,* ed. R. Pazzelli and M. Sensi, 181-201. Rome: Analecta TOR, 1984.

Gill, Katherine. "Open Monasteries for Women in the Late Middle Ages and Early Modern Italy: Two Roman Examples." In *The Crannied Wall: Women, Religion and the Arts of Early Modern Europe,* ed. Craig A. Monson, 15-47. Ann Arbor: University of Michigan Press, 1992.

Gilliat-Smith, E. *Saint Clare of Assisi.* London, 1914.

Guarnieri, Romana. "Beghinismo D'Oltralpe e Bizzochismo Italiano Tra Il Secolo XIV e Il Secolo XV." In *La beata Angelina da Montegiove e il movimento del terz'ordine regolare francescano femminile,* ed. R. Pazzelli and M. Sensi, 1-13. Rome: Analecta TOR, 1984.: Trans. Roberta Agnes McKelvie, "Beguines Beyond the Alps and Italian *Bizzoche* between the 14th and 15th Centuries." *Greyfriars Review* 5 (1991): 91-104.

Goodich, Michael. *The Ideal of Sainthood in the Thirteenth Century.* Stuttgart: Anton Hiersemann, 1982.

Gustaw, Romuald, O.F.M. *Klasztor I Kosciól sw. Józefa SS. Bernardynek w Krakowie 1646-1946.* Biblioteka Krakowska Vol. 105. Krakow: Towarzystwo Milosników Historii i Zabytków Krakowa, 1947.

Gustaw, Romuald and K. Kaczmarczyk. *Katalog Archiwum Bernardynek w Krakowie*. Lublin: Nadbitka z Czasopima Archiwa, 1970.

Hay, Denys. *Europe in the Fourteenth and Fifteenth Centuries*. London: Longmans, 1966.

—. *The Church in Italy in the Fifteenth Century*. Cambridge: Cambridge University Press, 1977.

Hearder, H. and D. P. Waley, eds. *A Short History of Italy from Classical Times to the Present Day*. Cambridge: Cambridge University Press, 1966.

Heffernan, Thomas J. *Sacred Biography: Saints and Their Biographers in the Middle Ages*. New York/Oxford: Oxford University Press, 1988.

Henderson, John. "Confraternities and the Church in Late Medieval Florence." In *Voluntary Religion*, ed. W. J. Shiels and Diana Wood, 69-83. Oxford: Basil Blackwell, 1986.

Herlihy, David and Christiane Klapisch-Zuber. *Tuscans and Their Families: A Study of the Florentine Catasto of 1427*. New Haven and London: Yale University Press, 1985.

Hofer, John. *St. John Capistran, Reformer*. Trans. Patrick Cummins. St. Louis: B. Herder Book Co., 1943.

Holzapfel, Herbert, O.F.M. *Manuale historiae Ordinis Fratrum Minorum*. Fribourg, 1909.

—. *The History of the Franciscan Order*. Trans. A. Tibessar, O.F.M. and G. Brinkmann, O.F.M. Illinois: St. Joseph Seminary, 1948.

Hughes, Dian Owens. "Invisible Madonnas? The Italian Historiographical Tradition and the Women of the Medieval Italy." In *Women in Medieval History and Historiography*, ed. Susan Mosher Stuard, 25-57. Philadelphia: University of Pennsylvania Press, 1987.

Hunt, Noreen. "Enclosure: II." *Cistercian Studies* 22 (1987): 129-51.

Iriarte, Lazaro. *Franciscan History The Three Orders of St. Francis*. Trans. Patricia Ross. Chicago: Franciscan Herald Press, 1982.

—. "Evoluzione storico del francescanesimo: secoli XIII-XV." In *Anno V di formazioni permanente*. Unpublished manuscript of the Tertiary Fransciscans of Blessed Angelina, Foligno.

Kantak, Kamil. *Bernardyni Polsce I 1453-1572*. Lwow: Nakladem Prowincji Polskiej OO. Bernardynów, 1933.

Katalog Archiwum Bernardynek w Krakowie. Biblioteki i Muzea Koscilene, Tom. 20, ed. Romuald Gustaw and Kazimierz Kaczmarczyk. Lublin: Nadbitka z Czasopisma Archiwa, 1970.

Kieckhefer, Richard. *European Witch Trials: Their Foundation in Popular and Learned Culture 1300-1500*. Berkeley: University of California Press, 1976.

Killen, Patricia O'Connell and John de Beer. *The Art of Theological Reflection*. New York: Crossroad, 1995.

Klasztory Bernardynskie w Polsce w Jej Granicach Historycznych. Ed. Hieronima Eug. Wyczawskiego, O.F.M. Krótka Historia Zakonu Braci Mniejszych. Cieszyn: Kalwaria Zebzydowska, 1985.

Kozminski, Honorat. *Swiety Franciszek Seraficki Jego Zycie*. Vol. II. Warsaw: Druk Piotra Laskauera i Spólki, 1902.

Labarge, Margaret Wade. *A Small Sound of the Trumpet: Women in Medieval Life*. Boston: Beacon Press, 1986.

Lambert, Malcolm D. *Franciscan Poverty: The Doctrine of the Absolute Poverty of Christ and the Apostles in the Franciscan Order, 1210-1323*. S.P.C.K., 1961.

Landini, Lawrence F. *The Cause of the Clericalization of the Order of Friars Minor: 1209-1260 In Light of Early Franciscan Sources*. Chicago: Franciscan Herald Press, 1968.

Larner, John. *Culture and Society in Italy 1290-1420*. London: B. T. Batsford, Ltd., 1971.

La "Supra Montem" di Niccolo IV (1289): Genesi e Diffusione di Una Regola. Ed. R. Pazzelli and L. Temperini. Rome: Analecta TOR, 1988.

Lawrence, C. H. *Medieval Monasticism: Forms of Religious Life in Western Europe in the Middle Ages*, 2nd ed. London and New York: Longman, 1989.

LeGoff, Jacques. *Medieval Civilization*. Trans. Julia Barrow. Cambridge: Basil Blackwell, 1989.

Levack, Brian P. *The Witch-hunt in Early Modern Europe*. London & New York: Longmans, 1987.

Little, Lester K. *Religious Poverty and the Profit Economy in Medieval Europe*. London: Paul Elek: 1978.

Lives of the Saints and Blesseds of the Third Order of St. Francis. Vol. IV. Taunton, England: 1886.

Lozano, John. *Foundresses, Founders, and Their Religious Families*. Trans. Joseph Daries. Chicago: Claret Center for Resources in Spirituality, 1983.

MacVicar, Thaddeus. *The Franciscan Spirituals and the Capuchin Reform*. St. Bonaventure NY: The Franciscan Institute, 1986.

McDonnell, Ernest W. *The Beguines and Beghards in Medieval Culture with Special Emphasis on the Belgian Scene*. New York: Octagon Books, 1969.

McLaughlin, Eleanor. "The Christian Past: Does It Hold a Future for Women?" In *Womanspirit Rising: A Feminist Reader in Religion*, ed. Carol P. Christ and Judith Plaskow, 93-106. San Francisco: Harper San Francisco, 1979, 1992.

—. "Equality of Souls, Inequality of Sexes: Woman in Medieval Theology." In *Religion and Sexism: Images of Woman in the Jewish and Christian Traditions*, ed. Rosemary Radford Ruether, 150-83. New York: Simon and Schuster, 1974.

McNamara, Joanne. "The Need to Give: Suffering and Female Sanctity in the Middle Ages." In *Images of Sainthood in Medieval Europe*, ed. Renate Blumenfeld-Kosinski and Timea Szell, 199-221. Ithaca: Cornell University Press, 1991.

Mancini, Giulio. "Memoria di frate Paoluccio Trinci." *Forma Sororum* 6 (1992): 296-310.

Matanic, Atanasio. "Il 'Defensorium tertii ordinis beati Francisci' di San Giovanni da Capestrano." In *Il movimento francescano della penitenza nella società medioevale*, ed. Mariano D'Alatri, 47-57. Rome: Istituto Storico dei Cappuccini, 1980.

—. "San Giovanni da Capestrano e la vita communitaria dei Penitenti francescani." In *Prime manifestazioni di vita communitarie maschile e femminile nel movimento francescano della Penitenza (1215-1447)*, ed. R. Pazzelli and L. Temperini, 81-90. Rome: Analecta TOR, 1982.

Mattioli, Lorella. "Le Terziarie Regolari Francescane della Beata Angelina e le loro Costituzioni." Dissertation submitted to the Istituto Superiore di Scienze Religiose di Assisi, affiliated with the Faculty of the Pontifical Lateran University, 1992; unpublished manuscript.

Migdal, Bogumil. "Bernardynki." In *Zakony sw. Franciszka w Polsce w Latach 1772-1970*, Vol. I. Ed. Joachim Bar, 26-50. Warsaw: Akademia Teologii Katolickiej, 1978.

Moorman, John. *The History of the Franciscan Order From Its Origins to 1517*. London: Oxford University Press, 1968; Chicago: Franciscan Herald Press, 1988.

Mulhern, Philip F. *Dedicated Poverty Its History and Theology*. New York: Alba House, 1973.

Neal, Marie Augusta. *Catholic Sisters in Transition from the 1960s to the 1980s*. Wilmington: Michael Glazier, Inc., 1984.

—. *From Nuns to Sisters An Expanding Vocation.* Mystic, CT: Twenty-Third Publications, 1990.

Neel, Carol. "The Origins of the Beguines." In *Sisters and Workers in the Middle Ages.* Ed. Judith M. Bennett, Elizabeth A. Clark, Jean F. O'Barr et al., 240-60. Chicago & London: University of Chicago Press, 1989.

Nigg, Walter. *Warriors of God: The Great Religious Orders and Their Founders.* Ed. and trans. Mary Liford. New York: Alfred A. Knopf, 1959.

Nimmo, Duncan. *Divison and Reform in the Medieval Franciscan Order From St. Francis to the Foundation of the Capuchins.* Rome: Istituto Storico dei Cappuccini, 1987.

Osheim, Duane J. "The Place of Women in the Late Medieval Italian Church." In *That Gentle Strength: Historical Perspectives on Women in Christianity,* ed. Lynda L. Coon, Katherine J. Haldane, and Elisabeth W. Sommer, 79-96. Charlottesville and London: University Press of Virginia, 1990.

Papi, Anna Benvenuti. *"In castro poenitentiae" santità e società femminile nell'Italia medievale.* Rome: Herder Editrice e Libreria, 1990.

Pásztor, Edith. "Per la storia dell'esperienza penitenziale francescana in Ungheria ne medioevo." In *Il movimento francescano della penitenza nella società medioevale,* ed. Mariano D'Alatri, 117-23. Rome: Istituto Storico dei Cappuccini, 1980.

Pazzelli, Raffaele, T.O.R. *St. Francis and the Third Order The Franciscan and pre-Franciscan Penitential Movement.* Chicago: Franciscan Herald Press, 1989.

—. *The Franciscan Sisters.* Trans. Aedan Mulaney. Steubenville: Franciscan University Press, 1993.

Peano, Pierre. "Angioni e Spirituali e la beata Angelina." In *La Beata Angelian da Montegiove e il movimento del terz'ordine regolare francesacno femminile,* ed R. Pazzelli and M. Sensi, 23-31. Rome: Analecta TOR, 1984.

—. *Les Religieuses Franciscaines: Origines, Histoire et Valeurs Constantes,* ed. J. de Schampheleer and J.F. Godet. Lens, 1981.

Peterson, Ingrid. *Clare of Assisi: A Biography.* Quincy, IL: Franciscan Press, 1993.

Petroff, Elizabeth Alvida. *Body and Soul: Essays on Medieval Women and Mysticism.* New York/Oxford: Oxford University Press, 1994.

Prescott, Orville. *Lords of Italy: Portraits from the Middle Ages.* New York: Harper and Row, 1972.

Quaife, G. R. *Godly Zeal and Furious Rage: The Witch in Early Modern Europe.* New York: St. Martin's Press, 1987.

Rènouard, Yves. *The Avignon Papacy 1305-1403.* Trans. Denis Bethell. Hamden, CT: Archon Books, 1970.

Rossetti, Felice. *La beata Angelina dei Conti di Montegiove.* Siena: Industria Grafica Pistolesi, 1976.

—. "La beata Angelina dei Conti di Montegiove: linea di una spiritualità." In *La beata Angelina da Montegiove e il movimento del terz'ordine regolare francescano femminile,* ed. R. Pazzelli and M. Sensi, 139-46. Rome: Analecta TOR, 1984.

Ruether, Rosemary Radford. "Misogynism and Virginal Feminism in the Fathers of the Church." In *Religion and Sexism: Images of Woman in the Jewish and Christian Traditions,* ed. Rosemary Radford Ruether, 150-83. New York: Simon and Schuster, 1974.

—. *Sexism and God-Talk.* Boston: Beacon Press, 1983; 1993.

Rule and Constitutions of the Bernardine Sisters of the Third Order of St. Francis. Reading, PA, 1963.

Sabatier. Paul. *Vie de S. François D'Assise.* Paris, 1894. Trans. L. S. Houghton. New York: Charles Scribner's Sons, 1894.

S. Bernardino-S. Giacinta 1426-1807: Notizie historiche. Ed. G. Regis. Viterbo: Tipografia Cionfi, 1907.

Schneiders, Sandra. "Contemporary Religious Life: Death or Transformation?" In *Religious Life The Challenge for the Future,* ed. Cassian Yuhaus, 9-34. New York/Mahwah: Paulist Press, 1994.

Schrader, H. J. *Decrees of the General Councils: Texts, Translation and Commentary.* New York: Herder, 1937.

Schüssler-Fiorenza, Elisabeth. *In Memory of Her: A Feminist Theological Reconstruction of Christian Origins.* New York: Crossroad, 1983; 1990.

Sensi, Mario. "Giovanni da Capestrano francescano." In *S. Giovanni da Capestrano nella chiesa e nella società del suo tempo,* ed. Edith and Lajos Pasztor, 21-53. Aquila: 1989.

—. "La Regola di Niccoló IV dalla costituzione 'Periculoso' alla bolla 'Pastorialis Officii' (1298-1447)." In *La "Supra Montem" di Niccoló IV (1289): genesi e diffusione di una regola,* ed. R. Pazzelli and L. Temperini, 147-98. Rome: Analecta TOR, 1988.

—. *Le Osservanze francescane nell'Italia centrale (Secoli XIV-XV).* Rome: Istituto Storico dei Cappuccini, 1985.

—. "Documenti per La beata Angelina." In *La beata Angelina da Montegiove e il movimento del terz'ordine regolare francescano femminile,* ed. R. Pazzelli and M. Sensi, 45-75. Rome: Analecta TOR, 1984.

—. "Il movimento francescano della penitenza a Foligno." In *Il movimento francescano della penitenza nella società medioevale,* ed. Mariano D'Alatri, 399-445. Rome: Istituto Storico dei Cappuccini, 1980.

—. "Incarcerate e recluse in Umbria nei secoli XII e XIV: un bizzocaggio centro-italiano."In *Il movimento religioso femminile in Umbria nei secoli XIII-XIV,* ed. Roberto Rusconi, 85-122. Regione dell'Umbria: La Nuova Italia Editrice, 1984. Trans. Edward Hagman, O.F.M. Cap., "The Women's Recluse Movement in Umbria during the 13th and 14th Centuries." *Greyfriars Review* 8 (1994): 319-45.

Shahar, Shulamith. *The Fourth Estate: A History of Women in the Middle Ages.* London and New York: Routledge, 1983.

Sheldrake, Philip. *Spirituality and History: Questions of Interpretation and Method.* New York: Crossroad, 1992.

Short, William, O.F.M. *The Franciscans.* Wilmington: Michael Glazier, 1989.

Simoni, C. *Il Castello di Monte Giove 'de Montanea.* Rome: 1925.

"Siostry Bernardynki w Ameryce." *Przeglad Katolicki.* May, 1933. 11-15.

Stewart, Robert M. *"De Illis Qui Faciunt Penitentiam." The Rule of the Secular Franciscan Order: Origins, Development, Interpretation.* Rome: Istituto Storico dei Cappuccini, 1991.

St. Francis of Assisi Writings and Early Biographies: English Omnibus of Sources for the Life of St. Francis. Ed. Marion Habig. Fourth Revised Edition. Chicago: Franciscan Herald Press, 1983.

Under the Shadow of the Almighty. [A Bernardine Sister.] Philadelphia: Jeffries and Mainz, 1951.

Vauchez, André. "L'Ideal de saintetè dans le mouvement femini franciscain aux XIIIe et XIVe siecles." In *movimento religioso femminile in Umbria nei secoli XIII-XIV,* ed. Roberto Rusconi, 313-23. Regione dell'Umbria: La Nuova Italia Editrice, 1984.

Vogt, Kari. "'Becoming Male': One Aspect of Early Christian Anthropology," In *Women: Invisible in Church and Theology,* ed. Elisabeth Schüssler-Fiorenza and Mary Collins, 72-83. Edinburgh: T & T Clark, 1986.

Waley, Daniel. *The Italian City-Republics*. 2nd ed. London and New York: Longman, 1978.

Weaver, Mary Jo. *New Catholic Women: A Contemporary Challenge to Traditional Religious Authority*. San Francisco: Harper and Row, 1985.

Wittberg, Patricia. *Creating a Future for Religious Life*. Mahwah: Paulist Press, 1991.

Yuhaus, Cassian, ed. *Religious Life: The Challenge for Tomorrow.* New York & Mahwah: Paulist Press, 1994.

APPENDIX A

PART I

Mark of Lisbon (d. 1591)

Chroniche degli ordini instituiti dal P.S. Francesco (Venice: Paulo Ugolino, 1597-1608), fols. 27-28.

At this time, the Third Order of our Father St. Francis began to become a "religion," as [it did] in the following way for the sisters with the profession of the three essential vows in the city of Foligno in the province of St. Francis: there came to Foligno a Lady called Angelina, Countess of Civitella in Abruzzo, accompanied by a few relatives, who were inspired by the Holy Spirit to live a strict and holy life with the habit and Rule of the Sisters of Penitence; and receiving into their company a few other Ladies and young girls, in a short time they created a numerous congregation, living in a monastery called St. Anna.

Because they placed themselves under obedience to the friars of the Observance, they received assistance and protection from them; wherefore in a few years there arose in many places other monasteries of Observance, and imitators of the Order and Rule of [the monastery of] St. Anna in Foligno. One of them was established in Florence, called St. Onofrio of Foligno, and it was founded by one of the companions of the said Angelina. There were also the monastery of St. Quirico in Assisi; St. Margaret of Ascoli; St. Agnes of Viterbo; St. Anthony of Perugia; St. Elizabeth in L'Aquila, which was later ruined; St. Mary in Ancona, and St. Clare in Rieti.

These monasteries lived under some statutes and concessions obtained from Popes Martin V and Eugene IV. Among other concessions, there was one that the ministers and the discreets elected by the other sisters could hold a chapter every three years, choosing a Minister General, who with the other sisters [discreets] went to visit all of the above-mentioned monasteries, and in them chose officials, appointing them to offices as suitable, and correcting and removing [those found incompetent] from office, as did the Minors their brothers; this was done with great edification of all the sisters.

The care and thought for these religious was no small aggravation to the Observant Friars, since many times they caused afflictions and disturbances to religion, as has always been [the case]. And therefore Blessed Bernardine of Fossa wrote, saying:

> Other grievances the friars bear on their shoulders, that is, the care of Monasteries of nuns of the Third Order, who give them the greatest distress. Fraternal charity is good and of great merit; good and well-ordered charity that begins from within oneself. To be thoughtful of religious is good and meritorious, but also very grave and dangerous.

These words left in writing by this good religious were a strong warning to the friars, the prelates of the Observance, for several reasons, but particularly [for] the pride which ruled in these religious because of the privileges they had obtained; and more, for the danger that their spirits ran to visits. So the friars held Chapters [and] procured and obtained from Pope Pius II [letters] revoking from the nuns the privilege of electing the minister general and the permission to visit the other monasteries. And from that time they [had to] begin to live as other religious. The nuns were displeased by such a prohibition, wherefore they did not fail to trouble the friars; and so a few of these monasteries cut themselves off from obedience to the friars.

But turning to the blessed Angelina, first mother of these religious, we know that her body is buried in Foligno in the church of the Friars Minor. There is no legend of her life. Nevertheless, what one can see from her picture in the chapel where she is buried, serves sometimes for a written narrative, and according to the account of persons worthy of belief, this blessed servant of the Lord, before she took the habit of the Third Order, was accused before the King of Naples, to whom she demonstrated her innocence, carrying coals of fire before his majesty in the folds of her clothes, without anywhere burning her clothes at all. After having received the habit, she was not only persecuted again, but was beaten for being completely devoted to works of piety: [including] visiting the sick and restoring many to health, [even] reviving a dead boy with her prayers.

After her death she was honored by our Lord with many miracles, because many years later, the walls of the tomb exuded drops of blood; and one time it seems that she appeared to a man devoted to her, telling him to inform the friars that they should remove her body from that place, and care for it with reverence, which they immediately did, placing it in a casket, wrapped in silk cloth. Today, the people still show great veneration.

Translation by Roberta A. McKelvie, OSF

APPENDIX A

PART II

Ludovico Jacobilli

Vite de Santi e Beati dell'Umbria (Foligno, 1656). "Vita della B. Angelina Contessa di Civitella d'Abruzzo, Institutrice delle Terziarie Claustrali di S. Francisci in Osservanze e Fondatrice del Monastero di S. Anna di Foligno, e d'altri 15 Monasterii nell'Umbria, Marca, e Toscana," pp. 33-35.

Blessed Angelina was born in 1367 of the noble Lord of Monte Giove, a *castello* situated ten miles from Orvieto. Her father was called Giacomo Montemarte of the Counts of Corbara, and of Titignano; possessor of these *castelli* [followed by 31 names] and other *castelli*, and villages in the territory of Orvieto, Perugia, Todi, Camerino, and the wetlands of Siena.

Her mother was called Anna, daughter of Giacomo of Angiolello Burgari of the counts of Marsciano of Perugia, who was a man much-esteemed, and who had governed the cities of Lombardy for the Duke of Milan; he possessed the titles of the Count of Marsciano, Monte Giove, Migliano, etc. [list of thirteen names] and other *castelli*, and villages in the territory of Perugia, Todi and Orvieto. This Angelina was a niece of Blessed Nallo or Reginaldo of Orvieto, O.P., who was the son of Count Farulfo of Titignano and died in holiness at the convent of Piperno, where he was prior, on 19 April 1348, as [recorded] in the *Diary of the Saints of Todi.*

At the age of twelve, Angelina made a vow of virginity, and at fifteen she was married to John of Termis, Count of Civitella of Abruzzo. She lived with him in perpetual virginity and after his death she took the habit of the Third Order of St. Francis. In company with some relatives, she distributed all of her paternal inheritance to pious places for the love of God. She was most deeply enamored of virginity, exalting this virtue greatly and inducing many virgins to make the vow.

She was falsely accused before Ladislaus, King of Naples. He was internally disposed to burn her [at the stake]. But, inspired by the Holy Spirit, Angelina carried burning coals in her mantle, unharmed, before the King, in order that he start the fire; when he saw the miracle, he was pacified. She had other persecutions and tribulations, which she suffered with admirable patience and example. She had great charity and humility; she used to visit the sick in hospitals and at home, consoling their spirits; she was accustomed to bless with charity their bodies and brought health to many of them. She resuscitated the only son of a Lady of Naples and did other marvelous acts.

She acquired many souls for God; and with the permission of Pope Urban VI in 1385, confirmed by Boniface IX, in 1395, instituted the reform of the nuns of the Third Order of St. Francis in enclosure with the three essential vows. Through the inspiration of God, she founded the first monastery in Foligno in 1385, under the title of St. Anna, mother of the mother of God. Fifteen others were erected in diverse parts of Italy: in 1387, the monastery of St. Clare in Rieti; in 1390, the monastery of St. Margaret in Ascoli; in 1399, with the help of Blessed Margaret, her disciple, the monastery of St. Agnes in Foligno; and in 1400 the monastery of St. John in Todi, through Sister Lucretia di Simone, Countess of Genga, the widow of Count Federico of Marsciano, relative and disciple of the same Bl. Angelina. And from the same Sr. Lucretia, its foundress, this monastery was named "Lucretia" or "Lucretie." In 1420 the monastery of S. Onofrio in Florence was erected by four of her disciples, nuns of the monastery of Foligno; and so this one in Florence was said to be of Foligno; in 1422 the monastery of St. Cecelia of Città del Castello was erected, and that of St. Quirico in Assisi. In 1426 the monastery of St. Agnes (later called St. Bernardine) in Viterbo was established; in 1427, that of St. Anthony of Padua in Perugia; in 1429, the monasteries of St. Appollonia and of St. Margaret in Rome; in 1431, St. Catherine of Pusterno in Spoleto; in 1433, St. Elisabeth in Aquila, a new St. Mary in Ancona and S. Mary Magdalen in Piacenza.

Other monasteries were established after the death of Angelina by her disciples and nuns in diverse parts of Europe. We have found, at the present time under this Institute of Tertiaries of

S. Francis of the Observance, 135 monasteries in twenty-two separate Provinces of Europe, totalling 4,323 nuns. All [are] the fruits of the prayers and efforts of this Blessed, who was elected the first Minister General of all of this her congregation, with many graces and privileges obtained from Pope Martin V. She governed until the end of her life with highest charity, prudence, and universal profit.

She was the most clear mirror of every virtue. Her humility was admired, her fastings daily, her prayers continuous, her discipline frequent, her tears incessant and her charity most ardent. Therefore, such raving and anger arose in the Devil that she not only was persecuted by him but suffered horrendous temptations. In the end, the earth being no longer worthy of the heavenly "little angel" (Angelina), she was overtaken by a most grave and mortal illness and received the last holy sacraments. She called together all of her nuns, of whom with most humble sentiment she asked pardon, if against her will she had tested them. She encouraged them in perfect observance of the Rule which they had professed and above all encouraged them to be founded in charity, in their own abjection, and in contempt of earthly and transitory things. She asked that they be assiduous in prayer, the mine of all graces; she said to them that prompt obedience was the crown of every virtue. And she requested that they sequester themselves from the world, forever abhorring it, saying that the true Paradise was the monastery in which flourished observance, union, and charity. She concluded that they should imagine having her always present who said to them: "Daughters, be observant, be perfect." After blessing all of them with maternal affection, she remained kneeling before them, shedding incessant tears for the lost ones who were making her [too much of] a good superior and mother. Rapt in highest contemplation, in a wonderful way her soul left her for the bosom of her celestial spouse on 14 July 1435, at the age of 68 years....

Her body, with much pomp and a great crowd of people, was buried in the church of St. Francis in Foligno, where to the present it is kept in a place of honor for public veneration. The Lord God has worked through her many miracles at various times. In the *Martyrologio Francescano* the following words can be read:

> . . . Of Foligno in the valley of Spoleto, of Blessed Angelina of Corbara de Termis, virgin, who, though born of a noble family, having lost her husband, renouncing the world and the display of riches and despicable wealth, took up the habit of the third [order]: and first of all professing the three monastic vows, she began the sacred order [*religio*] of the Third [Order]; afterward, outstanding in the display of many virtues, she shone with miracles during her life and after her death until now.

This Beata is different from the other great servant of God, Sister Angelina da Teramo, a city of Abruzzo, who was a nun at S. Lucia in Foligno, and later sent with other sisters to reform the monastery of S. Cosmato in Rome. Taken ill there, she was visited by the Lord her spouse on the day of the Apostle Thomas, and revealed to her that on the eve of His birth of that year he would see her again in heaven; and so it happened on the 24th of December of 1459, in the same monastery of S. Cosmato, where she was honorably buried. A few authors have confused the life of this [first] Blessed Angelina, Countess of Civitella and of Termes, foundress of the Reform of the Cloistered Tertiaries in Italy with the other, Sister Angelina of Teramo, nun of the Second Order of St. Clare in S. Lucia in Foligno. They make of two persons, one; but it is wrong, as is shown [aove]; and we explain this even better and more diffusely in the special life that we published in the year in 1627 about this Blessed Angelina.

N.B.: On the margins of text for each page of the original text, Jacobilli identifies the ms. tradition/sources used for that section.

Translation by Roberta A. McKelvie, O.S.F.

APPENDIX A

PART III

Gaetano Moroni Romano

Dizionario di Erudizione Storico-Ecclesiastica. Vol I. 1840.

Angelina, blessed. Born in the year 1357, in Montegiove of Alfina, in the territory of Orvieto. Ever since her early years, she began to enjoy the sweetness of intimate union with Jesus Christ, and when only twelve offered him a vow of virginity. In accord with the will of relatives she was joined in matrimony, but never violated the obligation which she first had made with the Lord. After her husband passed to a better life, she gave her earthly goods to the poor, taking the habit of a Franciscan tertiary. Exercising the higher virtues for some years, she thought to reform the *monache* of the Third Order of St. Francis, and in 1385, backed by pontifical authority, erected in Foligno her first monastery. To the merit of her surprising activity, there soon were erected in Italy 20 other monasteries that she herself comforted with visits and words of life. Finished with her mortal career, crowned with glorious virtue, she died in the embrace of God on 14 July 1435, in the 78th year of her life. Her body was buried in the church of Saint Francis in Foligno, in a place of distinction.

Translation by Roberta A. McKelvie, O.S.F.

APPENDIX A

PART IV

L. Oliger

Dictionnaire d'Histoire et de Géographie Ecclésiastiques Vol. 3. Ed. Alfred Baudrillart (Paris: Librarie Letouzey et Ane, 1924): 53-54.

Angelina of Marsciano (blessed) foundress of a Third Order congregation of St. Francis, born at Montegiove (Umbria, Italy) in 1377—died in Foligno, 14 July 1435. Her father was the Count of Marsciano and her mother was from the Counts of Corbara. Raised piously, Angelina at the age of 15 was given in marriage to Count John [Giovanni], lord of Civitella in the Abruzzo, with whom she had lived for two years when death ravaged him. A widow at seventeen, she was received into the Third Order of St. Francis and devoted herself to a retired life with [other] honorable women, looking, however, to comfort the poor. As a result of her example and her exhortations, many young noble women entered the religious life, and for her influence upon them she was accused of witchcraft before Ladislaus, who wanted to burn her as a witch. When she made her way to the court of Naples, Angelina was able to convince the king of her innocence. But some time later she was nonetheless exiled from the kingdom. In 1395 she went to Assisi with her companions. There she was inspired to found the monastery of St. Anna. Many Italian towns, [including] Assisi, Florence, Viterbo, L'Aquila, would ask to establish monasteries of the same institute. Angelina consented to this and governed as superior general of the new foundations. The order of Third Order Regular, approved by the Church, spread more and more and in the 17th century. Jacobilli counted 135 monasteries, of which fifty-three were in Italy and twenty-nine in France. But already under Pius II each monastery, with an abbess at its head, had become independent. Angelina died in the 58th year of her life. She began to be venerated soon and Leo XII confirmed her cult. Her feast is fixed on July 15th.

Translated by Roberta A. McKelvie, OSF

APPENDIX A

PART V

Bullarium Franciscanum I, n.s., pp. 706-707.

1826. The faculty of electing a Minister General and Ministers of single houses is granted to Angelina of Marsciano of Foligno and to the Sisters of other houses of the Third Order. 1428, 19 August, Genezzano

To our venerable brother, the Bishop of Todi.

The character of the holy religious life, under which Our beloved daughters in Christ, Angelina of St. Anne in Foligno, Catherine of St. John in Todi, Ceccha of St. Honofrius in Florence, Paula of St. Margaret in Ascoli Piceno, Thomasia of St. Quiricus in Assisi, and Clare of St. Agnes in Viterbo, all houses of the Third Order of St. Francis and called the Order of Penitence, and Sisters that give devoted and zealous service to the Lord, deserves that we give favorable approval, in so far as can be with the help of God, to their pious and reasonable requests. On the part of these and other houses of the same Sisters a petition, lately presented to Us, held that they lately, with the hope of the approval of the Apostolic See, elected and unanimously accepted some religious Sisters of the same Order as Ministers or Administrators in each of these same houses with a view to the fruit of a better life by living honestly under the obligation of obedience, namely, under the governance of some superiors so that their living together might become more acceptable to God, and that they might be able to progress in this way of life more serenely and advantageously. They desire to continue religious life uninterruptedly under the obedience and governance of these ministers, thus assumed and to be assumed in the future. Therefore, a humble petition was made to Us on behalf of these Sisters that, keeping in mind what has been said above, and in behalf of their peace and tranquility, for the increase of their way of life and the laudable direction of those houses, it should be incumbent on the ministers, elected in this way and those who should be elected in the future for these houses, to exercise the duty of governing. Furthermore, as often as it happens that these houses lack ministers, the already-mentioned Sisters and those of the same houses, both in this first instance and in the future, shall elect and assume other suitable Sisters, professed in the Order, as Ministers in places that are without them, to whom the Sisters are to submit and obey in things that are honest and licit. These elected Ministers will be in charge of the houses in which they were elected, and of the Sisters of these houses, and will rule over and govern them. Also from suitable women who wish to profess this Order, the customary profession may be elicited through the Sisters of these houses and they may admit and receive these women into their houses. Furthermore, the elected Ministers and those elected in the future should elect another one as General Minister for these Sisters and houses, who should visit the Ministers and Sisters and correct and punish them for their excesses according to the canonical regulations. The General Minister thus elected shall receive any other Sisters of houses of this Order in parts of Italy, who of their own accord wish to come under her administration and care. Moreover, the Ministers and the visitators of this Order have the power of freely and licitly going to see the General and other Ministers of the houses of the Order.

We, therefore, looking favorably on such supplications, commit to your discretion through this apostolic document and we order that by Our authority you diligently inform yourself as far as each and every point is concerned, and if through such information you find that all the preceding can be done according to law and according to the regulations of the Order, upon which we tax your conscience, by that same authority you shall bestow the permission to elect Ministers for the present and future Sisters of these houses; and by the same authority you may concede to the Ministers and to the Sisters of these houses and to the houses themselves that they may perpetually enjoy and use all and every privilege howsoever conceded to other Sisters and houses of such an Order. Given at Genezzano, diocese of Palestrina on the 19th of August in the 11th year of this pontificate.

Translated by the late Canisius Connors, O.F.M., of St. Bonaventure Friary, St. Bonaventure University.

APPENDIX A

PART VI

Bullarium Franciscanum VII, pp. 715-716.

1843. The Pope orders Jordan, Bishop of Albano, Protector of the Order of Minors to make it clear that the Brothers and Sisters of the Third Order of St. Francis are subject to the direction of the superiors of the Order of Minors.1428, 9 December, Rome

To Our venerable brother Jordan, Bishop of Albano.

Although among the other vows of the regular observance the yoke of obedience, without which religious life is thought to be not real but feigned, holds first place and therefore it is incongruous and absurd that one would show himself as a religious by wearing the habit outdoors, but like a rapacious wolf utterly disdains to live the regular life and subject himself to your regular discipline. Indeed, a petition, lately given to Us on the part of our beloved sons, Anthony de Massa, Minister General, the Ministers Provincial and all the friars, contained the information that there are some people of both sexes, both ecclesiastical and secular, in various parts of the world who, under a veil of sanctity, are wearing a gray habit conforming, at it were, to the habit of the Friars Minor, and are assuming a name taken from blessed Francis. They identify themselves as members of the Third Rule of this saint, otherwise known as the Rule of the Penitents. Both because of privileges, they assert, given to them and also on their own authority they presume and assert that they lead a religious life sometimes in common, sometimes partly, under a norm of living, as if at one's own free choice and without due subjection to obedience. From this not only confusion and contempt of this Order is generated, but also simple people thus deceived are led into different errors and heresies, and many scandals and dangers to souls ensue. Therefore, on the part of the Minister General, Ministers Provincial, and the Friars a supplication was humbly made to Us that We deem it worthy to give Our attention to this matter at an appropriate time.

Therefore, attentively considering that it is incongruous that such people wear a habit that was given in respect to this saint, and that they presume to give themselves the name of the Third Order, yet think it of little value to submit to the jurisdiction or discipline of the superiors of the Order of Minors and are not otherwise subject to the Order, and wishing to come to grips advantageously with these things, We commit them to your attention that, if it is so, each and every Brother and Sister of the Third Order of St. Francis, otherwise known as the Order of Penitents, both present and future, of whatever degree or condition they are or wherever they are, are by Our authority subject to the same Order and its superiors in all things excepting always their form of living and staying together. You should decide whether they are subject to the Ministers General and Provincial according to circumstances, as other, true Brothers and Sisters are subject to this Order. By this same authority you should set up and arrange that the forementioned Ministers by themselves or by other who are suitable make a visitation of the Brothers and Sisters of the Third Order as often as it is expedient. These will correct and punish delinquents and transgressors for their faults, hear their confessions and enjoin a salutary penance and administer all the sacraments of the Church. The visitators shall also see to anything else that does not interfere with the observance of the life they live together. They also have the power to exercise jurisdiction over them by restraining objectors by ecclesiastical censures without publishing names. We repeal all privileges and all and any apostolic constitutions in so far as they are contrary to the foregoing.

Given at Rome at the Holy Apostles on December 9, 1428, in the 12th year of Our pontificate.

Translated by the late Canisius Connors, O.F.M., of St. Bonaventure Friary, St. Bonaventure University.

APPENDIX B

Characteristics of Tertiary Observance in Bernardine Houses Founded without Enclosure

Place	BF Ch.	Rule of 1289	Vows (2)	Alms	Work of Hands	Educ. of Girls	BVM Off.	Penit. Pss.	Off. of Dead	Visit Sick
CRACOW (COL.)	X	X	X		X		X			
CRACOW (KAZ.)	X	X	X	X	X					
CRACOW (AGNES)	?[1]	X				X	X	X	X	
WARSAW (1454)	X	X	X	X	X	X	X	X	X	X
WARSAW[2] (1594)	X	1521 *Rule*	X			X				
WSCHOWA	X	X								
KOBYLIN	X	X	X							
POZNAN	?	X	X		X	X				X
LWOW	X		X		X	X	?[3]			
KALISZ	X	X	X		X					
PRZEWORSK	X	X			X					
RADOM	X	X								
KOWNO	X	X								
KOSCIAN	X	X								
WILNO (ZARZ)	Called "bizochami" and "koletkami" Supported by benefactors									
BYDGOSZCZ	X		X							
LUBLIN	Information unrecovered at this time									
WARTA	X		X	X	X					X
TARNOW	X							X		

[1] Had own church from 1459.
[2] Founded for those who would not accept enclosure of original house in 1594.
[3] Sisters "recited prayers."

Pg 17 – Poverty